# Male & Female in Social Life

# Lloyd E. Sandelands

# Male & Female in Social Life

**Transaction Publishers**
New Brunswick (U.S.A.) and London (U.K.)

Library of Congress Number: 2001027887
ISBN: 0-7658-0083-7 (cloth); 0-7658-0877-3 (paper)
Printed in the United States of America

Library of Congress Cataloging-in-Publication Data

Sandelands, Lloyd E., 1955-
    Male and Female in social life / Lloyd E. Sandelands.
        p.  cm.
    Includes bibliographical references and index.
    ISBN 0-7658-0083-7 (cloth:alk. paper)—ISBN 0-7658-0877-3 (paper:
    alk. paper)  1. Sex role.  2. Sex differences (Psychology)  I. Title.

HQ1075 .S264 2001
305.3—dc21                                            2001027887

# Contents

# Acknowledgments

I have abiding debts. This book is a fruit of many conversations with people I am more than glad to call friends, especially Jane Dutton, Jim Walsh, and Monica Worline. I don't for a moment presume to speak for these friends, as they have done me the great favor of opposing many of the arguments and emphases of the book. Neither this book nor I would be without them. This book is also the making of several people, including Irving Louis Horowitz, Mary Curtis, and the staff at Transaction Publishers, and Nichola Hutchison and Susan Douglas at the University of Michigan. Thanks to you all.

# Preface

Sex—the fact we are male and female—ought to be a bigger idea in social science than it is. It is the first thing seen about us at birth, and the main thing we see in ourselves throughout life. Yet, with the notable exceptions of Freud, Frazer, Malinowski, Mead, Brown, and a few others, social scientists attach little significance to sex in the theory of social life. Some give sex short shrift because it rests uneasily with social values for equal opportunity and equal outcomes. Others obscure sex in talk about gender, which is a contingent distinction of culture rather than a universal distinction of biology. And still others mock sex as a neurotically over-simple category for analyzing a complex social world (see, e.g., Adler, 1978). This book is about sex and social life. It asks what the division of our species into male and female means for our lives together. It finds social life to be a massive detailing of sex.

Traversing today's battleground of sex one seeks cover in established scientific paradigms and nomenclatures. This book enjoys neither. Would that I could keep to a paradigm or vernacular, or keep to lab studies of brain physiology, or field studies of behavior, or ethnographies of cultures, or excavations of ancient societies, or even armchair speculations. But the story of sex and social life is too old and too subtle to reach by any paradigm or method. It ranges over evolution's entire expanse from cosmic beginnings to leading edges of human culture. Social life is a physical, chemical, organic, social, and mental phenomenon that developed over biologic, geologic, even cosmologic time scales. We must be ecumenical in our outlook.

The meaning of sex in social life is not so plain that we can read it from a survey or focus group, nor by an over-the-shoulder glance at our ape-ish ancestors, or even by peering farther back to their ancestors' ancestors' ancestors. In these we find only the latest advances of sex and society, the last few forks and turns of primate evolution. As Teilhard de Chardin (1959) reminds, to see our human core, we must look all the way back to the beginnings of matter, life, and mind. We are a late flower of an evolutionary tree whose fiber, from root to canopy, integrates these three orders of the universe. If our aim is to understand the blossom that is us, we must adopt an anthropic viewpoint that sees evolution leading to us.

Although our own species manifests more clearly than most the three great orders of the universe—matter, life, and mind—we barely understand these orders, and even less their relations. Beginning notoriously but not uniquely with Descartes, we have compartmentalized these orders and thereby have made their relations incomprehensible. Indeed, our concepts of matter, life, and mind contradict our basic belief in evolution. We agree that life was born of matter, and mind was born of life, but who can say *how* life comes of matter and *how* mind comes of life? Mind, we say, transcends life. Life, we say, transcends matter. It seems you can't get there from here. Smuts (1926, p. 10) recaps the dilemma:

> If Evolution is accepted, and life and mind are developments in and from the physical order, they are in that order, and it becomes impossible to continue to envisage the physical order as purely mechanical, as one in which they have no part or lot, in which they are not real factors and from which they should be logically excluded.

In this book, I reclaim the outlook on evolution, championed by Smuts, Alexander, Morgan, Haldane, and Teilhard de Chardin, that integrates matter, life, and mind by seeing each in the others. What distinguishes late products of evolution from early ones is not the fact of life or the existence of mind, but the prominence of these aspects. I accept the view that all things have space, time, life, and consciousness. This is not to deny the obvious, that a person has more life and mind than say a rock, but only to affirm that among matter, life, and mind there are no logical breaks or contradictions, only lapses in our ability to discern continuities.[1]

Sex is a crucial dynamic in the evolving matrix of matter, life, and mind. At the minute scale of cells, sex means isogamy: two kinds of cells—a solitary, large, and stationary egg, and millions of small motile sperm. At this scale we see life and mind at the moment of conception, at the moment the egg "chooses" a single sperm to fertilize it. At the larger scale of mature animals, sex means dimorphism: two body plans differing in size, dominance tendency, hormones, promiscuity, reproductive organs, and orientation to offspring. At this scale we find life and mind everywhere as males strive to outwit one another and females size-up winning males. Sex is an amalgam of mental, biological, and physical means and motives.

Sex unites us with other animals. Like other animals, we are divided most plainly by sex. Male and female differ in body and attitude. And like other animals, our social life is underwritten by the complementarities of sex. Male and female dance their differences. Sex also distinguishes us from other animals. Unlike other animals, we extend sex into realms of mind and society. We turn sexual division into consciousness and into a distinctive social order. Thus, the division of sex that links us to other animals also explains what makes us human. This book stakes a bold claim that sex is the main factor that explains our social life. Baldly put, social life is for sex and sex is for social life. This book puts sex at the center of social science.

I imagine this book will find critics. Some may identify my assertions about sex and social life as motivated (either politically or psychically) and on that basis argue they are not to be taken seriously. The strong form of this criticism appears in those schools of post-structuralism and post-modernism that regard all the world as text and make everything in it an interpretation rather than a truth. On this view, my assertions express only personal values, not settled facts (which do not exist). A weaker and barely more respectable form of this criticism is that because we can never be certain of truth, we should discount anyone so arrogant to claim it. Either way, I hold out for the logical possibility that I could be *both* motivated and correct.

In a variation on the above, others may find my claims about sex and social life proof of cultural bias. They may see conservatism in the book and complain that this might be expected from a privileged agent of the culture. And after a quick check of a dust-jacket photo that finds me male and seemingly of European descent, they may feel they have all the evidence needed to convict. For these critics the book is suspect because it finds truth in prevailing social categories and arrangements that *they choose* not to endorse. Perhaps they may dismiss the book as "male backlash" at just and overdue reforms of male dominated society. This criticism has an obvious problem and an unobvious problem. The obvious problem is that even if it is granted that men and women differ in power, it does not follow that these differences are unnatural or even unjust. As we will see, males and females have different kinds of power that stem from different roles in reproducing the species. The unobvious problem with this criticism comes in unsaid but clearly implied premises that: (a) males have it all over females in this life; (b) that males do not deserve what they have come into; and (c) that males get and keep their advantage by oppressing females (e.g., in books like this one). I sincerely hope that this book goes some of the way toward debunking these premises, all of which are false and dangerous.

Others still may fault my claims about sex and social life for resting on sex differences and sex relations that are too pointed and too finely drawn. They may point out that there are few blacks and whites about the sexes; many more shades of gray. There aren't just males and females, but all kinds of blending, and even third sexes that are neither male nor female (see, e.g., Herdt, 1996). They may point out too that there is much more about the sexes that cannot be catalogued and described, that the sexes and their relations are more mysterious than settled, and forever thus. And on these bases they may accuse me of exaggerating differences and relations. In these charges the critics have my sympathy, for they are surely correct in their assessment that sex is more vague and more mysterious than I can say in this book. I accept this criticism as a caution about any attempt to talk about a human nature too subtle and too beautiful for words. But that does not make the effort less worthwhile. It is not like us to let even the unspeakable go without saying. We do the best we can, and so do better than we would otherwise. This book does not step lightly in the wood of sex—it crushes important growths under foot and machetes trails barely suggested by the lay of the trees. The book seeks comprehensive truths, recognizing that to find them it may have to sacrifice details. If this book does not honor the fullness, variety, and mystery of sex, at least it pays tribute to the centrality and importance of sex in social life.

And finally, there are those who may dismiss my claims about sex and social life as essentialist, as if that, too, were evidently disqualifying. Put starkly, this criticism finds claims of essentials false on their face. It finds that nature is full of exceptions and for any given process or function there are alternatives. Thus, where the features of the sexes are not rigidly fixed (even chromosome typing is problematic) and where differences between the sexes admit exceptions, there can be no simple or strictly determinative relationship between sex and social life. This criticism often takes the form of finding exceptions to supposed universals, where a single counter-example suffices as reproof. For example, where many studies of primates point to certain evolved characteristics of humans (such as that males are larger than females, or that males mate more promiscuously than females, or that females take primary responsibility for raising the young), critics find one or a few (often remote) examples that do not fit the pattern and on that basis propose to defeat inferences of evolved continuity (see, e.g., Hrdy, 1981). This practice, which is more influential than logical, has been called by a few exasperated workers in the field the "pick a primate" fallacy.[2]  Or again, where studies of world cultures suggest universals such as patriarchy and sexual division of labor, critics find one or a few "devastating" counter-examples. Even when these counter-examples are later found to be mistaken, as happened in the case of matriarchy, the retractions are rarely forthcoming and they rarely enjoy the visibility or force of the original and well-celebrated report.[3]  Indeed, as Goldberg (1993) has pointed out about college social science textbooks, some errors are so cherished that they are preserved in print as books go through one "updating" revision after another. This book trades in essential propositions that cannot be refuted simply by enumerated exceptions. My claims about sex and social life are general rather than absolute. Sex can be an essential factor of social life even when some females are bigger, stronger, more ambitious, and more dominant than some males; and some males are more caring, nurturing, and responsive to children than some females. The sex differences that define social life have many exceptions. Yet, it is because males generally exhibit one set of sensibilities and actions while females generally exhibit another set of sensibilities and actions, that certain social arrangements emerge and are maintained (arrangements that are bound to be oppressive to some). Furthermore, being aware of these tendencies, males and females stereotype the sexes and together build cultures to support the stereotypes. Sex is essential because sex differences are statistical (of average tendency). The laws that relate sex differences and social life are universal because they trade in differences of average tendency. In this respect they are like Boyle's laws relating the temperature and pressure of gas in fixed volumes. It is no more an argument against the claims in this book to say that sex cannot explain social life because some women do not differ from some men on some variable of interest, than it is to say that molecular activity cannot explain gas pressure in a cylinder because not all molecules contribute equally to the behavior of the gas. Indeed, the example of gases reminds us that the behavior of a system of agents can differ dramatically from the behavior of individual agents taken singly.

I welcome the criticisms above, and for two reasons. First, these criticisms would come from those for whom the book is intended. A science advances through the back and forth of assertion and criticism. To be rejected is to have played a part, and I would like nothing more than to play a part. Second, as I have pointed out, these criticisms can be answered. If the reader will grant my answers, at least provisionally, then the ideas of this book stand a chance of living a fruitful life in the larger conversation.

# 1

# Introduction

This book is about sex: about what sex means in our lives. This book tells an old story about males and females. Males compete to woo, females wait to choose. It is a story to describe the dynamics and the forms of our social lives. It is a story to describe why and how we play. It is a story to describe why and how we establish pair bonds, families, male and female groups, status hierarchies, and divisions of labor. It is a story to put at the center of a science of social life.

## Images

Leave it to the immersed reflections of artists, rather than the sterile dissections of social scientists, to bring sex to light. Aristophanes tells Plato in "The Symposium" what love is: Love is the urge to reunite what Zeus tore asunder when he split a hermaphroditic human race into male and female halves.

> And so, gentlemen, we are all like pieces of the coins that children break in half for keepsakes—making two out of one, like the flatfish—and each of us is forever seeking the half that will tally with himself. The man who is a slice of the hermaphrodite sex, as it was called, will naturally be attracted by women—the adulterer, for instance—and women who run after men are of similar descent—as, for instance, the unfaithful wife....

> Now, supposing Hephaestus were to come and stand over them with his tool bag as they lay there side by side, and suppose he were to ask, Tell me, my dear creatures, what do you really want with one another? And suppose they didn't know what to say, and he went on, How would you like to be rolled into one, so that you could always be together, day and night, and never be parted again? Because if that's what you want, I can easily weld you together, and then you can live your two lives in one, and, when the time comes, you can die a common death and still be two-in-one in the lower world. Now, what do you say? Is that what you'd like me to do? And would you be happy if I did?

We may be sure, gentlemen, that no lover on earth would dream of refusing such an offer, for not one of them could imagine a happier fate. Indeed, they would be convinced that this was just what they'd been waiting for—to be merged, that is, into an utter oneness with the beloved.

And so all this to-do is a relic of that original state of ours, when we were whole, and now, when we are longing for and following after that primeval wholeness, we say we are in love. For there was a time, I repeat, when we were one, but now, for our sins, God has scattered us abroad, as the Spartans scattered the Arcadians. Moreover, gentlemen, there is every reason to fear that, if we neglect the worship of the gods, they will split us up again and then we shall have to go about with our noses sawed asunder, part and counterpart, like the basso-relievos on the tombstones. And therefore it is our duty one and all to inspire our friends with reverence and piety, for so we may ensure our safety and attain that blessed union by enlisting in the army of Love and marching beneath his banners....

But what I am trying to say is this—that the happiness of the whole human race, women no less than men, is to be found in the consummation of our love, and in the healing of our dissevered nature by finding each his proper mate. And if this be a counsel of perfection, then we must do what, in our present circumstances, is next best, and bestow our love upon the natures most congenial to our own.[1]

Aristophanes' strange tale resonates to modern ears. We recall Zeus' punishment when thinking our true love our better half. And remembering the original joy of the race, we feel whole in his/her arms.

James Brown, proclaimed "Godfather of Soul," sings of a man's world made for woman. In his hit song co-written with Betty Newsome titled "It's a Man's, Man's, Man's World" he finds that man struggles and strains not for himself but for woman's love and the welfare of children. No woman, no life, no point.

This is a man's world. This is a man's world
But it wouldn't mean nothing, nothing
Without a woman or a girl.

You see, man made the cars
    That take us over the road
Man made the train
    To carry the heavy load
Man made the electric lights
    To take us out of the dark
Man made the board for the water
    Like Noah made the ark.

This is a man's, man's, man's world
But it wouldn't meaning nothing, nothing
Without a woman or a girl.


Man thinks about a little bitty baby girl
    And a baby boy.
Man make them happy
    Cause man made them toys
And after man make everything
    Everything he can

You know that man makes money
    To buy from other man.

This is a man's world,
But it wouldn't mean nothing, nothing, not one little thing,
Without a woman or a girl.

He's lost in the wilderness
He's lost in bitterness
He's lost, lost, ...


And Thurber and White (1929) joke about an opposing current of change in women's liberation that wastes away the differences that intrigue the sexes.    They find modern man and woman comically stranded upon a barren island of sexual equality.

So matters went. Man, we have seen, had begun to develop himself so that he would be attractive to Woman, and in doing so had made Woman of doubtful attraction to him. He had become independent. He had become critical. He had become scared. Sex was awakening and it was all Man could do to keep from laughing.


Woman, on her part, saw dimly what was going on in the world. She saw it through the sweet haze of Dream. She caught glimpses of it in the mirror of her Narcissistic soul. Woman was at the crossroads. She had many ways open to her, but she chose one: she chose to imitate Man. At a time when sex was in transition, she had the bad judgment to begin a career of independence for herself, in direct imitation of her well-meaning mate. She took up smoking. She began to earn money (not much, but some). She drank. She subordinated domesticity to individuality—of which she had very little. She attained to a certain independence, a cringing independence, a wistful, half-regretful state. Men and women both became slightly regretful: men regretted that they had no purple tail to begin with, women that they had ever been fools enough to go to work. Women now "understood life," but life had been so much more agreeable in its original mystery. (Pp. 99-100)

Here then are three images of sex in social life—images of the origins of love, of the meaning of life, and of the comedy of modernity. I take my cue from these and other images to look at social life through the focusing lens of sex. But in taking my cue I come to sex not as an artist concerned primarily for its feeling, but as a scientist concerned primarily with its structure and dynamism. I want to describe how sex defines our life together.

## A Philosophical Challenge

Science seeks our social life in evolutionary comparisons, either to primates like us, such as the chimpanzee and baboon, or to hominid species more like us still. Such comparisons hint at sex's role in social life.[2] In sexual dimorphism (particularly the fact that males are generally larger and stronger than females) we imagine a basis for patriarchal society. In sex differences in reproductive strategy (particularly the fact that males compete for access to choosy females) we imagine a basis for male status-seeking and for female solidarity and social sensitivity. And in sex differences in reproductive investment (particularly the fact that females put more time and energy into offspring than males) we imagine a division of labor which orients males outside the group to tasks of hunting and defense and orients females inside the group to tasks of raising offspring and keeping peace.

I use the word "imagine" in talking about sex in social life because that is what we have to do. Our evolutionary comparisons do not reach back far enough to tell us about sex. Present almost from the beginning of life on earth, sex is far older than hominid, primate, or even mammalian phylogeny. Sex is so much a part of the fabric of life, and we are so removed from its origins and effects, that we strain to see its importance. Our evolutionary comparisons are not deep enough to find important differences and are not tuned to detect similarities. Our method thus blinds us to sex's deep and abiding influence upon vertebrate, mammal, primate, and hominid life. We have come into the room late to hear the last few words of evolution's epic tale, having long ago missed the crucial part about sex. Our challenge is philosophical. We need a framework of ideas to think about sex in human social life. With this book I seek such a framework.

Ernst Mayr (1991) called life "one long story." It is one very long story. It is a story of the planet and indeed of the cosmos, a story with no discernible beginning and perhaps no end. Life grew from particular conditions of matter and energy. It is the tallest of tales—of cosmology, geology, chemistry, biology, anthropology, and psychology—of which we know only the barest outlines. We know that organic chemistry came with a soup of inorganic matter, temperature, and lightning. We know that the first living cells came with chains of simple proteins. We know that nucleated cells came with symbiosis of procaryotic cells. We know that sex came along as a variation on cellular reproduction. We know that frolicsome play took the field with mammals with brains that needed time to mature. And we know that self-dealing consciousness announced itself only with the very highest primates. This tale is too tall to tell in any single book. In this book, I tell a shorter story about how sex, one of evolution's oldest and greatest innovations, plays out in human social life. Mine is not a typical story of evolution that describes the appearance of a particular life form in terms of its adaptive fitness relative to rival forms. Rather, it is a story that describes how a single feature of our species life—sex—makes the dynamics and forms of our social life.

Compounding the philosophical challenge before us are two further facts of evolution that uniquely frustrate accounts of our social life. One is reflective consciousness. Unlike the social life of most animals, which can be traced to thoughtless biochemical processes, our social life is complicated by our thinking about it. We live among symbols and meanings that sometimes matter to us as much as our importuning bodies. Another, related to the first, is individuality. Our thinking takes a life of its own—a life of mind. Thinking for ourselves, we live as individuals unbeholden to the group or species. Thus, our humanity is twofold, made of two distinct orders of life—one of the species and expressed in sexual biology, the other of the individual and expressed in the free and lively use of ideas. Where an individual life develops, it is an alternative to species life. Reflective consciousness and individuality mean that our social life is not the genetically coded action pattern of other animal species (compare bees, or fish, or birds), but instead a series of games played by partly self-motivated players. Our social life is wildly more various and extensive. We enact innumerable games in which players play innumerable roles.[3] This creates conflicts between species needs and individual wants that are unprecedented in the natural world.

We are the only animal to think about, question, and sometimes refuse biology.

These two further facts of evolution make it difficult to parse and reconcile the contributions of biology and culture to our social life. Our social life has *both* a biological aspect evolved over tens if not hundreds of millions of years *and* a cultural aspect evolved over perhaps the last 2 or 3 million years, mainly the last 100,000 years with the rise of language, and acutely in the last 3,000 years of Western civilization. It is silly to say social life is fixed in the genes and therefore not in our power to modify. It is no less silly to say social life is but a moment of culture and therefore completely in our power to modify. Such assertions make good copy and invite raucous controversy for those spoiling for a fight, but add little insight. In this book I describe human social life as a play of biology that echoes in culture. I begin with and emphasize biology because that is the part of social life most shortchanged in our thinking today.

## The Argument

This book builds upon two evolutionary principles, visible throughout the cosmos. One is *growth through differentiation* of form. Things grow by differentiation, by which the whole divides and disperses its activities to specializing parts, thereby enhancing its efficiency and welfare. A tree, for example, reaches as fully as possible into the sky above and ground below to take what it needs. An integral and balanced whole throughout, it grows by elaboration, as root divides from root, limb from limb, and branch from branch. The tree is the model *par excellence* of evolution—be it that culminating in the material diversity of the periodic table of elements, or the organic diversity of flora and fauna, or the psychic diversity of feeling and idea—which is why its image figures powerfully in our thinking about evolution. When we turn specifically to human evolution, we find sex an early and basic branching. The sexes are big limbs that divide the trunk of the species and that must balance to maintain the working integrity of the species. We should be grateful for the division and its differences. In division goes life—*viva la differance*.

A second evolutionary principle, related to the first, is *involution of the whole in parts*. Parts take on the character of the whole. This happens even while, and indeed because, parts branch from one another. In taking a definite place among the others, each part speaks for the whole. We tear a branch from a tree and find a model of the whole. The branch has its own life—it sprouts, grows, dies, and falls—but could not live but for its connection to the whole, on which it depends for root sustenance. In just this way, each of the sexes claims a separate existence and life while taking its place with its opposite in a sturdy unity of the species. As elementary divisions of the whole, the sexes require and anticipate each other. In each there is evidence of the other. In each there is a basis for the other. The sexes "know" how to relate because they have never not related. They "understand" one another at basic levels of design and function because they evolved as the design and function of a single organism.

These companion principles—of growth by differentiation and of involution of the whole in parts—attest to the main fact and *sine qua non* of evolution, that unity reigns throughout. From the big bang forward, from earliest cosmos to latest development of mind and culture, evolution has been one incomprehensibly massive detailing of the cosmos. Though we are pitifully imperfect observers, unable to keep hold of the whole, we can find it in the parts. In Wordsworth's wonderful turn of phrase, despite our murderous dissections, there is in each part always "a brooding presence of the whole."

I argue that sex—a fact far older than we—is the mainspring of our social life and the factor that tells us the most about its dynamics and forms. The basic forms of our social life—of female care of young, female mate choice, male competition and hierarchy, same-sex grouping, family, individual, and bureaucracy—enact a reproductive regime in which males come together to compete for access to females who come together to support male competition and to nurture young. Males scrap and claw to be superior in status hierarchies, but almost always according to rules of fair play known and abided by all. Females jostle for resources to conceive, harbor, give birth, nurse, and nurture offspring, usually while sharing responsibilities and load. Males enjoy the power of superior size and status-seeking ambition. Females enjoy the power of reproductive centrality and mate choice. Together the sexes define an unconscious logic of complementary capacities, orientations, and powers. This logic of sex, I argue, is also the logic of social life. Sex produces and reinforces social life, which redounds to produce and reinforce sex. Feminist critics of modern society are firmly put to say that men and women take their cues from an already formed social world. However, these critics are on shakier ground when they conclude on this basis that social arrangements are no more than cultured conventions.[4]

I state the argument that social life is sex boldly for two reasons. First, raised eyebrows invite conversation. Ideas advance by active questioning that airs differences. Second, putting the argument boldly makes clear the conditions for rejecting it. I make two testable claims: (1) sex is a precondition of human social life; and (2) the primary features of human social life—its dynamism and organization—are implied by the strategy and possibilities of sexual reproduction. Thus, regarding the first claim, where one sex is missing (as for example in homosexual communities, or in prisons, or during protracted separations of the sexes), or where the sexes are not differentiated, we should find either social disintegration or creation of substitute sexes to maintain social life. We should find homosexual males and homosexual females divided between recognizably masculine and feminine roles. We should find in prisons or during protracted separations that some males and some females take on (either by force or preference) personae and mannerisms of the opposite sex. And in groups that limit or minimize sex differences we should find a compensating fantasy life (in art, ritual, sport, fashion, perversion, and criminality) that preserves the idea, if not the active aspiration, of distinct and complementary sexes (e.g., a $15 billion cosmetic industry for women, a flourishing trade in violent sports among men, obviously sexed movie icons such as John Wayne and Audrey Hepburn). Regarding the second claim, we should find no basic feature or principle of social life that cannot be traced to sex. Thus, a seemingly neutral principle of organization, such as the economic division of labor described by Adam Smith and later by Emile Durkheim, expresses the dynamics of sex. This book confirms these expectations, and more besides. And finally, this book shows that the cumulativeness of evolution—the fact that new forms are built up from old forms—makes it unlikely that any future social life will fail to bear the impress of sex.

To be sure, the basics of my argument are not new. As the book makes clear, these basics appear in antiquity in the philosophy of Plato and mythology of Ovid and in modernity in the anthropology of Mead and soul music of James Brown. I claim no endorsement for the argument by these or any other writers. Indeed, certain elements of my argument come from feminists such as de Beauvoir and Firestone, from whom any endorsement would surely be a long time coming. Late in my writing, when the book was nearly complete, I came across a charming volume by Kenealy (1920) which startled me with a thesis close to the one I had been at pains to construct:

> *Natura simplex est*, said Newton, *et sibi semper consonans*. (Nature is simple and always agrees with herself.) Bewilderingly multiple in her phenomena, she is superbly simple in her principles. By the operation of her one great Law of Gravitation, she sustains the mighty Solar system—and brings the apple to the ground. By the extension, counterpoise and co-operation of one Primal Cosmic Energy—with its dual impulses, Centripetal and Centrifugal—she has generated all the diverse marvels of a Universe. And in view of her simplicity of Principle, it is conceivable that the Duality of Sex may be an extension into Life of that same principle of Duality which characterises the vaster Cosmic phenomena.

> If this be true, Man and Woman are the complex resultant of infinitely many and varied evolutionary differentiations and associations of the two modes of Primal Energy. If so, the principle of Sex must have existed before Matter; must have been inherent in Creation before Creation began to evolve. And if so, Evolution would seem to have had for its purpose the ever further and fuller manifestation of these dual and contrary inherences in terms of Life and Sex. While to judge by effects, it has had for its means such ever more intimate and intricate co-operations of these as have resulted in the progressively diverse and complex developments found to-day in Human Life and Human Sex-Characteristics. (P. 34)

Although I did not write this book with Kenealy's thesis in mind, with a few changes of terminology and an eye to extending it into the realm of social science, it can be read as a detailing of her thesis. I likewise find in sex a cosmic principle of duality, and likewise find in this duality the basics of social differentiation and organization. However, whereas Kenealy's aim was more political—to identify feminism as a basic threat to British society—my aim is more scientific—to describe how the sexes conspire to organize our lives together.

## Plan of the Book

The book is built around five chapters that describe four "moments" of human social life. These are not moments in a temporal sequence, but points in analyzing social life. I leave for another day the question of what if any sequence connects these moments. I present them in an order I hope will make my argument easiest to follow.

I begin in chapter 2 with the first moment of social life—*unity*. I show that the unity of species explains how species develop and profit from biological and cultural divisions. Species divisions and dynamics manifest and maintain an abiding unity. In chapter 3, I turn to a second moment of social life—*division*. Finding sex the primary division of our species, I link the intricate complementarities of human male and female bodies and minds to the demands put on our species to cope with circumstances of the Pleistocene era during which most of our species' evolution occurred. I note how these complementarities are evolved from a reproductive strategy that importantly includes sexual selection of males by females. Chapter 4 brings me to a third moment of social life—*play*. I define play broadly as the defining dynamic of life. Where there is a contest of opposites there is play and where there is play there is life. In this chapter, I identify sex as the main play of the species and thereby the principle basis of social life. In chapters 5 and 6, I describe the fourth and final moment of social life—*order*. I argue that our most basic social arrangements, including female mate choice, male contest, female care of young, sorority and fraternity, family, bureaucratic organization, and even the individual, are produced by the play of the sexes. Social order, I argue, is the hard shell left behind by the living play of sex. Chapter 5 presents a three-part theory of social order based on the play of the sexes. Chapter 6 supplies argument and evidence in support of this theory by showing how disruptions or distortions in the play of the sexes bring compensating changes in social order. I conclude in chapter 7 with a summary of the book's main points and with a few thoughts about directions for further inquiry and reflection.

# 2

# Unity

*"When studied narrowly in himself by anthropologists or jurists, man is a tiny, even shrinking creature. His over pronounced individuality conceals from our eyes the whole to which he belongs; as we look at him our minds incline to break nature up into pieces and to forget both its deep inter-relations and its measureless horizons: we incline to all that is bad in anthropocentrism. And it is this that still leads scientists to refuse to consider man as an object of scientific scrutiny except through his body."*
— *Teilhard de Chardin, 1959, p. 35*

### Dark Matter Mystery

The common is always obscure. As the fish would be last to discover water, we are last to discover the sea of sociality around us. We are tied to others everywhere all the time. Seated before my computer at the university I am wired to legions seated before theirs. Great libraries and data bases, records and reflections on all matters human, lie at fingers' beck. Marching my office walls are phalanx upon phalanx of book and journal, invitations all to the thought and feeling of others. A swivel of a chair finds photograph, painting, print, statue, and cartoon — soulful communiqués from inner worlds. To my right a desk clock leaps hash mark to hash mark, a reminder of who I am and where I am supposed to be. Next door are parallel societies, the same as mine only completely different. Across the hall, a living breathing secretary aids and abets my commerce with others, via meeting, correspondence, office appointments, telephone, fax, inter-office mail, and preparation of course materials. Floors below dozens of faculty and staff repeat the drill, while hundreds of students take in and challenge all that comes their way. Never mind the newspaper I glided over this morning, the lecture I will give this evening, the signs I will read driving home or the radio that will keep my company along the way. Why is our human life so saturated with others?

11

Our sociality is doubly impressive for its exquisite design. Human society is all complementarities and reciprocal differences, worked out in thorough detail. The mating pair divides male and female—in physique, psyche, function, and role—in a dance of life choreographed in evolutionary time. Family divides husband, wife, and child according to role, rights, and duties. Other groups divide leader and follower, and grade one another in shades of status. Work organizations divide functions and distinguish tasks in smallest detail. In Adam Smith's famous example, eighteenth-century pins were made in eighteen steps, each performed by different persons linked in a complex interdependence. Somehow, these intricate coordinations are brought off without a hitch—trains run nearly on time, food arrives fresh to market, power and water answer to a switch or knob, new products meet the demands for them, there are teachers for students, police for criminals, celebrities for the faceless, and politicians for the voiceless. Needs are filled, questions answered, problems solved. It is a dazzling fittingness. How does it happen?

The intricate coherence of social life puzzles because we lack the imagination to see it. Most of social science sees social life as a play of persons.[1] Persons are granted group-forming powers of social concern, attraction, and mutuality. Groups are analyzed as selfish persons linked by exchanges (cf. Homans, 1950; Gouldner, 1960; Blau, 1955; Thibaut & Kelley, 1959; March & Simon, 1958; Axelrod, 1984). Such a focus on persons led Hobbes (1651/1958) long ago to the idea that groups form as people seek a sovereign authority to avoid an otherwise inevitable nasty and brutish war of all against all. Economics today views groups similarly as expressions of individual interests. Arrow (1994, p.3) describes the view this way: "The individual in the economy or in the society is like the atom in chemistry; whatever happens can be described exhaustively in terms of the individuals involved." Individuals coalesce, interact, and organize to meet personal needs. The group, on this view, is a working out of personalities, a play of individual psychology. The focus on persons makes the group a derived fact, an agglomeration of other things rather than a thing itself.[2]

By seeing social life as a play of persons, social science cannot fathom its intricate coherence. There is nothing in individual will or activity to account for the integrity of the whole. The problem is not that social science is young and has not had time to develop its understanding. The problem is essential. Social life cannot be glimpsed in the motives and activities of persons. The limitations of this viewpoint appear in today's two leading theories of social life—sociobiology and complex systems theory. Neither theory describes how social life comes to have the forms it does; and this because neither theory supplies a definite concept of the social whole. These failings call for a book like this to broaden our view of social life.

*Sociobiology*

Sociobiology explains social life by natural selection. The idea, in broad stroke, is that where social behavior is an advantage in the struggle for existence, genes for such behavior multiply in a population (E. Wilson, 1975; Williams, 1975; Dawkins, 1989). According to E. Wilson (1975), social behavior enhances reproductive fitness of species in eight ways: increased defense against predators, increased competitive ability, increased feeding efficiency, penetration of new adaptive zones, increased reproductive efficiency, increased survival at birth, improved population stability, and modification of the environment. Where these enhancements are substantial enough not to be offset by advantages to asocial or antisocial behavior, species evolve a social life.

There is no reason to question sociobiology's axiom that social life evolved by natural selection. But there is reason question sociobiology's conception of social life and its theory of *how* social life evolved. Sociobiology conceives social life as individual altruism. Individuals behave altruistically when they act in ways that sacrifice their own reproductive fitness in favor of the reproductive fitness of others. Examples of altruism notoriously include extreme measures, of mothers who go without food so that their babies can eat, men who risk life in battle for their country, strangers who leap into frozen ponds to save a drowning child, and couples who defuse the population bomb by limiting their own offspring. But examples of altruism also include mundane courtesies, of the millions who give to charities, of even greater numbers who wait their turn in lines, put newcomers at ease with a smile, open doors for the elderly, whisper in theaters, apologize for mishaps, and bus their trays in cafeteria. For sociobiology, the puzzle is to explain how people can behave unselfishly when nature is supposed to reward them for maximizing their own welfare and, specifically, their own reproductive fitness. If individual reproductive interests were all, altruistic behavior should not survive in a population.

This puzzle of altruism has been answered three ways. The oldest answer, group selection, begins with Darwin. Darwin was perplexed by sterile castes of social insects, such as ants. Here are individuals who cannot reproduce and yet are allowed by natural selection. This led Darwin to suppose that the family can be the unit of natural selection if it brings reproductive advantages to its members. Where a family benefits from an individual trait such as sterility, that trait can be reproduced. Group selection was later formalized by Wright (1945), Williams & Williams (1957), Hamilton (1975), and recently by Sober & Wilson (1998) in mathematic models which identify conditions of group composition, group separation, and group mixing, under which altruistic behavior can evolve.

A second answer to the puzzle of altruism was suggested by Hamilton (1964) who found hidden reasons for altruistic behavior in the genes that individuals carry and promote. According to Hamilton, genes have a selfish interest to build and manage bodies that promote copies of themselves, *wherever they appear*. Where other bodies share the same genes, it can be to a gene's reproductive advantage to risk one body for the sake of another. This should be particularly the case for closely related kin such as a child, sibling, or cousin who are likely to share the same genes. Thus Hamilton predicted and found that altruistic behavior is more often directed toward relatives than toward strangers. In this "gene's eye" view, natural selection rewards not only the reproductive fitness of individuals, but more directly and inclusively, the reproductive fitness of genes distributed across individuals. This is natural selection by inclusive genetic fitness, or "kin selection."[3] This view of altruism rooted in inclusive genetic fitness has been trumpeted by Dawkins (1989) in his immensely popular writings on the selfish gene. According to Dawkins, because genes are the ultimate units replicated from one generation to the next, evolutionary theories of social life must focus on the gene, and particularly on the gene's selfish concerns to make copies of itself in future generations. Because natural selection deals in genes, not in the individuals who carry them, it can produce individuals who cooperate with kin that share their genes, to the point even of self-sacrificing altruism.

The third answer to the puzzle of altruism comes in Trivers' (1971) theory of reciprocal altruism, an idea that brings us full-circle to return altruistic behavior to individual self-interest. Trivers shows that what looks like individual self-sacrifice is actually individual self-promotion. Altruism, according to Trivers, is based upon a buried reciprocity in which help is given in the tacit and largely unconscious expectation that it will be returned sometime in the future. Thus a person dives into icy waters to save a stranger because it increases the likelihood that a similar favor will be returned. Multiplied in a population of interdependent persons, this reciprocity produces norms of helpful and cooperative behavior.

These answers to the puzzle of altruism explain social life by suggesting how social concern can evolve as an individual trait. These answers remove the most obvious objection to sociobiology that individual behavior is not always selfish. We now see how kindness toward others can evolve by natural selection operating on multiple levels, from the microscopic level of genes to the macroscopic level of groups.[4] But having explained how an individual trait of social concern can evolve, sociobiology poses a new puzzle: How does social life come of such an individual trait?

*Criticisms.* The central flaw in sociobiological reasoning about social life becomes clear as we press for details about how individual social concern makes social life. To put the flaw succinctly, no such details are offered, and no such details can be found. No arithmetic of individuals, not even of individuals concerned for one another, adds up to social life. In a phrase, you can't get there from here.

Sociobiology's failure to account for social life is revealed in its idea of the group. The group rarely appears, except in models of group selection. And where it appears, it lacks all integrity, wholeness, organism, feeling, and life. It does not look much like the groups of our daily experience—a family, a church group, and class in school, a romantic attachment, a work group, a nation. Even Sober & Wilson (1998), who have gone farthest to develop a unified theory of social evolution that combines genic-, individual- and group- level processes of natural selection, picture the group as an atomized collection of individuals. They define group as a set of individuals who influence each other's fitness with respect to a certain trait but do not influence the fitness of those outside the group with respect to that trait. They represent the group mathematically as the frequency of a certain individual trait. And they define group fitness as a function of this trait frequency. But this is not a real group, it is a mathematical construct. All real things are whole, they are more than a collection of parts. Wilson and Sober's group is precisely a collection of parts; of individuals and ultimately of genes.

Sociobiology cannot conceive of the group apart from individuals or genes because it starts with the idea that evolution is motivated and moved by the reproductive selfishness of individuals or genes. Regarded as a truism, reproductive selfishness is sociobiology's great unexamined assumption. It is arguably a myth. Recall that individual selfishness was the problem that theories of altruism were invented to answer. These theories tell us individual selfishness is not all, that there is room for individual altruism made by gene selfishness and/or by group selfishness. But having called individual selfishness into question, these theories invite us to question all selfishness. Why confine our doubts to one selfishness? Today, the strongest claim for reproductive selfishness is made on behalf of genes, which are supposed by the likes of Dawkins (1980) to be ruthlessly concerned for their legacy. But viewed closely, Dawkins' "selfish gene" seems more certainly mythical than the selfish individual it supplants. Selfishness is not a property genes can have. Genes do not operate alone, but only in collaboration with others. If a gene could selfishly put its interests ahead of those of other genes, it would doom the organism as surely as a similarly motivated combat soldier would doom his platoon in battle. Genes do matter in life, but not separately and not selfishly. Genes play out in *patterns over time* with innumerable other factors in the growth and development of the organism. These patterns over time, not particular genes, are more or less fit to conditions of life. And these patterns over time, not particular genes, are reproduced and confirmed in succeeding generations.[5]

This is not to deny that reproductive success by an individual or by a group means that certain protein complexes, genes, gene sequences, chromosomes, and genotypes survive into succeeding generations while others do not. Rather, it is to question whether these survivals explain social life. There is nothing new in the truism that people look or act this way in groups because genes for looking or acting this way are reproduced. We want to know why social life takes one form and not another, why social forms/groups have certain inner dynamics and not others, and how social forms/groups change over time. Claims that the forms of social life evolved from selfish individuals or genes sound like explanations, but they bring no understanding.[6] Lay aside the argument above that selfishness may not exist, we still want for a theory to describe the link between selfishness to social life.

*Complexity Theory*

Complexity theories of social life join sociobiology in the idea that complex wholes are made of and by simpler parts. It likewise describes social life as a composition of selfish parts. Individual actors, called agents, take selfish actions that coalesce to form a larger whole. And this theory likewise speaks of evolution. Social life, it says, emerges and develops through time.

The disarmingly simple idea that complex forms are born of simple parts has been invoked by biologists and social scientists to explain social behavior such as flocking birds, schooling fish, foraging bees, and even people in crowds (Yamori, 1998). Social forms such as a flock, school, hive, or crowd are described by rules for behavior followed by individual organisms. When there are sufficient numbers of organisms and they have sufficient time to interact, they enact regular patterns, such the graceful flying V of migrating geese or the nervous darting mass of minnows at a pond's edge, or a moving wave of football fans in a stadium.

Perhaps the best known and most influential application of complexity theory to human social life appears in a 1984 book entitled *The Evolution of Cooperation* by Robert Axelrod. Axelrod poses the Hobbesian puzzle of how cooperation can occur among selfishly motivated individuals. His solution to the puzzle comes in the fact that where many real world situations reward antagonistic behavior in the short run, they reward friendlier behavior in the long run. With the help of computer models of such mixed motive situations, Axelrod elucidated conditions under which benign cooperation emerges and crowds out antagonistic cooperation. Egoistic actors will be kind to others in games that continue into an indefinite future and in games where the long-term payoffs for being nice are greater than the long term payoffs for being mean. In a compelling illustration of this dynamic, Axelrod shows how live-and-let-live warfare emerged between English and German forces along battle-field trenches of World War I. Sworn enemies ostensibly dedicated to killing one another, German units and English units figured out ways to "cooperate" to limit aggression and injury. This cooperation took the form of deliberately shooting their rifles over each other's heads and by making their artillery salvos harmlessly predictable in time and location. In the hell of protracted trench warfare, they figured out how to make their lives longer and more bearable.[7] Axelrod shows how this is an example of a mixed motive game with an indefinite future where the long-term payoffs for being nice to one another exceed the long-term payoffs for being mean to one another.

Recent years have seen a merging of complexity theory and sociobiology. Models of complex systems are becoming more biological in flavor and design. In particular, the similarities between agents and genes in the etiology of structure and behavior is leading scientists to models of complex systems that incorporate features of genic variation and natural selection. In the case of Holland's (1992) genetic algorithm, for example, computers now simulate complex social systems that adapt to changing circumstances through variation and natural selection of agents. In a manner of speaking, agents become the genetic code of complex systems. Such models are offered with the hope that computer programs can someday look, act, and evolve like living things.

*Criticisms*: Complexity theory appears to answer the question left open by sociobiology; namely, "*How* are groups made by genetic elements?" In the principle that complex order emerges from simple actions taken by simple actors, complexity theory seems to promise missing mechanisms of social life. Indeed a number of scientists suggest that the two approaches be married to form a new science of evolution (see, e.g., Holland, 1992).

If only that were possible. Complexity theory is no more able to describe social life because it likewise lacks a definite conception of the group. Indeed, its main liability recalls that of sociobiology; namely its supposition that the group is a collection of individuals. Complexity theory purports to account for the group by rules that specify individual behavior. But a closer look at the rules finds otherwise. The rules presuppose the group they are invoked to explain. Typically the rules operate upon actors who are already grouped in time and space. And typically the rules apply to actors who are assumed to want to interact with others, who are assumed to know with whom to interact, and who are assumed to know how to interact. That is a lot of assuming. Taking Axelrod's (1984) simulation as an example, its rules apply to actors already locked into a mixed motive game in which their partners and their joint payoffs are already given by their place in the social landscape of the simulation. These rules do not make the group, they presume the group. Axelrod's simulation is not a story about the origins of cooperation as he says, it is a story of how a pre-existing cooperation changes over time (from being unfriendly to being friendly). In his example of live-and-let-live trench warfare, a cooperation of mutual assault is transformed into a cooperation of mutual care. The two instances are connected by a single social norm of tit-for-tat reciprocity. One good turn or one bad turn deserves another. Not in this case, nor in any other case I am aware of, do theories of complexity say how the social whole and its abiding norms come about. The group does not emerge *ex nihilo* from individual behavior.

Complexity theory's missing conception of the group appears as a lack of production values. The theory offers no way to distinguish real groups from mere patterns of individual activity. Models of complexity generate patterns of individual activity—a few that might be recognized in other settings or even in real life, most that would not. But models of complexity do not say, and indeed can not say, when a pattern of individual activity makes a greater entity or whole, that is, when it makes a group. The greater entity or whole must be read into a pattern by an observer who sees in it something more than individual activity.[8] Pushing the matter further, we find the idea of pattern itself a mystery. When does individual behavior make a pattern and when not? What justifies the article in the phrase "a pattern"? Pattern is a magical word that elides the distinction between part and whole, that assures us that parts add up to a whole. At one moment we see that parts make a pattern (here our eyes are on the parts). At another moment we see that a whole is made of a pattern (here our eyes are on the whole). We do not realize that in moving between the two we treat two different ways of seeing as if they are one. Parts do not make a whole, at least not without our unwitting help.

Thus we see in two leading theories of social life—sociobiology and complexity—a steadfast image of social life comprised of individuals. Both theories claim to reduce social life to individual life with no loss of understanding. I am hardly the first, and will not be the last, to point out that the individual-centered approach to the study of social life cannot succeed. Durkheim (1893/1933) made it plain long ago that there can be no accounting for the social whole in terms of individual parts. To interact at all people must already want and know how to get along with one another. They must already be socialized members of a civil society.[9] Arrow (1994) echoes the point, finding that economic models are founded on unanalyzed social wholes. The market that enables pricing and exchange is a social institution beyond individual design or choice. To these observations I add a commonsense one of my own. If social life were only individuals acting on their own behalf, it should look different. People should be more evenly distributed in space and time; a random walk of actors who collide, interact, and bounce away. There should be more similarity and more self-sufficiency. And although we might find some mixing to meet individual needs, there should be little and only accidental coherence. There should be indifference to association *per se*—a person could as easily be alone as in league with others. Certainly there should not be our actual togetherness and dependence on others, which on this account are gratuitous. How does it happen that we are always and everywhere together—on the road, on the train, bus, or airplane, in the café, theater, library, bar, classroom, shopping mall, or at home in the family kitchen? And why is solitary confinement the most feared punishment of all?

Social science faces a mystery similar to that facing astronomy today. Astronomy is baffled by the coherence of the visible universe. Its luminous elements do not have sufficient mass to account for their associations. Stars coalesce in galaxies and galaxies clump in textures and movements that are beyond current physics to explain. This has led to a fantastic postulate of non-luminous dark matter, coextensive with luminous matter, to explain the integrity of the cosmos. Calculations suggest that this as yet undiscovered dark matter may comprise upwards of 90 percent of the universe—a humbling if not chagrining realization for astronomers. Social science is, or should be, likewise baffled by the coherence of human society. Its obvious elements, persons, do not have the motivations or skills to account for their togetherness, let alone for their intricate patterns.  Perhaps it is not far-fetched to suppose that an analogous dark matter, beyond the visible spectrum of persons, accounts for human society.

## One Humanity

Our social life is not only or even primarily the multiplicity imagined by economists, sociobiologists, and complexity theorists.  More than that, it a living unity, an organism.  However, to see this we need to look at social life in a new way—with the new eyes that come of a fresh imagination.  In particular, we must let go the prejudices,  perhaps especially rife in the West, to see social life in terms of individuals.  We must let go the tendency to project our own valued individuality into the facts before us.  As a start to this end, I suggest a little thought experiment.  Imagine how our social life might look to an alien intelligence seeing it for the first time.  Looking us over, what would an alien intelligence see?

### What Alien Eyes Might See

To begin, let's acknowledge that unless a good deal more intelligent that we, an alien intelligence might also be amazed by the complexity of our social life.  Probably it would see few unexcepted principles of order and a greater number of general trends.  Almost certainly it would see things we cannot see, or at least things we do not ordinarily see clearly.  With a viewpoint unfettered by personal concerns, I imagine this alien intelligence would see more coherence and more organism in our social lives than we do.

First off, an alien intelligence would see that we are a single species made of many members.  Where we speak metaphorically and often hopefully of the family of man, an alien intelligence would see this as a literal truth.  Probably this intelligence would be less impressed with distinctions of race and ethnicity that matter to many people today and more impressed by the commonality across such distinctions.

Second, an alien intelligence would see that our species is divided into two body plans, corresponding to what we call male and female sexes.  These body plans serve complementary functions for the species: one oriented to adventure, group defense, and sexual initiative; the other oriented to mate choice, gestation, nurturing offspring, and making a home.  These body plans have different physiology and different needs.

Third, an alien intelligence would see that species members are often grouped in time and space according to body plan (sexes).  It would note that young males play together and young females play together—in nursery schools, on playgrounds, in games—and that these groupings are rarely breached.  It would note that this pattern continues, albeit with many more exceptions, into adulthood, as older males group in sporting contests, on expeditions, in construction crews, on the battlefield, in business and government organizations, while older females group in schools, nurseries, in community activities and services, in the home.  Grouped in such activities, males and females do different things—males competing with each other for status in formal hierarchies, bound by rules and by honor, and engaged in projects that reach outside the home into the larger world; females joined in support networks in domestic tasks of childcare and homemaking.  It would note that in addition to forming same sex groups, males and females form pair bonds, of varying intensity and length.  The pair bonds often result in sexual intercourse and in some cases yield offspring.  Where there are offspring they are almost always attended by adult females.

Fourth, an alien intelligence would see that much of the activity and life of the species is concerned in one way or another with the interplay of the two sexes and with the interplay of the different groupings they define.  Much of what males and females do is connected to the interests and activities of the sex-based groups they form.  Males and females face different demands from their same sex peers and from their opposite sex partners.  Indeed, social life consists largely in participating in and reconciling the demands of these two kinds of groups.

And finally, being perceptive, our alien intelligence would see cross-currents that add turbulence to the pattern above.  One cross-current is homosexual pair-bonding.  Homosexual males and homosexual females relate in ways that both resemble and differ from heterosexual males and heterosexual females.  Yet, even here, where its means and effects are inverted, sex remains an organizing principle.  A more important cross-current is formation of individual lives to rival the life of the species.  Certain persons, in certain parts of the world, in certain historical periods, march to their own drummer, according to private imperatives that are beyond the group.  Our alien intelligence would perhaps find it remarkable that these individual lives—a late and partial development of a few persons in a few areas of the world—are the main focus of human social science.

If there is a signal lesson to be taken from our alien informant it is this: that human nature is dual.  We are not simply individual lives connected by self-interest.  We are also parts of a species life defined by and animated by sex.  We are each an individual person, of distinctive mind and personality, *and* we are each part of a living species made of sex defined groups.  Nowhere in the animal kingdom are individual and species life so clearly bifurcated.  A social insect, for example, knows only the life of the species.  An ant does not act alone—it runs errands for the colony, its grocery list written in chemical markers.  By comparison, and to the chagrin of parents, schoolteachers, and social planners, we are not so regimented.  We also act on our own, on rival directives of personal will.

Langer (1962) introduces the concept of *individuation* to reckon with this duality.  Individuation is the extent to which the life of a species is fulfilled by its members.  The life of an unindividuated species is spread out among its members and comes into focus only when considering the species as a group or whole.  Langer (1962) gives the example of the honey bee.  Its life belongs principally to the colony.  The colony forages, the colony builds a nest, and the colony reproduces.  The individual bee can do none of these things.  It has a place in these activities that depends largely on its sex and size, but it has no say in how or when these activities occur.  The beehive, according to Langer, is no conspiracy of cooperating bees.  As bees lack the freedom and ability as individuals to behave any other way, they cannot choose to cooperate.  In contrast, the life of individuated species, such as our own, is concentrated more fully in its members.  To a degree unprecedented in the animal world, we take personal responsibility for the life of the stock.  We choose where and how to live and we choose whether and how to cooperate with others.

In her reflections on human nature, Langer (1962) emphasizes the individuated part of our nature (in particular our ability to think for ourselves) at the expense of the un-individuated part of our nature, perhaps because she was keen to emphasize fundamental differences between our social life and that of other animals.  Nevertheless, we are also an un-individuated species. We cannot reproduce alone. This fundamental business of the species is spread out over two physically distinct organisms, male and female. Thus our individuation is irremediably partial. Yes, we can decide many things in life for ourselves, about what to do and how to live (more than any other animal by far). But we cannot decide for ourselves to reproduce. We cannot decide to be attracted to the opposite sex and to be oriented (in one degree or another) to procreating and nurturing offspring. As an individual, I can act as I please. But as a male I cannot help but be attracted to females, be competitive with other males, or be tender to my children. I can be socialized to resist these impulses. I can even try to sublimate them in myself. But I cannot choose not to have them. When it comes to sex, there truly is a lesson in the birds and the bees.

We are both an individuated animal *and* an un-individuated animal. With individuation comes the question of how to divide life between self and group. We take part in two lives, distinct and interdependent. We play our part in vital group activities such as reproduction, food-gathering, and defense even while we break away to build a life of mind for ourselves. And to the degree we develop the latter we must be socialized to do our duty in the former.[10] Integration of these two lives is rarely perfect—the balance lopsided by too much or too little individuality.

Our social life is puzzling to think about because while it is divided along the two tracks of individual and species life, our thinking tends to follow one track or the other (indeed, it is characteristic of a track of thought that it does not announce or admit alternatives). How easy it is to forget that modern ideas of human nature are just that, modern ideas. We see the individual as a life apart from the species and, in a breathtaking denial of evolution, assume it has always been this way and could only be this way. We do not see that a substantial individual life is a late and contingent development of Western culture. More important, we do not see how the bedrock unity of the species makes possible and gives shape to individual life. We do not see how this bedrock unity keeps people working on behalf of the group instead of spinning-off into egocentrism.

In this book I emphasize the life of the species over the life of the individual. I do this not because species life is necessarily most important (though I believe it is), but because it is the life that most needs emphasizing in social science today. Too much theory centers on the individual and not enough on the social whole (Sandelands, 1998). Thus I dwell on the unity of the species, on the oneness that permits us to speak meaningfully of humankind. I show that focus on the species is necessary to understand how its division between male and female plays to bring order to social life. In this I follow Teilhard de Chardin (1959) who saw unity as a universal principle and the key to understanding all development, from the origin of the cosmos, through the onset of organic life, to the appearance of society and mind.[11]

*With Our Own Eyes*

It is one thing to suppose that a clear-eyed alien would see a species life to rival our individual life. It is another thing to substantiate this species life with evidence of our own. What is to say that there is such a life? To be sure, we cannot see a species like we can see a person. Mankind is one of those facts, like love or play, that we know without having anything to point to. Occasionally, we feel its shadows in the body (in our physiology, comportment, gesture, and expression), or we notice its reflections or echoes in collective action. In the pages remaining in this chapter I call attention to shadows, reflections, and echoes of our species unity. I note how this unity—our *humanity*—appears in feelings, forms, and symbols. I do not aim to make a comprehensive accounting, but only to make real the idea that our species is a form of life.

*Feeling.* We know the species—our kind—intuitively, in feelings. We feel it in the power of a crowd, the effervescence of a Pentecostal gathering, the anticipations of sexual union, the camaraderie of a well-functioning team, the community of a town ravaged by calamity, or the calm of a family gathered round an evening fire. We feel that we are not alone and that we are part of something greater than ourselves.

However familiar such feelings may be, they are notoriously difficult to comprehend. Without some "thing" to point to we despair of finding a respectable basis for them. Indeed, in doubting moments we can wonder whether these feelings are real (see, e.g., Allport, 1927). Almost defensively we disparage brotherhood as myth, crowd power as projection, and domestic bliss as wish. Of the last we may even ask, with the song, "what's love got to do with it?" And yet, at the same time, we doubt our doubts. The feeling of "we-ness" that warms us in a family or community or crowd is too familiar and too compelling to be a sentimental figment. In its embrace we do not just think there is a life greater than us, we are more sure of it than even ourselves.

Our difficulties with species feelings are compounded by an impoverished conceptual vocabulary. Words such as organization, group, community, and society convey little of the whole and its feeling, but more a cold multiplicity. We speak of an organization of work roles, a group of friends, a community of scientists, a society of elites. We have to go back to the ancient Greeks to find species feeling named, as Eros. Plato (1892), in the Phaedrus, defined "Eros" as love of the divine realized in love of others. The immortal soul flashes in others—in their beauty, truth, and good. Love emancipates the soul-stuff that gives life to our bodies, releasing it from its corporeal prison, and connecting it with the one Soul. Love, for Plato, whispers unity, whispers immortality. In our own day it is the agnostic Freud who sees in love a human unity. With his epochal idea of "libido," Freud claims the plenum of energies that spring from all that is comprised under the word "love," including "on the one hand self-love, and on the other, love for parents and children, friendship and love for humanity in general, and also devotion to concrete objects and to abstract ideas" (p. 28). That Freud saw love tending toward sexual expression may have upset his readers, but it does not upset his wider conception of love as "the power ... which holds together everything in the world" (p. 31).[12]

The feeling of oneness with others is doubtless universal, albeit bent and channeled by culture in myriad ways. In the ancient Pagan West and in the East today, this feeling was and is kept simple and impersonal. Humanity is a diffuse oneness, integral with nature. Persons are "members" of the body of humanity. In the early years of Christianity, this feeling was concentrated and projected upon a personified monotheistic God "who so loved the world that he gave his only begotten son." Based on the model of Christ's love for his people, love for humanity became love for other persons—to love one's neighbor as oneself. In a further development of European Christianity, brought in the twelfth century by the heretical Cathars of France, and made popular by touring Provençal troubadours, this neighborly love was distilled into romantic love for a single other (one's "true love") (see de Rougement, 1940). Today in the West, and particularly in the United States, romantic love increasingly takes the perverse guise of selfishness (see Lasch, 1979). Thus, what began as undifferentiated love of humankind (*Eros*), became love of persons (*Agape*), was then transmuted by Catharism to become love of a person (*Amour*), and has now (finally we suppose) reached its limit of concentration as love of self (*narcissism*). Humankind's basic love and original oneness has been parsed and particularized by culture. In the West especially it has been made strange and exceptional. Gone is the feeling of oneness, the basic love of kind. Love comes as a surprise, as something that befalls us (as if a disease or ill-wind), or as something we fall into (as if a pit or a bad way).

*Form.* Where there is a feeling there is a form—some "thing" felt. In literal terms, of course, all we ever feel is our own bodies. But perception is figurative; it reports not on the body but on "facts" pressing on the body from outside. Among these facts are the forms we call matter, life, and mind. As Teilhard de Chardin (1959) suggests, and Langer (1967) affirms, the cosmos is an integrated development of these forms. We know matter as it contacts and interacts with our physical bodies. We know life as a dynamism of matter, as a play of acts or forces. Life wiggles. And we know mind as a play of life. Mind wiggles smartly. Life and mind thus are not new things on the scene, but forms that have always been there to be discovered. As the cosmos grows more complex and dynamic, its physical, living, and mental forms show more clearly. Joining Teilhard de Chardin and Langer, I argue that we rely on feelings to tell us about all things. Some things seem physical objects; other things register as lives; and still other things impress as minds. Our humanity appears in all of these forms.

A virtue in this ecumenical idea of form is that it frees us to consider as real things we know to have life or mind, even if we do not know they have substance. We can speak of things that wiggle or even that wiggle smartly even when we cannot see or touch them. There may be many such things to be told. To wit, the field of physics is today baffled by atoms that somehow retain their integrity after having been split into constituent particles. In one recent report, nuclear protons split and separated by several miles remained "connected" in their behavior. The particles travel similar paths and make the same turns, as if aware of and alive to one another. Here is a living and mindful form never before physically confirmed. Likewise, the field of microbiology is today perplexed by the social behavior of bacteria. Studies find that bacteria, such as E. Coli, coordinate their actions as a group to defend against outside threats. They draw together into clumps in which bacteria on the outside shelter bacteria on the inside (Budrene & Berg, 1991). This surprising behavior by bacteria once thought solitary has elicited odd talk about group life and mind from reductionist biologists. Here again is a living and mindful form never before physically confirmed.

Turning to our own species, we likewise come to forms of group life and mind that we have a hard time confirming as physical objects. There are tantalizing hints, to be sure. One is the change that comes over a person when entering a group. Alone a person may be free, willful, and self-sufficient. But in a boisterous crowd, a close family, or a lover's embrace, he/she may lose shape and identity as a drop in a pond. No longer self-sufficient and self-directed, he takes the attitude and activity of the group as his own. The transformation can be for good or ill. It is there in the solidarity of prayer in church and combat unit in battle as well as in the atavistic conformities of fascism and angry mobs. The life and mind of the group appear as the independent life and mind of the individual disappear.

Then there are phenomena of social facilitation (Zajonc, 1965) in which basic life processes appear more plainly in groups than in individuals. Alone, an ant or termite makes few halting movements to build a nest. But joined with others the same ant or termite works dramatically harder to the same end. Alone, we eat a modest quantity of food. But joined with others, we eat dramatically more (here is a lesson for dieters). The same goes for arousal, activity level, sex, and aggressiveness. One gets the feeling our bodies belong more to the group than to ourselves and that we are most alive when gathered with others.

Or consider the special instances of identical twins and feral children. Identical twins are the closest of all human beings. Sprouting from a single seed, they develop from the same genetic blueprint and share an intimate gestation. This aboriginal unity remains over a lifetime. Identical twins are notoriously more concerned than other siblings to hold onto their connection—if not literally by constant companionship (which is not unusual), then symbolically by means such as dressing alike, sharing likes and dislikes, and even by choosing similar mates (who in a surprising number of cases are themselves twins). Connection is apparently sought and realized even by twins reared separately. Studies find even these "individuals" connected in numberless ways—sharing lifestyles, tastes for sound, color, hobbies, food, and mates.[13] We are reminded of the split atom, mentioned earlier.

At the opposite extreme are those unlucky children who, by unhappy circumstance of abandonment or neglect, grow up without substantial contact and connection with others. Among such cases are two that have been extensively studied and reported in the scientific literature: Victor, the Wild Boy of Aveyron, described by Itard, and Genie, a young woman of Temple City, CA, described by Rigler, Curtiss, and others (Rymer, 1993). Although these children are remarkable in many ways, their absent humanity impresses and disheartens most. Despite the best efforts of loving caretakers to reach and reform them, these children are cut-off irretrievably from the group. They cannot feel for others or even recognize in others feelings they have themselves. They act with other persons as they do with objects—with a cool curiosity about size, texture, and feel, and after a while, with remorseless indifference. What is more, and perhaps related, these children cannot formulate and use symbols in ways that are generative and productive. They can repeat words and associate them with objects, but cannot arrange words in meaningful syntax. They cannot make sentences. These last require a desire to communicate (to make one's feelings and ideas known to others) and a capacity for conversation and relationship. We learn from feral children, in yet another way, that our most human qualities—of empathy, affiliation, language—are not individual achievements, but makings of a social life with others. These are qualities of the species, not of individuals alone.

Occasionally, we discern outlines of the group in collective behavior. This is a point on which social animals vary considerably. Eusocial insects, such as the ant are densely massed in colonies of as many as 20,000,000, while the primate orangutan lives out its days alone and meets its opposite member only rarely in a sexual interlude. But these dramatic variations cannot obscure the unity characteristic of all animal species. Even the orangutan steps with its fellows. The adult male orang maintains a large territory in which one or more female orangutans reside. He knows this, she knows this, and both work to keep it that way. He and she move in concert. Even in this sparsest of animal societies, behavior cannot be understood apart from the group. For our own species, as for the orangutan, attraction not contact is the measure of unity. Just as contact with the earth does not mean that it attracts us more strongly than it attracts the orbiting moon (indeed, we know to the contrary that gravitation is a constant function of mass and distance), our contact with others does not mean that we are more strongly attracted to them than to orbiting others. As with gravity and the moon, where the rival force of angular momentum makes attraction and underlying unity harder to see, so the rival force of individuation makes our attraction and underlying species unity harder to see. Although we humans are a highly individuated species, our groups are not for that reason less unified.

Finally, there is growing evidence to indicate a physical substrate for species life and mind. Studies of brain anatomy and physiology point to a brain built for group life (Brothers, 1997). It now appears that the human brain is specifically designed to detect and respond to the sights and sounds of other people. Infants attend most closely to visual stimuli that look like faces (Goren, Sarty, and Wu, 1975). Primate studies point to specialized neurons that mediate between social situations and behavior (Brothers, 1995). These socially responsive neurons appear to have evolved to handle specific social stimuli such as hand and facial gestures, movements of others, and touch.[14] And, turning from anatomy to physiology, it now appears that two neural peptides—oxytocin and vasopressin—are substantially responsible for organizing and regulating group life, interestingly on what appears to be a sexual basis. Where these neural-peptides recruit and orient male energies to sexual initiative, competition, and communal defense, they turn female energies to sexual receptivity and maternal behavior. Across a range of mammalian species these neural peptides regulate recognition and memory for others, play, agonistic behavior, grooming, partner preferences, affiliation, and social influence.[15] Moreover, these processes are socially contingent. The neurophysiology of the male is controlled by co-present females and competing males, that of the female is controlled by co-present males, competing females, and suckling young. Social isolation depresses the level and functioning of these neural regulators in both sexes. Although we think of the brain as an individual organ, it is looking more and more like an organ of the species.

In sum, we are beginning to see that there are real forms to go with our real feelings of species life. These feelings and forms define a field for study that can yield new insights about social life. Yet with feelings and forms we continue to labor under the handicap of not having simple objects to study. What could be more vague than feeling or ideas of form? We need things to point to, things we can look at and talk about together.

*Symbol.* Langer (1976) points out that we are able to get along apart from others to the extent we are able to assuage our basic need for the group. We do this, she suggests, by inventing and using symbols of the group.

> With the overgrowth of mental functions in hominid phylogeny ... the need of contact between individuals, found in all degrees in various animals, undergoes a change from bodily contact to mental contact. Communion becomes an elaborate emotional need, in which the simple impulses to grooming, clinging or going to sleep in each other's arms are gradually replaced by symbolic collective acts ... the mental contact among the proto-human beings which displaces the constantly needed physical contact of gregarious simians is most readily made by celebration, dance, choric shouts and gestures, centering around some symbol of potency. By such acts all the participants are joined in one performance and feel themselves as one. (Pp. 302-303)

Following Langer, I exhort social scientists to find the group in the symbols people use to keep the vague feelings and forms of groups in mind (Sandelands, 1998). Symbols objectify the group. We see and feel the group in gestures, such as smile, wave, kiss, bow, threat, that express dynamics of social life, such as openness, approach, affection, deference, hostility. Occasionally, we see and feel the group in collective gestures of concerted movement and sound. These can be impressive tokens of unity. And they can be highly satisfying. One thinks, for example, of stadium chants or parades or protest marches or even funerals. These productions offer the pleasure of having inner feelings outwardly confirmed.

The clearest symbols of the group appear in art, which is made to reckon with feelings of social life. Compared to language, art fares better with the group because its live abstractions and all-at-once syntax of opposition and movement better fit the living form of the group. Group feelings are richly abstracted in ritual, religion, song, game, dance, myth, and poesy. We find them in Christian symbols of the church such as Christ, bible, and cross; in the rules of soccer;

in the enigmatic smile of Leonardo Da Vinci's Mona Lisa; in the figures and movements of a square dance; in John Lennon's and Paul McCartney's self-described "silly little love songs." These symbols represent the group by objectifying its feelings. With these symbols we have something to look at, point to, talk about, and savor together. We enjoy the boisterous songs of the tavern and repentant hymns of church because they make togetherness real. Art's main function (minding its expression as myth, ritual, play, and religion) is to express social unity by recapitulating its feelings in objective forms.

One of art's most compelling symbols of humankind is the body, particularly the female body. Ancient cultures built cosmologies around images of the female—no doubt because her body is most obviously involved in the life of the species. Goddess images were made to represent the world and all its parts. As we are all children of a flesh and blood mother, so too is everything else. Community is mother, world is mother, universe is mother. Even Christianity which, with the help of the ancient Hebrews, replaced Mother Nature with an abstract and distant male sky God (a God who made the world but resides in heaven), symbolizes the church with images of the female body. Echoing its origins in paganism, which everywhere celebrated the female body as an image of humankind, the biblical Gospel of Luke celebrated the virgin birth of Christ (and thereby the birth of us of us all) from Mother Mary. This is imagery of the birth of spirit from nature. We are all of mother and all of nature. The Virgin Mary is no ordinary Mary, but Mother Mary. Her body, like that of Christ, is a flesh and blood symbol of our human kind. Even more simply than Christ, whose life is the story and image of spiritual redemption through bodily suffering and death on the cross, Mary symbolizes in one person the birth of immortal life of spirit from a mortal body.

Christianity generalized the body image to include the male body, which in the figures of Christ and Adam became images of mankind as a whole. Writes Brown (1966, p. 83):

According to St. Thomas Aquinas, "many men are derived from Adam, as members of one body"—*tanguam membra unius corporis*; and, "the human race is to be considered as one body, which is called the mystical body, whose head is Christ himself, both with regard to the souls and with regard to the bodies"—*et quantum ad animas e quantum ad corpora*. The mystical body is not, because mystical, therefore nonbodily. And St. Augustine: "the whole human race which was to become Adam's posterity through the first woman, was present in the first man." "We all existed in that one man, since, taken together, we were the one man who fell into sin." Even as in Hebrew Adam is mankind in one; and the man Adam. "All mankind, whose life from Adam to the end of this world is as the life of one man."

## Brown (1966) continues:

And the resurrection is the resurrection of the body; but not the separate body of the individual, but the body of mankind as one body. The fall of man is the fall into division of the human race, the dismemberment of the first man, Adam; and the resurrection or rebirth through the second man, Christ, is to reconstitute the lost unity.

The social unity celebrated in religious symbols of body appears today in the irreligious precincts of modern psychoanalysis. Here Brown (1966, pp. 86-87) translates the Christian ideal of the one body (of Christ, of the church) into a goal of the modern secular religion of psychotherapy:

The goal of psychotherapy is psychic integration; but there is no integration of the separate individual. The individual is obtained by division; integration of the individual is a strictly self-contradictory enterprise, as becomes evident in the futile attempts of the therapists to define "what we mean by mental health" in the individual person.[16] ... The integration of the psyche is the integration of the human race, and the integration of the world with which we are inseparably connected. Only in one world can we be one.

But among psychoanalysts, Jung makes the most resonant claim for social unity. Jung sees the human race united by ancient and pervasive similarities in ways of feeling, thinking, and acting. Each person realizes in his/her own way psychic tendencies/faculties that belong to the species and that arose in its archaic past, presumably by evolution. These tendencies, he argues, make up the collective unconscious. According to Campbell (1973):

If it were possible to personify the unconscious, we might think of it as a collective human being combining the characteristics of both sexes, transcending youth and age, birth and death, and ... practically immortal. ... it would be exalted above all temporal change; ... it would be a dreamer of age-old dreams; and, owing to its immeasurable experience, an incomparable prognosticator. It would have lived countless times over again the life of the individual, the family, the tribe, and the nation, and it would possess a living sense of the rhythm of growth, flowering, and decay. (P. 12)

Thus we see the unity of the group in symbols of various kinds. I argue elsewhere, in Sandelands (1998), that the primary function of art in human culture is to produce symbols of the feelings and forms of group life. Through art, group feelings and forms which are otherwise difficult to see and talk about are rendered in objects or performances that can be seen and talked about. Through art, the group assures itself of its existence (a real symbol indicates a real group) and of its permanence (an enduring symbol indicates an enduring group). This explains the meaning and function of monumental symbols such as the Egyptian pyramids, Aztec burial mounds, the stone statues of Easter Island, or skyscrapers of today. And this explains the meaning and function of more modest symbols such as a totemic carving, a gemstone amulet, or a royal crown. Symbols thus join and corroborate intuitions of social unity in the scattered feelings and forms of group life described above. Among feeling, form, and symbol we have bare hints of the group, to be sure. But we have evidence enough to carry the supposition that the human group is a unity over and above the persons it includes.

## Unity and Order

I take unity to be a defining property of our species and indeed to be a defining property of all species. Animals cooperate in many of the basic tasks of life, such as foraging for food, defending the group, reproducing the species, and nurturing the young. These co-operations are species solutions to the struggle for existence. Thus it is common for species members to help one another and uncommon for them to kill or injure one another. I argue that altruism is not a puzzle of strangely motivated individuals, but an abiding principle of species life. Upon the species unity identified in this chapter, I build the central argument of this book that sex is the primary and most far reaching division of our own species and as such is the most far reaching basis of its life and order.

As I have shown, attempts to explain human social life are hampered by a reductive standpoint that finds its forms (of cooperation, mating pair, group) a reflection and negotiation of individual persons. In contrast, I see social life from the standpoint of the whole. In my view, the forms of social life carry the unity of social life forward through differentiation of parts. The mature elm tree is a marvel of balance and organization, all the more when we consider its humble origins as a seedling. It is a unity that has been massively differentiated and organized through time. This unity is truly mystifying if looked at from the standpoint of individual leaves. How could so many leaves come together around so many twigs, around so many branches, around such a well-balanced system of limbs, and all in respect to a single trunk?  We don't think to explain a tree by its leaves.  Why do we think to explain an equally differentiated human society by its individuals?  Unity is not evolution's achievement, but its precondition.  Unity is not for any theory of evolution to explain.  Unity has no ultimate explanation because it has no alternatives.  The best a theory of evolution can do is explain how a unity takes the form it does.[17]  In the chapters that follow I describe how the unity of the human species is organized on the basis of sex.

# 3

# Division

Life is made of integral divisions. A seed branches upward to find air and sun and downward to find water and nutrient. An embryo divides to articulate a body of blood, organ, vessel, nerve, bone, and muscle. The integrity of seed and embryo is not undermined by division but enriched by it. Growth comes by division of the whole. And so it goes with our social life, which likewise begins simply— as human unity—and likewise takes shape and life in division. The great division of humanity is sex—the branching of male and female.

## Again, Images

Sex divides the species. In the East, sex is Yin and Yang, the basic opposition of life. Female Yin is dark, cold, moist. Male Yang is light, warm, and dry. Together the two generate the phenomena of nature. Their duality is elegantly rendered in the ancient emblem of the T'ai-chi tu (the word meaning "the great map of the poles") (figure 3.1). In the West, sex is order and chaos, a duality epitomized in mythic Greek figures of Dionysius and Apollo that in many ways recapitulate the older Yin and Yang. Dionysius is chaos, impulse, feeling, and nature (dark, volatile, watery, indecisive). Apollo is order, idea, reason, and society (light, established, landed, resolute). As Paglia (1990) shows, these two figures pervade the traditions of Western literature and art.

Art captures sex in images we understand. Sex plays in myth, painting, music, and dance. Greek mythology is largely an explication of sex. In the tales put to pen by Ovid (see Hughes, 1997, for a fine English translation), males impress females while females preoccupy males. She lures him. He chases her. But she and he are

37

ambivalent prizes, too much to resist and too much to handle. She and he are drawn together in an explosive chemistry that produces children and all manner of other havoc.

Figure 3.1

Source: Arnheim, R. (1966). Toward a psychology of art. Berkeley, CA: University of California.

The Greeks identified the female with bounty, indeed with life itself. She is arbiter of life, who gives and takes away. Ceres, wife of Jupiter, was the first to split open the grassland with a ploughshare, first to plant corn and nurse harvests, first to give man laws. She is also the first to visit plague and pestilence, first to break ploughshares with her bare hands, and first to lay the fields barren by forbidding them to bear crops. The female is not a lesser power to be taken by the male, but an equal if not superior power to be wooed and won. Her sexuality is more considered and deliberate than his. Cyane, the fountain nymph of Sicily, sees tradition in her own case. Of her husband she says: "He did not carry me off in a violent passion. He never alarmed me. He was gentle. And after a courtship of prayers, I was willingly won" (Hughes, 1997, p. 53).

The Greeks identified the male with initiative and pursuit. His sexuality is visual and immediate. He rarely decides for love, but falls into it. Pluto comes across Proserpina in a glade: "In a sweep of a single glance he fell in love and snatched her away—Love pauses for nothing" (p. 52). Through their tales, the Greeks delineated the sexual paths of hero and fool. Evil Pluto snatches Proserpina (daughter of Jupiter and Ceres) to hell, only to have the fates divide her between hell's dark and the day's light. Arethusa's naked beauty beguiles the lusty river god Alphaeus who chases her madly across hill and dale, only to have his exertions stymied by goddess Diana who steps in, first to hide Arethusa in a shrouding mist, and later to divide Arethusa from Alphaeus by a gorge. A game and determined Peleus struggles to gain Thetis (daughter of Proteus), to succeed only by terrible efforts to hold her steady as she runs through her many hideous shapes and colors. Poor Actaeon the hunter was done in by the bad luck of stumbling across the naked goddess Diana in the wood. Taking vengeful offense, she changes him into a deer to be hunted and consumed by his own hunting party. An arrogant Hippomenes takes fleet Atalanta's challenge of a footrace, to win her horrible heart or to die. But having won the race with the help of love goddess Venus, he is turned by Venus into a beast for not showing sufficient gratitude. Good Pygmalion, living in a wasteland of hard-hearted women, imagines for himself the perfect woman sculpted in stone. Many devoted offerings, sacrifices, and prayers later, his fondest wish for life is answered by Venus who brings his cold statue to life. And then there are the naive or foolish who refuse the female. Young Hermaphroditus refused the water nymph Salmacis only to be overwhelmed by her suffocating attentions.[1] And Narcissus spurned the chattering Echo only to die a terrible death in self-reflection.

Sex is no less part of folk art today. As a case in point consider the American folk dance, the Virginia Reel, whose sexual imagery I described in an earlier work (see Sandelands, 1998). This three-part longways or square dance begins with a set defined by a line of men opposing a line of women partners (figure 3.2a, adapted from Mayo, 1948). The first part of the dance is performed by the head (first) and foot (last) couples and consists of a series of meetings at the center of the set alternating between the head gent (for gentleman) and foot lady and head lady and foot gent. These meetings take several forms, beginning with *greetings* (bow and curtsy), progressing to *balances* (movements forward and away), and then to *arm swings*, and ending with a *doe-si-doe*. The second part of the dance involves the entire group. It begins with the lead couple joining hands and sliding down the inside of the set and back. This is followed by the *reel* (figure 3.2b), in which lead couple join right arm in right arm and swing each other a half-turn clockwise. They then break and join left arm in left arm with the opposite sex member of the second couple and swing a half-turn counter-clockwise. These new couplings then break and the lead pair turn next to the opposite member of the third couple, join right arm in right arm, and swing a half-turn clockwise. This pattern continues down the line. Upon reaching the end and completing the reel, the head couple slides back up the set to their original positions. The third and final part of the dance is the *march* (figure 3.2c). Head gent and head lady lead their respective lines in backward arching circles that peel away from each other and bring the lead couple to the foot of the set, whereupon they form an arch with outstretched hands under which the trailing couples rejoin and pass on their way to forming a new set. This leaves the lead couple at the foot of the set and puts the second couple now at the head of the set. From here, the three parts of the dance (greetings, reel, march) are repeated until all couples have served in the role of head. The dance ends with all gents joining hands and all ladies joining hands and moving forward together to the center of the set to meet and honor their partner.

Here, in a simple dance, go powerful images of sex in social life. Consider first the dance's basic figures, which are basic figures of human social life. In the set of the dance there is a figure of the community as a whole, of two parallel lines joined in gaze. In the lines of gents and ladies there are figures of fraternity and sorority. And in varied couplings of gent and lady—the abiding partnership and momentary flings with others—there are figures of the reproductive pair. When dancing among these varied groups it is impossible to feel alone—one is included in many ways. Then there are the dance's exhilarating tensions, each distinctively felt, of which I emphasize three. First, there is the opposition of male and female that appears in the many ambivalent contacts between them—of gaze, greeting, circling, doe-si-doe, promenade, and bridge formed over others. These contacts announce complementarity and attraction,

## Figure 3.2

Source: Mavo, M. (1948) The American square dance. New York:Sentinel, (figs 50, 51, 52 53)

as boy and girl meet.  But they also proclaim difference and repulsion, as boy and girl wander apart with other places to go, things to do, people to see.  Male and female meet, orbit briefly, and then fly away.  They meet as if drawn together, they break off as if to answer other voices, particularly those of their respective fraternal and sororal groups.  It is an old story between the sexes, a bittersweet opposition—happy and sad, lustful and disgusted, forgiving and vengeful, dynamic and  stable, riven by resentment and transcended by love.  Second, there are tensions between and among the groups defined by sex, particularly between the pair and  fraternal/sororal groups.  When the sexes pair off they stand against the men's and women's groups from which they came and against the community as a whole (Freud, 1922/1959).  This tension is symbolized at the start by the line-up of men facing a line-up of women.  Brothers together, sisters together, each group fixed on the other.  One imagines that if the two lines were pulled just a little farther apart, or if the male and female lines were packed just a little more tightly, there would be no dance at all—rather the standoff of a junior high sock hop with boys huddled on one side of the gym, girls on the other, separated by incomprehensible distance.  This tension is symbolized also by the march, just after the reel.  Male and female groups turn their backs on each other for a moment to reclaim their solidarity in self-contained circles before relinquishing that solidarity as partners find one another for a promenade under the arch formed by the lead couple.  And this tension is symbolized in the closing of the dance, whereupon males join hands and females join hands and move as lines together to honor each other in the center of the set.  Here the connection of attraction between sexes is juxtaposed against the solidarity within sexes joined by hands.  These are brief and subtle moments, to be sure, but in their play of forms they evince a range of familiar feelings—of illicit pleasures of defiance in pairing, of resentment or envy toward those who thus defy the larger groups, of longing to return from the pair bond to the group of men or group of women.[2]  And third, there is a tension between sexual monogamy and polygamy.  We see its symbol first in the opening movements of the dance as head and foot couples exchange partners for a series of greetings (a series whose stylized movements go from a  distant bow and curtsy, to face-to-face approaches, to a dallying swing, and finally to a doe-si-doe) that allegorize sexual intercourse.  We see it later in the reel as head gent and head lady alternately dally with opposite-sexed members of other pairs and with each other.  These exciting moments of feigned infidelity lend interest and value to the partnership, somewhat in the way flirting does.[3]  The dance is a game played with sexuality, all in good fun.  The dance, unlike real life, ends safely by resolutely honoring partner.

These examples of myth and dance portray social life as a play of sex; as a play of the most basic division of the species.  This is their excitement, their charm, and their truth.  To be faithful to this truth of social life, social science must account for the play of sex.  It must see how sex brings life, form, and meaning to human experience, and how, by dividing the species, sex organizes the species.  And social science must do these things while avoiding two pitfalls.  First, it must make enough of sex to see how its division sparks and plays in social life.  It should not sacrifice sex differences at the altar of political equality.  And it should not be carried away with pseudo-scientific figments such as the rational individual or selfish-gene which have no sex.  Second, social science must not make so much of sex that it no longer sees how its manifold differences play together to define the species.  It should make no place for any male or female chauvinism that declares the sexes irreconcilable.  The sexes play as in a game, not as enemies sworn to victory, but as good sports interested in the play itself.

## A Singular Moment of One Long Story

Sex ranks with the great moments of natural history—with the earlier development of eucaryotic (nucleated) cells among procaryotic (non-nucleated) cells and with the later appearance of symbolic thinking in humans.[4]  Sex is both a noun and a verb.  As a noun, sex is a quality that distinguishes one half of the species from its other half.  Between male and female are natal differences of form and activity as well as engendered differences of feeling, belief, attitude, and behavior.  These differences make an exquisite complementarity.  As a verb, sex is an act that unites male and female parts in intercourse.  To have sex is both to be distinct (as male or female) and to overcome distinction.  The wisdom in the word "sex" comes in its pairing of division and unity and its pairing of substance and activity.  Sex differences potentiate sexual relations that reinforce sex differences.

Sex embodies the basic principle that life takes form and energy from division. In living things, division means polarity, tension, and dynamism. To survive, a divided whole must coordinate its parts. Where the whole is parsed and specialized its parts must be integrated. Where once went the solidarity of an unbroken whole now goes the solidarity of interdependent parts. Indeed, life is perhaps best defined by this living division. As we see the health of a tree in its branching and buds we see the health of our own species in its branching and buds, sex being a main branch with many buds.

The organic division of sex brings texture and nuance to species life. There are conflicts to be sure. Male and female lead different lives with different aims. Wilson (1975) describes sex (incorrectly) as a shearing force to be overcome in social evolution. Human bonds, he suggests, are formed between individuals in spite of sex and not because of it. Wilson finds that courtship mixes aggression and attraction and that intercourse overcomes antagonism at considerable expense of resources. But Wilson's sociobiology under plays sex's contribution to the solidarity and life of the species. According to Freud, all social attraction—all that can be subsumed under the heading of love—is born of the complementarities of sex. Sexual desire is an acute attraction. A great many other attractions arise as displacements, projections, or sublimations of intercourse. By dividing the interests and labors of the species between members, sex holds the species together by requiring members to work together to survive. With division of the whole comes adaptation of every part to every other part. Each has its place in the whole.

Still it must be asked, "Why sex?" Why a division of species into male and female parts? Sex has been explained by its effects on the number and diversity of forms. Sexual reproduction recombines genes to produce more varied genotypes—thus enhancing the species chances of adapting to unsteady or changing circumstances (Williams, 1975; Holland, 1992). Sex has also been explained by its role in selecting adapted phenotypes—thus providing the species a mechanism for matching genotypes to circumstances. This is the process of sexual selection described by Darwin whereby females consort preferentially with males they judge most fit.

More important than these explanations for sex, even if less emphasized by biologists, sex promotes adaptive social order (a point to which we will return with a vengeance in chapter 5). Along with the alien intelligence visited in chapter 2, we find groups of many kinds based on sex. Females act together—to play dolls or house in childhood, to coordinate estrous cycles, to bear and nurture children, to manage male sexual interest, and to reinforce male hierarchy. Males act together—to establish a status hierarchy, to muster sexual initiative in the face of frustrations, to venture from the home for resources, and to defend the group against enemies. And these sex groupings interact in varied ways to fit the species to its circumstances. We see this particularly as conditions of life change, as they did for our hominid ancestors some 3 to 4 million years ago when they left (or were driven from) the safer and more abundant biome of the forest for the more dangerous and hardscrabble biome of the savannah. Tiger (1969), among others, speculates that adaptation to this new life was enabled by a primate sexual organization that linked males in robust status hierarchies around a leader and that linked females in mutual tasks of childcare and mate selection. Males were pre-adapted to a new life that demanded collective hunting of other animals for food and collective defense of the group against predators. In the millions of years since the move to the savannah, male anatomy, physiology, and psychology evolved to specialize in concerted group activity. Females were likewise pre-adapted to a more complex social and material life that demanded more intensive care of young who needed more time to learn and grow into adult groups. In the intervening millions of years, female anatomy, physiology, and psychology evolved to specialize in protracted child rearing and education. Thus a social organization rooted in sex allowed our ancestors to leave the trees for the savannah and set in motion a path of development that culminated in modern *Homo sapiens*.

Of course, there can be gains in sexual division and social order only so long as the sexes maintain the integrity of species and particularly their capacity to reproduce. Sexual division comes with problems to solve. One is *attraction*—divided sexes must seek one another to combine. Another is *transportation*—divided sexes must surmount distances and barriers. A third is *selection*—divided sexes must find the best combinations. And a fourth is *support*—offspring must survive to reproduce. These problems may be best met on the model of two kinds of organisms; one to take primary (but not sole) responsibility for bridging distance and for overcoming boundaries, another to take primary (but not sole) responsibility for combining genes intelligently and making fruit of their union. Among mammals, where this model is generic, we call the one male and the other female.

The problems of reproduction (attraction, transportation, selection, and support) appear in virtually every detail of our own human lives—from the dance of sex cells at conception, to the impulses and movements of adult bodies in intercourse, to the folkways of courting and domesticity that underlie pair bonding and family life. In the moments leading to conception millions of sperm race a large distance for a small chance to be incorporated by the egg to fertilize it and set a life in motion. This story in microcosm—of male interest, activity, and contest and female attraction, discernment and nurturing—is paradigmatic. We see its elements in singles bars, on playing fields, in families, in political arenas, in business and commerce, in the arts. Crude but largely correct to say, in body and mind the male is essentially an elaborated sperm—he is designed for contest and courting, moved by hopes of being chosen, and in body and mind the female is essentially an elaborated egg—she is designed to have and hold, moved by the demand to choose well (Symons, 1979). To see only this much about the sexes is to understand a great deal about the social life they together define.[5] Theirs is a deep history of productive reciprocity that can be traced back millions of years. We may think sex a personal affair, or at most an intimacy of two, but its full measure is the social organization of the species.[6] Sexual desire is not simply an individual hankering, it is the will of the group.[7] The social world is based on sex, is for sex, and runs on sex.

## The Great Divide

There is no good way to tell the story of sex. The object-predicate syntax of language obliterates species unity and sexual mutuality by calling attention to the sexes singly. We refer now to the male and now to the female, but never to the two at once and never to the two as one. With this hazard in mind, I tell the story of sex as a story of the body, as a story of the ways female and male participate in species life and particularly in its central enterprise of reproduction. I observe that female and male play different parts—that it is more the female's part to choose suitors well and to care for offspring and that it is more the male's part to show off before females and to support and defend the group. It is a grandmother's argument, old-fashioned and familiar, but not wrong or less valuable to repeat for that reason. We think ourselves solo acts—individual and unbeholden. Our bodies know better.[8]

My argument forsakes many subtleties. Even while concentrating upon reproduction, I trace only the boldest lines of a rich and complicated story. There is more than one way to solve reproduction's problems of attraction, transportation, selection, and support. Depending on circumstances, female and male can exchange or even reverse parts, can substitute for one another, and/or can meet each other half way in sexless androgyny. And there is no simple way to parse female and male traits. Each sex has sensibilities and traits of the other (as indeed they must in order to understand and cooperate with one another). Thus, whereas females are most concerned with choosing well and taking care of children, they also do better by showing well. Attractive females have more options than unattractive females. And likewise, whereas males are most concerned with showing well, they also do better by showing warmth to females and children. It is not just in the movies that the sensitive male holds his own against more macho rivals.

And for the moment, my argument under-emphasizes collaboration within each sex. Males and females play their parts in groups. Males do their thing with other males. They gather to compete for status. Thus organized they move in concert in adventure, work, and defense of the group. Likewise females gather to manage male attention, to defend their mating prerogatives, and to reward male status. And they collaborate to mind the kids. In chapter 4, I show how males in groups and females in groups collaborate to meet basic needs of the species. There I make it clear that male character and female character are established not only by relations between male and female but also by relations among groups of males and among groups of females.

Finally, my argument offends modern ideas of progress and possibility. Advances in culture and technology make all but the simplest declarations about the sexes seem dated. Reproductive science brings choices about who has babies when and how. Women need not give up a life outside the home to carry and care for babies. Indeed, we can imagine a day when bearing and rearing children

are delegated to a cadre of reproductive workers.[9]  Machines elimi-
nate jobs better performed by one sex or the other.  Women work in
war machines while men tend household appliances.  All the while
mass media intrude upon privacy to rob us of the secrets and mysteries that intrigue the sexes.  It is tempting to think these changes
real and tending to interchangeable equality of the sexes.  But I argue that our bodies, which stand at the end of hundreds of millions
of years of life on earth, are not so pliable.  Modern ideas of progress
and possibility are wind-blown ripples at the river's surface.  Running more slowly are deep currents of the body that carve the hills
of social life.

*Female*

The female is called to choose suitors well and to bear and raise
children.  Though she may not always welcome these imperatives,
nature has built her to answer them.  Her body harbors the nutrient-
rich egg, of which she makes very few available to be fertilized in
her lifetime.  Once fertilized the egg consumes her body as the fetus
takes shape at her expense.  Even when pregnancy is deferred, she
is reminded of her biological destiny in monthly blood, bloat, and
cramp.  The female knows one tyranny of nature.  She knows what
it means to be dominated by the life of another person.  Some la-
ment this as unfair, seeing in the female body a limiting persecution
(e.g., de Beauvoir, 1952).  Others find compensation in this, seeing
in the female body a reproductive centrality of unshakeable meaning (e.g., Horney, 1967; Paglia, 1990).

That nature has built the female to care for young is obvious of a
body that makes and harbors nutrient rich eggs, that houses the complex machinery of gestation and childbirth, and that produces milk.
Throughout pregnancy, she and her offspring are identified as a single
protoplasm.  After parturition, she remains at the center as the locus
of milk and succor.  Her body responds to the infant in a way his
does not.  Bringing baby to breast initiates a distinctive physiology
mediated by neural hormones of oxytocin and vasopressin that lets
milk down, slows breathing and heart rate, and diverts body heat to
the chest (thus calming and comforting the child).  In the male these
same hormones regulate aggression.  Female physiology is supple-
mented by a powerful psychology that keeps her focused on child
and childcare.  Compared to the male, she is more child-entered

(Berman, 1980; Pryce, 1995; Whiting & Whiting, 1975), more sensitive to other's feelings and needs (Hoffman, 1977; Gilligan, 1982), more concerned to establish supportive relationships that bear on child rearing (Willingham & Cole, 1997; Geary, 1998), and perhaps for these reasons, better liked (Eagly, Mladinic & Otto, 1991). This psychology gets an early start in female play which is distinctively centered on childcare, romance, and sororal relationships (Erickson, 1963; Lever, 1972; Sachs, 1987).

In view of the female's substantial investments in reproduction, nature has also built her to choose sexual partners wisely (Hamilton, 1964). Her health and indeed that of the species depend on it. She is not so promiscuous as the male (Kinsey, 1953; Buss, 1994) and selects her consorts upon a more thorough evaluation of character (Daly & Wilson, 1983; Symons, 1979; Buss, 1994).[10]  Where he is happy to find any partner, she wants just the right partner. She looks for suitors with good genes to produce strong healthy children. And she looks for suitors willing and able to support her and the children through long vulnerable periods of gestation and child rearing. As these qualities of the male can be more or less hidden or feigned, she must find ways to discover them. Healthy genes may be gleaned from physical cues (e.g., energy, size, speed, strength, clear complexion, bright eyes, lustrous hair, body symmetry, an erection) or inferred from comportment (e.g., confidence, aggressiveness, ambition, personality, humor). Generous and reliable support may again be gleaned from physical cues (e.g., achievements, acquired and defended wealth) or they may be inferred from comportment (e.g., generosity, gift-giving, competitive zeal, undivided attention, interest in children). Given her need to choose wisely, and the difficulties of doing so, the female is a reluctant consort who responds to male urgencies only when she is ready. Nearly all of this femaleness is unconscious, most of it rooted in the body. She cannot help it that she is slower to attract and slower to arouse sexually (Kinsey, 1948, 1953; Symons, 1979). She cannot say why she is moved by the sustained attentions of males with energy and staying power (though these are clues to his vitality, reliability, and intentions).[11] And she cannot say how, through the machinery of orgasm, she "decides" whose sperm she will help along in the journey to fertilize the egg.[12]   What is true of sexual response and orgasm is true of courting generally. She must be wooed. The adage to make him wait is not only or merely a cultural precept, it is written into female biology.

Although the female could perhaps gauge the male on his individual merits, she does better to compare him against others to find the one who meets her needs best (Symons, 1979). Thus, she has an interest in staging and judging male contests. She wants males to show themselves as fully as possible in competition—ideally as many males as possible, ideally the best males possible, and ideally in competition for her alone. This brings out the flirt in females and rewards that coquettishness that males find irresistible and exasperating. Thus females have an abiding interest in male power and in the hierarchies that define and regulate it. The American diplomat, Henry Kissinger, is reputed to have said that power is the ultimate aphrodisiac. I take him at his word. Power indicates resourcefulness. The most powerful males are the winning males. They have the spoils of victory and presumably the wherewithal to garner more.[13]   And thus females compete with other females who are likewise oriented to the winners of male competitions. Where one monopolizes male attention others lose out. Females accommodate this competition by forming a social order of their own, akin to the male status hierarchy but less formal and rigid. It is a competition marked and shaped by painful understanding that female chances rest in part upon a time-limited youthfulness and attractiveness. Males compete for access to as many females as possible, though their struggle is most acute for the most attractive females. Females compete for the reliable and exclusive  attentions of the best males. The one contest is generic and mannered, focused on an abstract idea of winning and based on clear rules abided by all. The other contest is more particular and more ruthless, focused on a concrete prize and settled by whatever means necessary.

Perhaps our most compelling portrait of the female comes painted by psychoanalysis—that excessively disparaged school of depth psychology originating with Freud that traces the interplay of animal impulse (id), individual selfishness (ego), and conscience (superego) in individual life. In the dynamics of id, ego, and superego we can distinguish male and female patterns. The female psyche is dominated by instinctive concerns of the id for the welfare of offspring. Take away or harm her baby and you see a most fierce and ruthless passion. She is passionate too about sex, not only for its pleasure, which she takes in greater or lesser degree, but even more for its cementing of male-female pair bonds. The female develops an ego to support these instincts. She is selfish and deliberate about the resources and protections needed to bear and raise children. She is keen to mate a resourceful and generous and reliable male (Buss, 1986), to the point even of limiting her matings to secure his undivided attentions and resources. Her sexual jealousy centers on emotional rather than physical infidelity, her dread worry is that he and his resources could be lost to another (Buss, Larsen, Westen & Semmelroth, 1992). And because the female's place in species life is secured by her centrality in reproduction, her ego is less absorbed than is the male's with compensatory concerns for social status and hierarchical position (Mead, 1949; Gilligan, 1982). Compared to the male, she is not as much driven to distinguish herself from others. She does not work so hard to define her individuality. And she does not care so much about the social rules that define and regulate the social order (Freud, 1963; Gilligan, 1982; Chodorow, 1989). In Freud's terms, she does not develop a sharply differentiated ego and superego. The super-ego, according to Freud, develops from castration anxiety stemming from the Oedipal complex. Women, who do not have a penis to begin with, or a rival father to lop it off, and whose pre-Oedipal attachments to mother preclude a clear-cut Oedipal resolution, do not develop a super-ego of the same strength as men. Her super-ego, he wrote, is not "so inexorable, so impersonal, so independent of its emotional origins as we require it to be in men" (p. 182). Thus:

> Character traits which critics of every epoch have brought up against women—that they show less sense of justice than men, that they are less ready to submit to the great necessities of life, that they are often more influenced in their judgements by feelings of affection or hostility—all these would be amply accounted for by the modification in the formation of their super-ego which we have already inferred. (P. 182)

While not disputing Freud's conclusion about women's morality in relation to men's, feminist psychologists such as Gilligan (1982) and Chodorow (1989) finds its origins elsewhere, in the intimacies of maternal care. Throughout maternity, mother and daughter see themselves as alike and as continuous. This leads the mother to identify with her daughter and the daughter to identify with her mother. In contrast, throughout maternity mother and son realize their opposite sex and sooner or later realize their need to separate.

Thus, where a daughter's development means primary love and an empathic tie with mother, a son's development means separation from mother and defensive firming of ego boundaries. Compounded over years of development and reinforced by the ways of society this initial difference in mothering produces females more attuned to the experiences and needs of particular others and less impressed with abstract rules of society and males more attuned to social definitions of identity and status and less moved by the experiences and needs of particular others.[14]

Female nature is expressed fully in the young woman with an infant, when her physical and psychological capacities are most in play. Things change as she ages and especially as her children grow into independence. For the female, menopause and the empty nest are existential challenges not easily met by a biology geared for reproduction. Her body is for reproduction and melancholy is the day when that function is passed along to the next generation.[15] And it is perhaps an ambivalent consolation to the female that as her children mature their attachments trace a wider arc beyond her. Her unasked for liberation comes tinged with the resentment that others take her place. She needn't worry of course, for the others are always day trips. Attentions and affections always return to her. She is home base.

*Male*

While the female waits at the center of reproduction the male ventures in from the periphery. He has not the sober responsibilities of mate choice, pregnancy, and child rearing, but instead an unholy ambition to sire all the children if he could.[16] The male compensates for his smaller part in the biology of reproduction by taking a larger part in the social psychology of reproduction. He takes his place in species life through dominance contests with other males. Whereas purpose and meaning come to her as a birthright, they come to him by effort of ambition. Thus, the male knows a different tyranny of nature than the female. He knows what it is to have to win a place in a group and thereby to win a place in the arms of a receptive female.[17] He finds that always having to prove himself is both a freedom and a curse. He is free to earn his stripes in a wide world. In simple societies his stature may depend on who brings home the biggest game or who is the greatest warrior. In complex societies his position may be a broader question of who brings home the biggest paycheck or who achieves the most in his field of endeavor. Either way he is cursed by the insecurity that comes from the cold fact that he is always to be chosen. The un-chosen have no mates, leave no heirs, die without trace.[18]

Nature has built the male to impress and take initiative with females. To him fall the reproductive tasks of wooing the female, bridging the distance between them, and helping her with childcare. As part of this mandate, nature has also built the male to join other males in occasionally dangerous activities of hunt and group defense. He has the capacity and desire to divide and coordinate activities with other males. This is facilitated by a specific ability and inclination to take direction from a leader. Through submission to a leader, males concentrate energies in group action—such as to corral and mob a beast of prey or to repel an attacking enemy. Intelligent cooperation makes the human male a pack-hunting and pack-warring animal, able through group action to make up in willfulness and strength what he lacks individually.

The male part of species life calls for a particular physiology. The male must have the energy and focus and resolve to succeed in contests with other males on the one hand, and to hunt and defend the group on the other hand. He needs a physiology that concentrates attention and energy for narrow purposes and for short periods of time. He is helped by the hormone testosterone which recruits and projects energies outward and which spikes rapidly upward when confronted by a receptive female or by a prey or by an enemy (Archer, 1991; Booth, Shelley, Mazur, Tharp, & Kittok, 1989; Mazur & Booth, 1998; Mazur, Booth & Dabbs, 1992). This compares to a female physiology based on different hormones which orient attention and energies inward for mating, gestation, and care for young. Built for contest, the male is quicker to act (Moss, 1974; Goleman, 1996), more energetic (Maccoby & Jacklin, 1974), more aggressive (Moyer, 1974; Palmer & Tilley, 1995; White & Burton, 1988), more violent (Daly & Wilson, 1983; 1990; Wrangham & Peterson, 1996), and more likely to be exhausted when his furious energies are spent. He pays for his alert readiness to compete and for his rapid turns of energy with a more vulnerable, hazardous, and abbreviated life (Daly & Wilson, 1983).

What is most remarkable about male physiology is its modulation. To win the female the male needs to be vigilant, energetic, and persistent. But at the same time the male must measure his ardor in pursuit of the female. He must not hurt her and he must abide by the rules by respecting her prerogative to decide the issue (even if it means redoubling his efforts another day).[19] The male must likewise modulate his responses to other males in the group. Strange to say, in view of his outward aggressiveness, he must be civil. He competes with other males for access to females, but within bounds that keep male groups intact by not allowing them to become injurious or fatal. He fights rivals bitterly in the courtroom, boardroom, seminar hall, or sporting stadium, but afterwards joins them for drinks or perhaps a round of golf (a fact that confuses many females upon entering the male realm).[20] Males contest for status more intensely and playfully than females. He thinks winning is everything, but only if it comes fairly and by the rules (Lever, 1972).[21] Social hierarchy comes naturally to the male. Compared to the female, he takes more interest and is more active in hierarchy (Eagly & Karrau, 1991; Eagly et al., 1994; Goldberg, 1993). We see this in male hierarchies that are more ordered, more finely graded, and more stable than female hierarchies.[22] Male chivalry thus extends to men as to women. There is too much coincidence in these two patterns to think they evolved separately. Male behavior with males reflects male behavior with females. In both instances there is a game to play—a game with clear rules and coveted prize. It seems likely that sex and play grew up together, each in support of the other. The affinities between sex and play are the subject of chapter 4, to which we will turn shortly.

Again perhaps our most compelling picture of the male comes painted by psychoanalysis, where again we come to appreciate the depths of animal impulse (id), individual selfishness (ego), and conscience (superego). Where female psyche is dominated by concerns for offspring, male psyche is dominated by concerns for status and power, particularly as these relate to mating. In his heart of hearts he seeks priority, to be first among his fellows. Take away his position in the group or diminish his standing and he responds with aggressive violence. Even more interested in sex than the female, he is almost exclusively after its carnal pleasures. Thus the male develops an ego around and in support of his different instincts. He is selfish and deliberate about making a place in the world. He is attuned to his status and seeks constantly to establish his priority among rivals. Indeed, no contest is too small or too arcane if by it there is an opportunity to win status. He endeavors to overcome female sexual reticence, to the point of undertaking long energetic courting to win her favor. His sexual jealousy, contrary to hers, centers on physical rather than emotional infidelity (Buss, Larsen, Westen, & Semmelroth, 1992). He dreads being cuckolded and played a chump by devoting his energies and resources to the care and upbringing of another male's child (Symons, 1979). And finally, because the male must work alongside the very males with whom he competes for status and access to females, he needs a powerful superego with which to channel aggressive impulses in playful and constructive ways. Males pay for their developed superego in the guilty torments of failing to live up to its stern values (Freud, 1963; Gilligan, 1982; Chodorow, 1989).

Male nature is most fully expressed in the young bachelor in his physical and sexual prime. This is when his ambitions are most acute and his willingness and ability to compete are strongest. Like the female, he changes with age—as his hormones slow as he settles into a more or less monogamous domestic life. In middle or late life he may begin to question the unconscious premises upon which his youthful striving was based. With his instincts fading, he may wonder why he cared so much about the contests of the schoolyard, workplace, ball field, battlefield, and town meeting hall. He may even wonder why he worked so hard to get the girl. At first his wondering may come as a crisis, as doubts undercut life's meaning. Later he may find peace in seeing that it was his part to play the game and do his best. Freed of his old anxieties, he can perhaps begin to enjoy the spectacle of younger men at play. He is ever the warrior, but with age he sits wisely on the sidelines.

## Unity in Difference

To speak of female and male separately is to speak a few truths and a great many lies. To distinguish male and female is to deny their mutuality. Yes male and female differ, but in ways that answer and reinforce one another. His body complements hers. Her mind complements his. Male and female connect and interpenetrate completely. Their intricate sure fitted-ness is made amazing only by our reluctance to see it. The sexes do not break the species, they dance the species, in steps and figures that support and sustain the whole.

Thus it is not mere poetry to say the sexes complete each other. They are as sides of a coin. In male and female alike we see evidence of the whole in the part—each is an involution of the whole. We see this in basics of body and mind where the shape and workings of the female appear in the male and the shape and workings of the male appear in the female.

*One Body*

The match of male body to female body is so extensive and so exquisite that if we squint a little and think about them the right way, we see them as jigsaw parts of a single body, as parts of a species body. We know this body in our bones, in the ease and comfort of lovers' embraces. Or with a little imagination we can recall Aristophanes' mythical image from chapter 2 of an eight-limbed hermaphrodite.

The bodily unity of the species begins with the female and is completed with the male. The cytoplasmic egg in which life begins is female. The womb in which life takes shape is female. And the developing fetus is female, unless and until it is transformed by testosterone into a male. Male and female are conceived and nurtured in a female milieu. Against this backdrop, the male is a hero's journey of departure and reconciliation, a branching from and return to the female. Testicular hormonalization is one branching. Birth is another. Leaving mother and home for life in wider society is another still. Each branching comes with a return and with synthesis of differences. The male must stay in touch with the female for the species to prosper. Male and female participate differently in this story though with certain overlaps. Both are born of mother and so share in her femaleness. But females, having the body for it, take femaleness farther. Both likewise depart from mother (at birth, in forming an identity, in leaving home and family) and so share in common maleness. But males, again having the body for it, take maleness farther. Nature provides the differences that draw the sexes together and the similarities that enable them to relate.

The common origin of the sexes in the female ensures that their differences unite as complementarities. These complementarities begin early in gestation in the play of fetal hormones. The development of male testes, signaled by his Y-chromosome, increases serum testosterone at a critical point in the formation and development of the central nervous system. Fetal testosterone promotes earlier and more extensive development of brain structures (primarily the hypothalamus) which later mediate dominance behavior. The male develops a brain sensitive to hormones that call for dominance tendency on occasions of status competition or mating (Collaer & Hines, 1995). He is wired for contest with males and for pursuit of females. The female, who is undisturbed by this flood of testicular androgens, follows a different path to develop brain structures which later mediate pregnancy and childcare. She develops a brain sensitive to hormones that call for nurturing succor on occasions of a child's cry (Skuse, James & Bishop, 1997). She is wired to have, hold, and care for offspring.

Fetal testosterone thus sets male and female on different paths—their bodies to answer different concerns of the species. His taller and more muscled body is fit to hunt and defend the group from predators. Her smaller more adipose body is fit to gestation and nurturing. His explosive physiology is geared to concentration, focus, and pursuit. He is made to hunt, fight, and court. Her measured physiology is geared to receptivity, temperance, and constant support. She is made to judge, receive, and nurture. This complementarity serves a species need to allocate energies efficiently. Where male energy is consumed by larger size and greater strength, female energy is consumed by an elaborate reproductive apparatus. Male and female are different body plans for different roles in the group. Each is a specialization that contributes to the species whole. Although these two body plans and roles may not seem so important or valid today, looking more broadly over the many hundred thousand years of human existence it is hard to imagine a more salutary division of the species.

The bodily unity of the species is perhaps most apparent in the complementarities of sex. His body fits hers. His organs fit hers.[23] Where his external genitalia are built to project outward, to bridge distance, and to penetrate barriers, her internal genitalia are built to choose or refuse, to receive, and to accommodate. And his sexual responses differ from hers in a surprisingly effective answer to the species need to match pregnant females with supportive males. Where his sexuality is concentrated in the body and in time (he is aroused easily and quickly, often upon no more than distal visual cues, and orgasm for him is an explosive ejaculation), her sexuality is diffused in the body and in time (she is aroused more slowly and less easily, often upon more proximal and elaborate stimulations of scent, touch, and attentive foreplay, and orgasm for her comes as a series of waves extended over time). To be sure, the two seem mismatched, as females often do not reach orgasm before the male ejaculates and withdraws. But nature cares not for persons, but only for species. Female orgasm facilitates movement of sperm through the vaginal canal into the uterus where it can fertilize the egg. The female body delays orgasm, not to frustrate the female, but to favor the sperm of the fittest, most resourceful, most caring, and most reliable males. Healthy, symmetrical males with energy and staying power stand a better chance of impregnating the female.[24]

*One Mind*

Mind is the capacity to make and use symbols in communication with others. Mind is a double movement of sensation and ideation. Sensation comes of the body's contact with the world, as a resonance of the body with movements and forces acting upon it. Ideation comes of the brain's juxtaposition and processing of sensations. From the most crude to the most discerning, ideas arise as paired sensations whereby one stands for the other as its symbol. To lift a somewhat prosaic example from an earlier work (Sandelands, 1997, pp. 138-139), consider the idea of a cow.

> One way this idea might come about is by interaction of bodily sense and visual sense, where these two senses work together to define an experience of a cow as an object having certain properties. In this marriage of senses, the object-ness of the cow originates not as a received property of the actual cow but as a feeling of the perceiver's own body projected on his or her visual image of the cow. The perceiver knows his or her own body to be a real object by its constant interplay of outside impacts and inside impulses. The perceiver imparts this personal bodily feeling of object-ness, together with closely allied bodily feelings of weight, balance, symmetry, and vitality, to the cow by assimilating them to his or her visual experience. As Sheets-Johnstone (1990: 59) puts it, "vision is *impregnated* with tactile values." The result: the cow is known as a thing in the world because this is how the perceiver knows him-or herself. At the same time, and by the same token, visual sense imparts properties of shape, color, depth, and "out-there-ness" to body feelings, thus conferring on the cow properties it did not have before. This interleaving of sense experiences results in an idea of cow that is more than a visual percept and more than a kinesthetic percept. It is a compound that supervenes over the two (as table salt supervenes over the poisons sodium and chlorine). It is also an idea that begs for a name, such as "cow" (which is why language has the object-predicate structure that it has). Behind idea and name are two symbols: the body symbolizes vision by associated bodily awarenesses with what the eye sees, and the eye symbolizes bodily feeling by associating a visual image with what the body feels. Working together the senses comprise the alchemy of symbols we call mind.

This double movement of mind, of sensation and ideation, recapitulates the sexes. Sensation is essentially female; it is a taking of
the outside world into the body as feeling. Ideation is essentially
male; it is concentration and projection of feelings to create a symbol, to create an idea that transcends feeling. I hasten to add, however, that to identify sensation with female and ideation with male is
*not* to find females incapable of ideation and/or males incapable of
sensation. Rather, it is to suggest that this two-fold movement of the
mind—one part receptive sensation and one part projective ideation—
originated with bifurcation of species into receptive female and projective male. Actual minds take shape in whole human beings—in
males who are part female and in females who are part male. Mind
belongs to neither male nor female, it is of male *and* female together.

A close look at males and females finds that they participate differently in the two movements of mind. Born alike of a female
mother, they share in her receptive sensibility. To a varying degree
both are open and sensitive to the world about them and so have
feelings to think with and about. But here special advantage goes to
the female whose more finely featured and inwardly oriented body
develops sensation and feeling to a greater degree. She appreciates
more hues of sense and feeling over a wider range of intensities.
Where a male hears only the wail of a child's cry, she hears a plead-
ing insecurity. Her greater sensitivity shows up in responsiveness to
light touch, subtle postures, and verbal nuances. Her body better
answers the quiet importuning of an infant child, better understands
and empathizes with subtly communicated feelings of others, and
better executes the fine motor skills required in domestic life. Thus
we should not be surprised that compared to males, females are more
emotionally intelligent (Goleman, 1996; Golombok & Fivush, 1994),
more responsive to infant children (Sears, Rau & Alpert, 1965;
Berman, 1980; Hoffman, 1978), more skilled in language (Halpern,
1992; Maccoby, 1998; Hedges & Nowell, 1995; Hyde & Linn, 1988),
and more adept in fine motor tasks (Maccoby, 1998).

By the same token, both male and female leave mother to make a
life for themselves. Both separate from mother at birth and to varying degrees both form a personal identity and leave home for a wider
life in society. These departures depend on forming and enacting
ideas about the world and about the self in relation to it. To the
extent males and females share in these departures they are likely to

develop a similar ideational capacity. But here special advantage goes to the male whose focused energies and outwardly oriented body develops ideas to a greater degree. As noted above, ideas result from concentration and projection of feelings onto one another. Concentration and projection are capacities for which the male body was built. These show up in superior ability to control and coordinate large motor muscles (e.g., in running, throwing) (Maccoby & Jacklin, 1974; Isaac, 1992; Watson & Kimura, 1991). These show up also in superior ability to control and coordinate abstractions, particularly those involving objects and/or persons in space and time (Collaer & Hines, 1995; Hedges & Nowell, 1995; Jardine & Martin, 1983; Maccoby, 1998; Stumpf & Eliot, 1995).[25]

Paglia (1990) epitomizes the psychic difference between female and male with a "genital metaphor" which we now see is no mere metaphor. For Paglia this metaphor confirms the female as mysterious. Her hidden genitals are hard to fathom or imagine. With them she takes the world in and makes it her own. Her power comes by assimilation, by taking in what comes her way. And for Paglia this metaphor confirms the male as obvious and forthcoming. Through his plainly visible genitals he asserts himself in urination and erection. He projects himself outward to make a mark (in the snow, with the female, in sport, society, art, or philosophy). This metaphor was demonstrated strikingly a generation earlier in Erickson's studies of sex differences in children's use of space in play (see Erikson, 1963). Erikson gave pre-adolescent children a set of wooden blocks to play with upon a table. He found that boys erected structures, buildings, towers, streets and that girls used the play table as the interior of a house with simple, little, or no use of the blocks. Boys intruded on play space with elements of height, downfall, strong motion, and channelization. Girls included in play space elements of breadth, enclosure, and stasis. According to Erikson:

> It is clear by now that the spatial tendencies governing these constructions ... closely parallel the morphology of the sex organs: in the male, *external* organs, *erectable* and *intrusive* in character, *conducting* highly mobile sperm cells; *internal* organs in the female, with vestibular *access* leading to *statically expectant* ova. Does this reflect an acute and temporary emphasis on the modalities of the sexual organs owing to the experience of oncoming sexual maturation? My clinical judgement (and the brief study of the "dramatic productions" of college students) incline me to think that the dominance of genital modes over the modalities of spatial organization reflects a profound difference in the sense of space in the two sexes, even as sexual differentiation obviously provides the most decisive difference in the ground plan of the human body which, in turn, co-determines biological experience and social roles. (P. 106)

And regarding social roles Erikson continues:

A boy's tendency to picture outward and upward movement may, then, be only another expression of a general sense of obligation to prove himself strong and aggressive, mobile and independent in the world, and to achieve "high standing." The girls' representation of house interiors (which has a clear antecedent in their infantile play with dolls) would then mean that they are concentrating on the anticipated task of taking care of a home and of rearing children. (P. 106)

Female and male emphases of mind thus come as a division and specialization of orientation and expertise. They come also as a trade off. His ability to control and coordinate ideas in constructive thought is bought at the expense of her rooted feeling and intuitive responsiveness. She feels more and stays in better touch with feeling, he feels less and uses feelings to make ideas to think through. Thus, where he may be exasperated by her inability to put feelings aside to act thoughtfully, she may be appalled by his willingness to make plans that are coldly indifferent to her nuanced feelings. How often his calculations leave her doubtful and uneasy, and how often her feelings and vague intuitions leave him doubtful and unpersuaded?

The unity of mind made by the sexes is confirmed in the fact that ideas function effectively only if they accord with feelings. Just as male must stay in touch with female, ideas must stay in touch with feeling. This is the recipe for all worthwhile thinking. Thinking is productive when it works with and upon feeling. The best ideas name rich experiences. Thinking is unproductive either when it ventures too much or too little from feeling. The world's libraries are overstuffed with such misadventures—with castle worlds of pure theory and murky swamps of personal feeling. Intellectual genius in science, literature, or art is rare because it requires both male and female sensibilities that rarely share each other's company in one body.[26]

United in body, male and female are united in mind.[27] Ironically, the latter is perhaps easier to appreciate because there is not the same obvious separateness and outward difference of male and female bodies to get in the way. We have to do less squinting to see the unity of male and female in mind. Indeed, in the similarities and differences of actual male and female minds we can come to know the fundamental nature of mind as a property of the species. Through the sexes we see into the life of the species. We see that the differentiation and complementarity of male and female originates in their common origins in the mother and in their branching from mother. Sex begins with unity.

## Involution of the Whole in Parts

Male and female answer each other at every point. Each implies the other. Each is an image of the other. Each involves the whole. Sex confirms the biologic principle that as things grow by dividing into parts, the parts retain connection to each other and to the whole. We are back to our two evolutionary principles—growth by differentiation and involution of the whole in parts—that are touchstones of this book.

Ontogeny is often said to recapitulate phylogeny. The sexual division that appeared early and instrumentally in the development of the species appears early and instrumentally in the development of the person. The person grows as does the species, as a play of male and female elements. We see this particularly in the family. Life begins in the uterine, in the oneness of the female womb. Development is a series of awakenings and departures—of birth, selfhood, adult autonomy, death. Underlying this eventful series are two sex-typed principles: a principle of consolidation represented by mother, and a principle of adventure represented by father. Mother provides a constant signal of unity and unconditional acceptance. Hers is the body and face of the species. Development is partly a process of generalizing the species feeling of "mother" to other settings. Nature is mother, church is mother, college is mother (*Alma Mater*), nation is mother, corporation is mother. These are images of the species, images of unity. Against this backdrop, father supplies a constant signal of separateness and contingent acceptance. As rival for mother's time and affections, father teaches the child that mother does not belong to him/her. By playful roughhousing, father emphasizes the world's hard outside realities and the need to face them on one's own two feet. And by his example of venturing out from the home, father teaches the child a lesson about personal identity. Thus, development also is partly a process of generalizing the feeling of separateness of "father" to other settings. Striving is father, contest is father, achievement is father, measurement is father, time is father, contingent love is father. These are images of the individual, images of division. Together these female and male principles define what attachment theorists such as Bielby call a "secure attachment." Children secure in their attachments, who feel they have a safe home base, are free to venture out to play, to explore, to distinguish themselves from others.

As I've shown, nature assigns the role of "mother" to female and "father" to male. Because the female is directly involved, bodily involved, in conception, gestation, and nursing, she is in a better position to convey and maintain the feeling of oneness and unconditional acceptance. She is in many ways as attached to baby as baby is to her. She feels separations the male does not. Mothers know postpartum depression. Mothers cry on the first day of school when child first ventures from home, and on wedding day when child leaves home for good. And it is indeed possible to have a face that only a mother could love. By the same token, because the male is peripheral in the reproductive process, and in many ways cut off from baby, he is in better position to convey and maintain the idea of separateness and conditional acceptance. Knowing what it is to have to earn his place in species life, he is able to pass his wisdom about this to the child.

The idea that sex involutes the whole in parts is epitomized in psychic development. For all the differences between male and female bodies, minds, feelings, and behaviors, there is but one psychic structure divided between id, ego, and superego that is shared by male and female. As we've seen, this psyche is enacted differently by males and females—with the female more identified with the body and the reproductive project and thus more alive to the id, and with the male more identified with status contests played fairly in a cooperative group and thus more attuned to the cultivated strictures of super-ego. Where the female ego is concerned to regulate and direct an id dominated by reproductive instincts, the male ego is concerned mainly to intermediate between the civilizing strictures of superego and animal impulses for sex and aggression. In this way the species polarity of male and female is reproduced in the psychic polarity of superego and id. Psychic structure recapitulates social structure. Inverting Freud's classic theory of group psychology, which finds social structure to follow psychic structure, I argue the causality runs the other way to find psychic structure follows social structure.

That males and females develop along sex-typed lines—where boys learn and take on the part of father and girls learn and take on the part of mother—can be no surprise. Boys and girls take the places their bodies and their worlds make for them.[28] This surprises only young liberal-minded parents whose ideas of gender equality rule out sex-typing as morally and politically dangerous. But with or without help the daughter plays at consolidation—in circles, at home, with dolls, in mother role play (Thompson, 1936; Erickson, 1963; Maccoby & Jacklin, 1974). Her development means learning the ways of the female at home and in the larger society. She may venture out from the home, but she is not pressed to do so. She is born into her element and ambit. And with or without help, the son plays at contest, differentiation, hierarchy, adventure, exploration (Scheinfeld, 1943). His development means claiming an identity apart from mother and apart from home (Chodorow, 1989). Somewhere along the line, often in rituals of puberty, he faces the existential crisis of finding his place in the world.[29] Finally, we can note that sex differences wax and wane through the life course. Sex differences between toddlers at age three differ from those between sexually active adults at age twenty-three and again from those between mid-lifers at age forty-three and late-lifers at age sixty-three. Where little girls and boys hardly notice or care for each other, adult women and men notice and care for nothing else. Then, again, older women and men may feel toward one another somewhat as they did as kids, indifferent if not mildly contemptuous. Coupling in later years is perhaps more a vestige of a bond formed and maintained in middle adulthood than a fact of sexual attraction. It is the comfortable path worn by a couple of "old shoes." This age related variability in sexual differentiation carries the interesting and testable implication that sex effects on social life wax and wane over the life span. One imagines that the reproductive years of young and middle adulthood are most influential in organizing the species because these are the years when sex differences are most acute.

# 4

# Play

## Viva La Differance

With division of a whole comes a play of parts. And with division of a whole comes life—*viva la differance*. Division is play is life. Perhaps nowhere in nature is this identity of division, life, and play more true and more evident than in the species division of male and female.

In light moments we may say that sex makes the world go round, but rarely do we appreciate how near the truth we come. In the next several pages I sketch some of the world-turning dynamics of sex. I begin with the play of male and female with and against each other— the so-called "battle of the sexes." I, too, call it the battle of the sexes to emphasize its conflicts, stresses and strains, but do so reluctantly, hoping not to crowd out the mutuality, cooperation, and good fun that join the sexes in one species. I go on to describe the mating games that take place within each sex separately. I show that the play of men with men and the play of women with women arise as further expression and support of the play between the sexes. I sketch these world-turning dynamics of sex as a prelude to chapter 5 in which I show how the play of sex explains the order of our social life.

### Battle of the Sexes

There is a battle of sexes—a play of sexes—to the degree sexes divide the life of the species. Where there are clear divisions of responsibility between the sexes—that is, clear sex roles—there are clear lines between them they must negotiate and cross for the good of the species. We have already seen how the battle lines between the human male and female are drawn in distinctive bodies and responsibilities. The female takes tasks of reproduction with body and brain built to direct energy to make eggs, carry fetuses, and nurse infants at breast. The male accepts tasks of support and defense of the group with body and brain built to focus and project energy in concerted group action. Between the two runs an ancient play and an ancient *quid pro quo*.

The story of the human battle of the sexes is thus the story of human sex roles. It is a story of biology and a story of culture. Biologists explain human sex roles the same way they explain animal sex roles, by the demands posterity makes on males and females. Trivers (1972), for example, finds that interest in and care for offspring follows investment in offspring. In almost all species the female puts more into offspring than the male. This is especially and universally true of mammals where the female makes a nutrient-rich egg, harbors a demanding fetus through gestation, undergoes an effortful childbirth, and nurses an infant after parturition, while the male makes millions of sperm daily and takes little time and energy to pass them around. According to Trivers, because the female mammal does not get many chances to conceive, and because each conception demands so much from her, she secures her posterity best by providing for offspring until they can reproduce. In contrast, because there is virtually no limit to the number of chances the male has to conceive and because each conception demands so little from him, he secures his posterity best by mating as many partners as possible. He does best to love them and leave them, especially when he can rely on his consorts to care for offspring after he's gone. Diamond (1997) describes the sexes as locked in a game of "chicken" in which each sex wants to foist the burden of childcare onto the other. The game, he finds, is hardly fair. Having more to lose than the male, the female is in a poor position to call the male's bluff by leaving children for him or others to care for (which is not to say that females do not sometimes do this). Dealt the weaker hand, according to Diamond, she accepts the burdens of childcare and home making, while he plays his cards in the wider world.[1] Indeed, if the male sticks around at all it is because he might win additional opportunities to mate the female or because he can increase his chances of paternity by jealously guarding her from other suitors.[2]

For biologists the question is whither this pattern of parental investment? Why did females inherit most of the machinery of reproduction, and males the problem of competing for access to this machinery? These questions tend to a theory of the evolution of sex differences in paternal investment, beginning with the first instances of male and female in sexually reproducing species. In chapter 3, I speculated that anisogamy of sex cells is an efficient solution to reproductive imperatives of attraction, selection, transportation, and support.[3] I now speculate further, with rule-proving exceptions acknowledged, that anisogamy forecast developments leading to distinctive male and female bodies and distinctive male and female roles. Around a large, stationary, precious egg, nature built female animals to guard the interests of the egg through careful mate choice and to harbor and nurture the egg once fertilized. Female body and mind are evolved elements of species reproduction. Around innumerable, small, mobile, expendable sperm, nature built male animals to take initiative to compete with other male animals to spread sperm as widely as possible. No less than the female, male body and mind are evolved elements of species reproduction. These are mammalian adaptations to the exigencies of reproduction. To these adaptations humans add unique flourishes of cryptic ovulation, continuous sexuality, face-to-face copulation, and pronounced monogamy, which together promulgate long term pair bonds which provide offspring a longer period in which to mature to a substantial intelligence.

While the human battle of the sexes unfolds within this broad biological outline, to understand its particulars we must look at how biological tendencies are shaped by learning and culture. As Mead (1949) says, "we need to think vividly, and yet at a comfortable distance, of the way our bodies have learned throughout their lives, how to be male, how to be female" (p. 5). Such vivid thinking at a distance about actual bodies in actual societies calls for sensitive comparisons of societies, one against the other—ideally, comparisons of societies different enough from each other to indicate which aspects of sexual roles and behavior can vary between cultures and which cannot. For such comparisons we turn to our leading anthropologists who by lived experience and intensive study know what it is to be male and female in cultures different from their own.

Perhaps the most comprehensive and best known anthropological study of the battle of the sexes is Margaret Mead's *Male and*

*Female*, published in 1949. Against the example of Western culture in the United States, Mead contrasts seven South Sea peoples: the Samoans, the Manus of the Admiralty Islands, the mountain Arapesh, the cannibal Mundugumor of the Yuat River, the lake-dwelling Tchambuli, the Iatmul head-hunters of the Great Sepik River, and the Balinese. Mead's study anticipates key conclusions reached in this book about how sex functions in organizing human social life. She begins as we have, with biology, noting:

> The differences between the two sexes is one of the important conditions upon which we have built the many varieties of human culture that give human beings dignity and stature. In every known society, mankind has elaborated the biological division of labor into forms often very remotely related to the original biological differences that provided the original clues. (P. 7)

And Mead finds, as we will later, that sex differences define social life by how they either limit or enlarge ways of meeting basic necessities of life, particularly those associated with reproduction. The limits on the ways of life, according to Mead, have primarily to do with the structure and function of male and female bodies:

> Because we are mammals, and male and female mammals at that, we have limitations, and we must know them, provide for them, keep them safely in our habits, if not continuingly [sic] and boringly in our minds. There are certain things that men cannot do because they are men, and women cannot do because they are women: begetting, conceiving, carrying, bearing, and suckling the next generation are divided differently. As the bodies of the two sexes develop, to be ready for their different roles in reproduction, they have basic needs, some of which are shared, some of which are different even in little children. All through our lives, the fact that we are creatures who are made not only to be individuals, but to continue the human race, is a persistent, unavoidable condition that we must meet. (P. 20)

Factors enlarging our ways of life, according to Mead, have also to do with the structure and function of male and female bodies. Because of their specialized bodies, male and female have specific potentials that they develop in greater or lesser degree:

> What are the potentialities of sex differences? If men, just because they are men, find it harder to forget the immediate urgencies of sex than do women, what are the rewards of this more urgent remembering? If little boys have to meet and assimilate the early shock of knowing that they can never create a baby with the sureness and incontrovertibility that is a woman's birthright, how does this make them more creatively ambitious, as well as more dependent upon achievement? If little girls have a rhythm of growth which means that their own sex appears to them as initially less sure than their brothers, and so gives them a little false flick towards compensatory achievement that almost always dies down before the certainty of maternity, this probably does mean a limitation on their sense of ambition. (Pp. 20-21)

The central place of sex in human social life is apparent in Mead's South Pacific cultures; in part because the body itself is apparent among these often scantily clothed peoples.[4]    Mead finds surprising variation among these peoples in how the sexes relate to one another and to their offspring.  Among the gentle Arapesh, men cherish and dote on their wives, women protectively fuss over their children, and the two are joined in strong family units.  Among the hostile Mundugumor, men and women confront each other as hostile opponents, lovemaking is like the first round of a bruising prizefight, men in groups prey upon miserable neighboring bush peoples, and women treat infants harshly and disdainfully.  Among the unhurried and un-intense Samoans, men and women live harmoniously in large family units, sexual relations are relaxed and informal, infants are cared for generously by the mother together with all the women in the community, and older children are treated softly and tolerantly by both sexes.  Among the energetic and hard-working Manus, men and women measure love for each other and for their children in goods exchanged, sexual relations and sexual attraction are devalued, and sex roles are only slightly differentiated (both men and women are involved, albeit somewhat differently, in core religious and economic affairs).  Among the swaggering and macho Iatmul, men gather in men's houses that are strictly taboo to women, women treat infants harshly and somewhat distantly, boys who begin life passively and femininely are rudely broken from home and hearth and brought into the men's group by arduous initiation rights, sexual relations between men and women are active and vigorous to the point of contention (a woman might seduce a man by questioning his manhood or by assuming an attack-able posture).  Among the retiring Tchambuli, women are confident, stern, and matter of fact, while men are artistic, skittish and wary of others, women deal confidently and gaily with their children and together form a great solid mass of the house, always together working briskly, while men wear lovely ornaments, do the shopping, paint and dance.  And among the Balinese, an elaborately ordered and somewhat impersonal social life locates women and men precisely in time, space, and caste.  Men and women are not much segregated and not much differentiated except as men sometimes have their ceremonies and women have their counterparts of them.  Sexual relations are light and without enduring warmth, and marriages are expected not to be enjoyed.

This variation in how the sexes relate to each other affirms the plasticity of the battle of the sexes. But it also confirms regularities in this battle that we may guess to be universals. Most impressive to Mead is that women assume primary if not exclusive responsibility for the young. She points out that in no civilization are infant young cared for by educated and responsible men. Even among the Mundugumor, whose women are as fierce as their men, and whose women and men alike detest children, women accept responsibility for the young. In this regularity, in which infant and mother forge intimate relation, Mead finds sexual and social destiny. The infant boy's intimacy with mother brings realization of sexual complementarity (felt by mother and son) that sets in motion his long difficult development of differentiation from mother. From this the boy learns:

> that he must make an effort to enter the world of men, that his first act of differentiating himself from his mother, of realizing his own body as his and different from hers, must be continued into long years of effort—which may not succeed. He still carries his knowledge of child-birth as something that women can do, that his sister will be able to do, as a latent goad to some other type of achievement. He embarks on a long course of growth and practice, the outcome of which, if he sees it as not only being able to possess a woman but to become a father, is very uncertain. (P. 157)

In contrast, the infant girl's intimacy with mother enacts a common female pattern (felt by mother and daughter) that calls not for a dramatic break from mother but relaxed acceptance of herself as a female like mother. Thus, the little girl meets no such challenge as the boy:

> The taboos and the etiquette enjoined upon her are ways of protecting her already budding femininity from adult males. She learns to cross her legs, or tuck her heels under her, or sit with her legs parallel and close in. She is dressed to enclose her further against attack, against premature defloration. Implicit in the abundant rules that are laid upon her, the prohibitions against the freedom, the exhibitionism, the roaming and marauding, permitted to her brother, is the message "It might happen too soon. Wait." ... So in Iatmul, in Arapesh, in Mundugumor, in Tchambuli, the little boy puts on a G-string when he feels like it, but the girl has a grass skirt carefully tucked around her diminutive waist. And as adolescence approaches the prescient signs that surround the girl increase: chaperonage will increase in those societies which value virginity, approaches from older men will increase in boldness in those societies which do not. Upon the initial uncertainty of her final maternal role is built a rising curve of sureness, which is finally crowned—in primitive and simple societies, in which every woman marries—with childbearing, with an experience that is so real and so valid that only very few and very sick women who are bred in societies that have devalued maternity are able wholly to disavow it. So the life of the female starts and ends with sureness,

first with the simple identification with her mother, last with the sureness that that identification is true, and that she has made another human being. The period of doubt, of envy of her brother, is brief, and comes early, followed by the long years of sureness. (Pp. 157-8)

A second regularity in the battle of the sexes, not emphasized by Mead but evident in her study and which we will have reason to feature later, is that men organize into groups headed by a leader. Together in hierarchies, men hunt, make war, build, and produce art. Mead shows that men's groups differ in activity, differ in how far they go to exclude women, and differ in how much they swagger. But always they make some part of the world their own in which they can compete and achieve as men, apart from women. Even the passive men of Tchambuli gossip and make their beautiful art as a group. According to Mead (p. 160):

In every known human society, the male's need for achievement can be recognized. Men may cook or weave or dress dolls or hunt humming-birds, but if such activities are appropriate occupations of men, then the whole society, men and women alike, votes them as important. When the same occupations are performed by women, they are regarded as less important. In a great number of human societies, men's sureness of their sex role is tied up with their right, or ability, to practice some activity that women are not allowed to practice. Their maleness, in fact, has to be underwritten by preventing women from entering some field or performing some feat. Here may be found the relationship between maleness and pride.

Finally, we can go beyond Mead to note a third regularity in the battle of the sexes that Mead found characteristic of several of her South Pacific cultures but not of contemporary Western culture. This is an orientation to the female and to an idea of superior female power. Mead finds this orientation and idea manifest in cultures that ritualize and celebrate male initiation into the society of men.

The basic theme of the initiatory cult ... is that women, by virtue of their ability to make children, hold the secrets of life. Men's role is uncertain, undefined, and perhaps unnecessary. By a great effort man has hit upon a method of compensating himself for his basic inferiority. Equipped with various mysterious noise-making instruments, whose potency rests upon their actual forms being unknown to those who hear the sounds—that is, the women and children must never know that they are really bamboo flutes, or hollow logs, or bits of elliptic wood whirled on strings—they can get the male children away from the women, brand them as incomplete, and themselves turn boys into men. Women, it is true, make human beings, but only men can make men. (P. 103)

But Mead does not find this pattern in Occidental cultures which, she contends, think of woman as derivative of and inferior to man. She cites the Biblical story of creation wherein God makes woman from

Adam's rib as symbolic of Western woman's plight of unsuccessful striving to imitate man's superior powers and higher vocations.

I suggest that Mead is mistaken in her comparison; not about South Pacific cultures, but about Western culture. Western cultures also rely upon rituals of initiation to separate boys from women and home and mark their entrance into the society of men—think of religious rites of passage (e.g., the Jewish bar mitzvah), fraternity hazing, or basic training in the military. And it is no stretch to see in celebrations of male power and achievement in the West the same fantasy structure—not of the mystical power of a bamboo flute or bull-roarer, but of the mystical power of an awesome feat of engineering (a pyramid, skyscraper, aqueduct, suspension bridge, archway or channel tunnel), gaudy and noisy machines (which women are supposed not to understand), and great political, economic and military organizations (which are intended to exclude women). Perhaps these objects have the same existential motivation; namely, to assert a manhood on par with womanhood. The psychoanalyst, Horney (1967), comes to this very conclusion about her clinical observations of men, who she says are typically persecuted by a fear of being rejected and derided, and which she traces to a mortal dread of woman and woman's power. She writes: "Is not the tremendous strength in men of the impulse to creative work in every field precisely due to their feeling of playing a relatively small part in the creation of living beings, which constantly impels them to an overcompensation in achievement" (p. 61). The celebration of male achievement and male values, and corresponding deprecation of female achievement and females values, by both men and women in the West, she believers, reflects an unconscious resentment against women. Leaving aside psycho-dynamics, which many readers today may regard skeptically, there is, again, the biology of sex that puts woman at the center and relegates the male to the periphery. According to the anthropologist, Fox (1994), male dispensability is a basic principle of primate social organization. In a memorable phrase, and with a nod to Samuel Butler, he writes that "a male is the female's way of making more females" (p. 13).[5] That men in the West might share anxieties and compensating motives with men in the South Pacific has also been suggested by classicist Paglia (1990) who issued the bold claim that Western art and indeed all Western civilization is largely male protest against superior female power.

Thus, if Western cultures appear not to join South Pacific cultures in venerating the female and the idea of female superiority, perhaps it is because Western male protest and myth-making has succeeded too well—so well that women today join men in believing his myth of superiority.[6] That Mead herself may have misread Western culture is suggested by a later preface to her book, written in 1962, in which she wonders if today's Western societies give too much emphasis to female sensibilities and so leave men in trouble.

> At this moment in history, young males are in a particularly difficult spot, threatened with a world-wide catastrophe which no individual heroism can prevent and without new means to exercise their biologically given aggressive protectiveness or desire for individual bravery. The necessary virtues of the present age are essentially domestic virtues, virtues that have long been regarded as more appropriate for women—patience, endurance, steadfastness. It is essential that the tasks of the future should be so organized that as dying for one's country becomes unfeasible, taking risks for that which is loved may still be possible. Athletics provide only a partial answer. Possibly the exploration of space, the depths of the sea, and the center of the earth, will provide a more complete answer. (Pp. xxvi-xxvii)

All told, while details of the battle of the sexes vary from one society to another, the outline of the battle is universal. Females coalesce to care for children, secure in their place at the center of species life; males gather in hierarchies to support the group and thereby find meaning for their existence. Females seek the most resourceful and reliable males; males compete for access to females and especially to desirable females. Cultures differ principally in how sharply they draw the lines between the sexes, in how adults and particularly mothers care for children, and in how masculinity and femininity are expressed.[7]

In Western culture today our most vivid accounts of the battle of the sexes draw upon these age-old and universal themes, particularly as they appear in the content and workings of psyche and culture. I think here of psychoanalysts such as Freud, and Reik, existentialist and feminist writers such as de Beauvoir, and cultural critics such as Paglia. From such writers we learn that male psyche translates social hierarchy. The male superego represents the leader; the male ego represents an individual self; and the male id is unreconstructed animal nature. Psycho-dynamic conflicts are acute in the male for whom dominance and identity are preoccupying concerns. The male worries his existence and place in the life of the group in a way the female does not. By contrast, these writers tell us that female psyche translates nature. Because the female is less in-volved in social hierarchy (because more involved in nature) her psyche is less sharply divided by superego and ego and less riven by conflicts. She is more in tune with nature; her body and feelings follow nature's rhythms more closely—moon, month, menses (same word, same rhythm). She is attuned in body and spirit to others, especially so to children. Freud was insightfully male to ask "What do women want?"—so strange is the female psyche to a differently oriented male psyche.

These psychic differences reverberate in a social life that opposes male and female interests in a powerful complementarity. Simone de Beauvoir compares the roles and opportunities of males and fe-males this way:

> It might be said that before procreating, the male claims as his own the act that perpetu-ates the species, and in doing battle with his peers confirms the truth of his individuality. The species takes residence in the female and absorbs most of her individual life; the male on the contrary integrates the specific vital forces into his individual life. ... The male is thus permitted to express himself freely; the energy of the species is well integrated into his own living activity. On the contrary, the individuality of the female is opposed by the interest of the species; it is as if she were possessed by foreign forces—alienated. (1952; pp. 26-28)

Camille Paglia (1990) frames the battle of the sexes differently than de Beauvoir, seeing in it not a liberating freedom for the male and an oppressive burden for the female, but a secure basis of mean-ing for the female and an anxious existence for the male. Men, she claims, are driven by their vulnerability and self-doubts into a social life beyond woman, outside the home, into culture, to find a place for themselves for the good of the species.

> From the beginning of time, woman has seemed an uncanny being. Man honored but feared her. She was the black maw that had spat him forth and would devour him anew. Men, bonding together, invented culture as a defense against female nature. ... And from this defensive head magic has come the spectacular glory of male civilization, which has lifted woman with it.[8]

According to Paglia, sex is metaphysical and existential for men in a way it is not for women. Women have no problem to solve by sex. Physically and psychologically they are serenely self-contained. This, she suggests, is why men are attracted to women. Woman personifies nature (mother nature). She is home base, even and es-pecially for a symbolizing and nature-transcending man. Woman is also alluring in her mysterious unconcern for the things men live for.  Although she values them in the male, she does not herself go in for identity, ambition, competitive success.  Self- contained and self-sufficient, she is what the male dreams of becoming.  To the male this looks for all the world like self-confidence;  in fact it is nothing of the kind because it involves less selfness.[9]

The robustness of human sex roles and relations across cultures and times calls into question arguments that the battle of the sexes is un-biological and therefore open to reform.  Hrdy (1981), for example, offers primate comparisons to question the biology of human sex roles and relations, noting that whereas large sex differences in size and strength (sexual dimorphism) may dictate sex roles and relations among chimpanzee, gorilla, and baboon, there are no comparable sex differences in size and strength to dictate sex roles and relations among humans.[10]  She is joined by others, such as Dinnerstein (1976), who remind us that in today's world especially there are few things one sex can do that the other sex cannot.  As the feminist, Gloria Steinhem famously quipped:  "There are few jobs for which a penis or vagina are required."  And indeed, excepting childbearing and breast feeding, anthropology shows there are few tasks not somewhere performed both by men and women.  In view of the sexes' mostly equal abilities these authors conclude that the sexual division of labor and the battle of the sexes are not God-given, but reflect men's deliberate historical oppression of women.  We now see some of the ways this conclusion is mistaken.  First, while men and women do not differ in size and strength as much as males and females of other species, they do differ in other respects such as brain structure and function (see note 53) that may matter as much or more to the sexual division of roles and battle of the sexes.[11] Second, while there are few tasks such as childbearing, nursing, and perhaps hunting that are necessarily sex-typed by being built into male or female bodies, a great many others may be sex-typed in less direct ways without malice.  Although both sexes can cook a meal, or scout for a hunting party, or change a diaper, or sharpen a spear, these tasks may be claimed by one sex or the other because they are associated (in time, space, sequence, requirements, opportunity) with other tasks that are built into the body.  And third, conclusions about what sex roles and relations should be cannot be drawn from premises about what sex roles and relations can be.  Moral values cannot be deduced from theoretical possibilities.  To agree that a great many tasks *can* be performed equally well by both sexes, is not to agree that these tasks *should* be performed equally by both sexes. One can, with Mead (1949), question the wisdom of equality as it is usually defined because it means loss of difference.[12]   The sex differences in behavior and role that define the battle of the sexes, she points out, are valuable resources that a species sacrifices at its peril.[13]

## Mating Games

As male and female eye and circle one another they begin the dance we call mating.   In the hoe-down of conception, a female egg metaphorically "chooses" a partner sperm among the many that have jostled and raced for the "honor." By choosing, the egg puts sperm in play. The mating dance is less metaphorical in courting as women, and to a lesser degree men, decide who they will mate. By making a choice, a woman puts men in play (they too must jostle and race for her honor). And by making a choice, a man puts women in play for his attentions—although women do not play with the same passion and initiative. Mate choices by males and by females are key elements in the play of sex in social life.

*Male Competition.*   Male competition for access to females is a pervasive theme of animal life. The variations upon this theme rest with how females choose males. As she chooses more widely and with more various criteria, his competitions become more contingent and complex. The hens of a chicken coop, for example, await the scuffle of roosters for primacy in the pecking order, and in virtually all instances mate the winner. Chickens lead a simple social life, organized primarily by a single pecking order.  Compare the baboon, one of our close primate relatives.  While the baboon female mates preferentially with the dominant male, she also mates furtively with other males when opportunity and desire allow (though this can be a risky proposition).  More empowered than the hen, the baboon female chooses not only when to mate but whom to mate (Smuts, 1985).  And for this, baboon social life is richer and more complex.  Mating is again guided by dominance hierarchy, but is influenced also by cross-cutting relationships.  Male baboons need not win the contest to gain the female, it can be enough to be liked. This gives the males reason to dote on particular females and leads to what may reasonably be called "friendships" (Smuts, 1985).  Coming to our own kind there is further erosion of the male status contest and further gain in friendship as the basis of mating.  Women enjoy

more choice in mating. Excepting cases of matchmaking or concu-
binage, women rarely have their sexual partners dictated for them
(and even then they can risk the sanctions of infidelity[14]). Women
can wait in hopes of attracting a dominant man, who will be attractive to others, or they can decide for a less dominant but more reliable friend.[15] For men, who are left to wonder what women want,
there is a pay-off to being dominant (dominance still means a greater
number and variety of consorts), but there is also a pay-off to being
an attentive friend. Her choice, his dilemma.[16] Should he concentrate his energies on the fight to succeed, or should he stay home to
devote himself to his sweetheart?

Female mate choices are particularly powerful in defining the activity of human males, who collaborate in these choices by estab-
lishing status hierarchies for choosing winning men. The process
unfolds as a game in which men play for status under the cooperation of rules. That men may often play this game as an end in itself
does not upset the point that its origins are in mating. However, and
unlike in other species, women's choices compel men to compete
all the time. Woman's continuous sexual availability and cryptic
ovulation confound men with many more mating opportunities than
any single man could control, much less satisfy. Mating is thereby a
preoccupying concern for all men. Where there are ongoing contests for every woman, every man has at least a chance to win somewhere sometime and a reason to compete everywhere all the time.
And so we find men in contests at every level and in every corner of
society. In the classroom, boardroom, courtroom, or drawing room,
on the polo field, campaign trail, beach, drag strip, or dance floor,
come opportunities to show off and impress—venues to perhaps
win the girl. It is reasonably suggested that the innumerable contests of social life sprout mainly from the sturdy stalk of male competition for the female. High school boys in Texas play football on
Friday nights, gangsters in Russia fight authorities for economic
control, captains of industry angle in China for market share, brothers in Cairo shout across a backgammon board, sociologists debate
fine points of theory in the *American Journal of Sociology*, subway
motormen in New York City race their trains from the 33rd Street
Station to 42nd Street Times Square, and fathers in Ann Arbor on a
father-daughter canoe trip break into a race as they return to the
dock. Although such games may seem remote from the reproduc-

tive project, the ballplayer, politico, capitalist, sibling, sociologist, engineer, and father (and we might as well throw in philosopher, impressionist painter, bull-fighter, fisherman, rock star, and construction worker) want the same thing—to impress and win the girl. It is a common mistake to think the many forms of men's play frivolous and not part of the serious business of mating and making a life. Workplace, ball field, and bedroom differ mainly in the weight attached to the games' outcomes. We admit as much when using each as metaphor for the others. American boys brag of sexual exploits in a baseball vernacular of bases reached and scoring. Barely older boys prate of business exploits in football terms or yet again in sexual terms.   A close look at motivations in these instances induces a surprising conclusion about what is serious and what is not. Writes Shaw: "Men trifle with their business and their politics, but never trifle with their games. It brings truth home to them. They cannot pretend that they have won when they have lost, nor that they have made a magnificent drive when they foozled it. The Englishman is at his best on the links and at his worst in the Cabinet."

Darwin coined the term "sexual selection" to describe reproductive competition within sexes, particularly among males. Males that win female favor pass their winning ways to future generations— such as size, strength, dexterity, or intelligence. This dynamic operates more stringently through female choice of males than the other way around because the contest between males is more decisive (Symons, 1979). Males vary widely in their chances to reproduce (a few enjoy many chances, while many enjoy few chances), whereas females vary narrowly in their chances to reproduce (it is rare that a fertile female cannot find a willing male). Thus, sexual selection operates mainly upon male variation.[17]  Thus, too, there is greater change in male character with changes in circumstances over time. As male variability is more assiduously selected, male characteristics are more assiduously culled and reinforced through time. This may be a key to the origins of sex differences. Sex differences could arise as more highly selected males diverge from less highly selected females.

*Female Competition.*   Although female competition for mates is rare in animal life, it is an important dynamic of human life. Women also compete for men. Modern women go in for clothes and cosmetics and augmenting surgery as part of the age-old female arts of attraction and flirting. Women keep a watchful eye on rivals. Such contest evokes in women some of the same striving for supremacy as men, but the parallel runs only so far because the contests are about dramatically different things. Women compete for resources from men, not for access to men. A woman can easily gain sexual access to a man (she is rarely refused). What she cannot gain so readily is a man's undivided attention and commitment of support. For this more difficult prize, which he relinquishes grudgingly, she competes determinedly and unsparingly.

The distinctive character of women's contests for men reflects the particular game nature asks her to play. As noted in chapter 3, a woman has much to gain and much to lose by her mate choices. Her life and those of her children depend upon finding a winning man who can be a good and reliable provider. Hers is a high-stakes and, she hopes, one-time contest with other females. As economic theories of games show, this sort of contest does not invite cooperative norms among players because there is little prospect that a kindness extended today will be returned tomorrow (cf. Axelrod, 1984). A woman does best to put her reproductive interests before all others. Compare this to the man who invests little in reproduction (essentially the time and energy for intercourse), and therefore can mate more indiscriminately. He might care only about youth, a pretty face, and a large hip-to-waist ratio (and as Symons, 1979 notes, even these values are overrated). He is in a low-stakes repeating game with other males. Economic theories of games show that this sort of contest can produce friendly competition (Axelrod, 1984). One man can give way to another today expecting the favor returned tomorrow. Comparing her and his contests, hers is notoriously less cooperative and less playful in spirit. Where his contests are often well-defined rituals guided by clear rules to distinguish winner from loser, her contests are more conflict ridden and rarely guided by clear rules. He can be sporting because he plays for smaller stakes in repeating games. Indeed, he must be sporting because he has also to work alongside his rivals in group tasks of hunt and defense. She cannot be so compromising because she is after bigger stakes in a contest that may not be repeated. Moreover, she need not be so sporting with a particular rival because she need not work with her afterwards.

This pattern of male playfulness and female seriousness in mating is corroborated by a number of observed sex differences. One is that men are more interested in playful competition than women. From early age, males compete more in their play (Parke & Slaby, 1983; Scheinfeld, 1943; Symons, 1979; Whiting and Edwards, 1988) and enjoy it more (Charlesworth & Dzur, 1987; Pitcher & Shulz, 1983). Another is that males put more stock in the outcomes of their games (Mead, 1967; Goldberg, 1993). Males use these outcomes to define status in the group and thereby to allocate resources (Palmer & Tilley, 1995). A third, that has already been mentioned, is that males are more controlled and cooperative in games than females. They care more about how games are played and particularly about following rules (Piaget, 1932; Reik, 1957; Lever, 1972). Where male contests tend toward impersonal rituals—of sport, commerce, jurisprudence—female contests tend to get personalized and to stray beyond convention or rule (Reik, 1957).[18] Not infrequently, women's contests involve what Crick and Grotpeter (1995) call "relational aggression." Comparing girls and boys over several years time, Cairns et al. (1989) found girls more likely to retaliate against others in conflicts by saying "I won't be your friend anymore," by excluding the other from the group, or by spreading negative gossip about the other in an attempt to alienate the other's friends. The frequency of these tactics among girls increased sharply with age. These tactics were almost never used by boys. And in her 1972 study of boys and girls games, Lever found that while boys often argued in their games about the rules (about who did or did not do what), these arguments rarely ended a game. Girls' quarrels, however, regularly ended their games—often with one girl marching away saying she didn't want to play anymore (often adding that she wasn't talking to playmates anymore either). Thus where male contest tends to be impersonal and figurative, female contest tends to be personal and literal.[19]

## Sex is Play is Sex

Looking at mating choices and behaviors of men and women together we see how finely adapted they are to each other and how they interact to create a social life of nuance, intrigue, and moral tension. The man is torn by competing impulses. Should he seek the sexual variety that comes of competing successfully against other men? Or should he devote himself to one woman to make sure his genes, and not some other fellow's, make it into the next generation? The woman is likewise torn by competing impulses. Should she flirt with several men in hopes of sharpening the competition between them? Or should she commit to one man to command more fully his attention and resources to help with the children? As we've seen, women's and men's mating choices affect the behavior of men with men and women with women. And these mating choices bring us back to the battle of the sexes. Men and women are locked in a contest, each trying to make the best for themselves. Men seeking sexual variety in short-term matings may feign the respectable posture of men seeking a long-term commitment (i.e., they pretend to be completely absorbed and in it for the long haul). Knowing this about men, women minutely examine men's behavior for clues about his intentions (Buss, 1994). Conversely, and not to be outdone, women seeking both sexual variety and a committed partner may cuckold a regular partner by taking a lover. New evidence suggests that women's sexual desire evolved not only to foster competition among suitors, but also among sexual partners. Women are more likely to stray from their regular partner to take a lover when they are fertile, and women are more likely to reach orgasm with a lover than with a regular partner (Baker & Bellis, 1995). As if knowing this about women, men appear to have evolved answers to this challenge to their paternity by (1) formulating semen that contains a spermicide to deter passage of other male sperm in the vaginal canal, and (2) dramatically increasing sperm count and seminal volume upon return of an absent mate (as if to reclaim paternity by force) (Baker & Bellis, 1995).

The more nearly we examine the interaction of the sexes the more clearly we see the connection between sex and play. In each we see the other. Freud (1922) put sex first in his social psychology, seeing in social life a field day of sexual interests. Huizinga, put play first in his cultural anthropology, seeing sex as one of the main things played. In both instances the image of male contest and female choice is the basic motif of culture-making play. Young boys in the sandlot imagine a watchful crowd that cheers every success. The crowd is an unconscious image of the female (Brown, 1966). And young girls at play with Barbie dolls imagine a flight of eligible suitors with a single Prince Ken doll to win the day. The sex of grown men is writ large in spectator sports—especially in such gladiatorial sports as football or ice hockey. Winners stand erect, shout, beat their chests, and with wild eyes and open arms race around the field hugging and jumping all over one another. One imagines they race out for sex. Losers stoop diminished and cover their head to avert weeping eyes. One imagines they limp home to mates as to mothers, not for sex but for consolation. Could this be why men play competitive sports so fervently, unselfconsciously to themselves and amusingly to women (Tiger, 1999)? The sex of grown women is writ large in the theater. The stage play is about relationships, about how to get along, about tragedy and comedy, and in the end about domesticity as the fair maiden extends her hand finally to her ardent suitor. For the actors, the stage play is not a competition, but a collaboration. It is about mutual support, about being open to others while at the same time pressing for one's needs. Where sport masculinizes its players, theater feminizes its players.

Perhaps because his sexual excitement is more easily provoked, more clearly concentrated in the body, and more plainly visible, we are especially cognizant of the sexual aspects of competitive play in males. Chimpanzee males in dominance fights often sport erections (de Waal, 1989). Men on a ball field or in a boxing ring stand erect over fallen enemies. Men in the heat of war recognize its sexual passions. Here, for example, is Junger (quoted in Thewelweit, 1987) referring to the Nazi blitzkriegs of Eastern Europe in World War II:

... when blood whirled through the brain and pulsed through the veins as before a longed-for night of love, but far hotter and crazier. ... The baptism of fire! The air was so charged then with an overwhelming presence of men that every breath was intoxicating, that they could have cried without knowing why. Oh, hearts of men, that are capable of feeling this! (P. 59)

Competition, be it in the guise of sport or war, demands of males the same sense and impulses as sex (see chapter 3). Both competition and sex involve concentration and focused projection of energies. No surprise then that males engage intercourse as barely concealed battle. Male sexual initiative—to approach, to bite, to penetrate—is cousin to male dominance tendency. However temporarily, he seeks to dominate the female in somewhat the way he seeks to dominate his male rivals. He wants to be on top, to have his way, to be the one. That sex can turn rough, that sex can shade into a hyper-masculine sadism and a hyper-feminine masochism, underscores the parallel between sex and competition. This parallel suggests a common evolutionary basis for competition and sex in the male psyche.

There are parallels as well between female play and female sexuality.  Girls and women play in and at relationships.  In girls play of "dress-up" or "house" or "school," or in girls play with dolls, or in older women's shared confidences, we see rehearsals and affirmations of the woman's role in domestic affairs or in sexual relations.  Often the focus in these interludes is upon the woman's role as caretaker (e.g., as mother or teacher) or as object and judge of male interest and courting (e.g., as Cinderella-like princess).  Women's sexuality reflects her play as nurturer and receptive judge of male initiative.  There is both an urge to mother the male and a desire to be impressed by male power (May, 1980; Wilson, 1978).  Her sexual response comes in waves that build-up slowly upon tenderness but amass to consuming force.  Judging from female erotica and clinical report, her sexual fantasies often run to being overtaken by a powerful male who, although considerate enough to not pre-empt her choices, has urges that are nearly indomitable (Friday, 1973; Wilson, 1978).  She wants to be taken, but on her own terms.  Thus, her sexuality is not allied with competitive play but with an internal play between giving and receiving, between choosing and being taken.  Sex demands of her a different sensibility and a different range of impulses than does competition.  Where her sexuality diffuses energy to anticipate and receive, competition concentrates energy to act against.  Where her sexuality opens the senses to respond, competition closes down the senses to take aim.

Thus men and women are joined in an elaborate game which pits them against each other and which puts them in certain relations to others of their sex.  Theirs is a complicated play of a mildly promiscuous species in which both sexes seek sexual variety (though perhaps the male more than female) and at the same time seek a monogamous pair bond (though perhaps the female more than male).  In chapter 5, I show that this complicated play of the sexes is responsible for our species' unique social order and intelligence.  I show that we are the animal we are because we are sexed the way we are.

## Conclusion

"The play's the thing," wrote Shakespeare.  And so it is with a social life that turns out mainly to be a play of male and female.  This play of the sexes explains our unique evolution as the thinking primate, *Homo sapiens*. We alone have brought the play of sex to the pitch of consciousness, into realms of symbolic activity, into language, art, sport, philosophy, mathematics, and science. Compared to other animals, we play more intensely and variously. Where animal play consists mostly of mock fighting by immature males, our play ranges from flirting to foreplay, from fighting to fantasy, from galumphing to goal scoring. Bear cubs play at combat. Men in shorts run wooden courts in large arenas to see which group of them can put a ball through an orange hoop more times in a fixed period of time. Women in leotards stage a dance of Swan Lake.

We play so intensely because sex is always in the air. Females of other species move between clearly marked periods of sexual receptivity. Women are continuously interested in and available for intercourse. And even though women are like other animals in being only occasionally fertile, they do not advertise this fact to men through genital swellings or other body markings.[20] Her continuous sexuality and cryptic ovulation keep men's sexual interest high and complicate their striving. With all women available for intercourse nearly all the time, there is constant room and reason for contest. No single contest could abide for all women of the group. There are too many mating opportunities with too many women for any one man or few men to monopolize. Thus, where men may know the male animal's concern for dominance, it is a more preoccupying concern that can be expressed in many more ways. Male walruses pound at each other on the beach during the rutting season, men sport in the marketplace, court room, town hall, art museum, seminar room, and athletic arena all the time. By keeping men's sexual interest high, women also elicit more from them than dominance play and sexual initiative. They recruit their abiding attention, friendship even. A less dominant man who lavishes more attention on a woman may yet win her favor. Human sexiness thus encourages intimacy between male and female. Reinforcing this, both sexes gain by monogamous commitment, he a regular partner and paternal certainty, she a reliable breadwinner for the family. Among primates, long term pair bonds and family life are peculiarly human.

It is this last point in particular that accounts for why we have made so much more of the play of sex than other animals. Men invest more in the lives of women and in the lives of children than do males of other species. This brings a more leisurely childhood with greater opportunity to play and to develop intelligence. At the same time, women demand more of men than do females of any other mammalian species. They mate preferentially with men who show best in contests of various kinds. What may have begun in prehistory with a few contests of physical strength or hunting prowess has given way to all kinds of contests of physical, mental, social, political, and economic ability. With the more complex social life made by these factors has come greater intelligence among men and women. These factors, and no doubt others, combine to make a reinforcing spiral. Increases in intelligence lead to more elaborate social life with more elaborate contests of intelligence and thereby to selection by women of men with greater intelligence. The result: a primate species driven to heights of intelligence through the intensity of its play. Huizinga (1950) recognized this when he renamed our species *Homo ludens*, "man the player."

To be sure, calls to study sexual play in social life ring hollow without substantiating detail. What is meant by phrases "sexual play" and "social life"?[21] How are these ideas related? This chapter suggests that these ideas mean substantially the same thing, that each furnishes a substantiating image for the other, and that by considering the two ideas together we can bootstrap our way to understanding both. When we see social life as a play of sex we see the cooperative antagonism of male divided against female. And when we see the play of sex as the basis of social life we recognize the place of play in nature, not as a frivolity of a few mammals or primates, but as a basic dynamic of species growth and development. As this chapter shows, the indistinct concepts of play and life come into focus as we turn to sex, which exemplifies both.

It was Huizinga's (1950) great insight to see play, and particularly the competitive game, as the germ of social life and social organization. Human society everywhere is played, often as a thinly veiled game:

> The view we take in the following pages is that culture arises in the form of play, that it is played from the very beginning. Even those activities which aim at the immediate satisfaction of vital needs—hunting, for instance—tend, in archaic society, to take on the play-form. Social life is endued with supra-biological forms, in the shape of play, which enhance its value. It is through this playing that society expresses its interpretation of life and the world. By this we do not mean that play turns into culture, rather that in its earliest phases culture has the play-character, that it proceeds in the shape and mood of play. In the twin union of play and culture, play is primary. (P. 46)

Huizinga ranges broadly over the world's cultures to describe the games that make and maintain culture. In so-called "primitive" cultures there are simple contests of physical strength, hunt, and spiritual supplication. Some of these surprise, as for example the Kwakiutl potlatch in which tribal chiefs contest for moral and spiritual superiority through prodigious destruction of worldly possessions. In "advanced" cultures there are more elaborate contests of jurisprudence, politics, and commerce. Some of these surprise no less, as for example the Protestant ethic for capital accumulation or our thoroughly modern potlatch of conspicuous consumption. Across his many examples, Huizinga finds a unifying agonistic principle. Culture begins and unfolds, he says, as agonistic contests played according to rules. Where this is not apparent in the practices and institutions that surround us, it is only because their original play character has receded into the background. Some contests are ritualized and celebrated soberly as sacred. Other contests are crystallized to become the ways of artistic, intellectual, economic, judicial, and social life.

Huizinga's thinking about play in social life meets ours in the connection he draws between fundamental divisions in archaic societies and the life of those societies. I quote him at length as he comes squarely to the focus of this chapter on the play of sex in social life:

> Anthropology has shown with increasing clarity how social life in the archaic period normally rests on the antagonistic and antithetical structure of the community itself, and how the whole mental world of such a community corresponds to this profound dualism. We find traces of it everywhere. The tribe is divided into two opposing halves, called "phratria" by the anthropologist, which are separated by the strictest exogamy. ... The mutual relationship of the two tribal halves is one of contest and rivalry, but at the same time of reciprocal help and the rendering of friendly service. Together they enact, as it were, the public life of the tribe in a never-ending series precisely formulated and punctiliously performed. The dualism that sunders the two halves extends over their whole conceptual and imaginative world. Every creature, every thing has its place on one side or the other, so that the entire cosmos is framed in this classification (p. 53). ...

> Along with the tribal division goes the sexual division, which is likewise the expression of a cosmic duality as in the Chinese yin and yang, the female and male principle respectively. These, alternating and collaborating with one another, maintain the rhythm of life. According to some, the origin of this sexual dualism as a philosophical system is supposed to have lain in the actual division of the tribe into groups of youths and maidens, who met at the great seasonal festivities to court one another in ritual form with alternate song and dance. (P. 54)

With Huizinga we are reminded of the American folk dance described in chapter 3, the Virginia Reel. We saw then that this dance engages males and females in basic movements and forms of social life. With Huizinga we now see that this dance ritualizes the play and life of the group. To call it *recreation* is to name a truth. This dance recreates the play and life of the group for all to see and remember. And with Huizinga, we are confirmed in thinking that social life arises as play and takes the form of a game. Looking in the direction pointed by Huizinga, this chapter has shown that our social life is substantially a play of sex and that this play takes the form of games, both within and between sexes.

# 5

# Order

I have come some way to describe sex in social life. Upon the ground of species unity, I have shown that the sexes play in a living dialectic. Female and male meet as *thesis* and *antithesis* in search of *synthesis*. This living dialectic, unlike the logical dialectic described by Hegel, does not rest with synthesis, but lives on in a continuing opposition of male and female. Sex intrigues and charms with provisional syntheses, in a *détente* that slips and shifts with time and circumstance.

With the play of sex comes the social order of sex. Play and order relate as process and structure—one cannot be separated from the other. Just as there is no process without structure, there is no structure without process. Thus far I have spoken of sex as a process visible in the battle between the sexes and in mating games within the sexes. In this chapter, I speak of sex as a structure visible in relations between the sexes and in relations within the sexes. I call attention to and systematize elements of social order that have been implicit in the discussion so far. I show how sex plays to define the human social order.

## Elements of Order

Our social life would be an easier study if she sat still. We barely catch a glimpse of her in movements of mating, family, and community. The task of coming to know her is something like that faced by an art critic coming to know a work of art. The critic looks into a work to delineate basic elements or themes and to describe how they interact to make a living whole. To be sure, his/her description is never perfect—the elements and interactions are not the living whole, but a parsing of the whole for the purpose of understanding.

In the same way, we can look into social life to delineate basic elements and to describe how they interact to make a living whole. And in the same way, we can admit that our description is never more than an imperfect parsing of the whole for the purpose of understanding.

How does an art critic interpret a work of art? How and where to begin? In his analysis of Picasso's painting, *Guernica,* Arnheim (1962) begins at the beginning of Picasso's creative process to identify themes as they are introduced and elaborated in the work. This developmental view eliminates the need to discover themes under layers of elaboration in the finished work. It also gives a better view of the artist's intents as they are worked out in the finished piece. I look at social life the same way, beginning at the beginning with the earliest human societies known, the Pleistocene hunter-gatherer tribes of the African savannah. Doing so, I hope to discover themes, present in human life from the outset, today buried under layers of social complexity.

Strictly speaking, there can be no beginning at the beginning. At whatever point we mark the break between our species and hominid, primate, and mammalian ancestors, we have an animal with an already organized social life. Thus, I begin with elements of social order inherited from our mammalian ancestors. I call this the primary or zoological order of human social life. I then turn to consider distinctively human elements of social order that evolved with migration of our immediate hominid ancestors from the safety of trees to the dangers of open savannah. I call this the secondary or archaeological order of human social life. I end with elements of social order that appear variably in human cultures. I focus particularly on elements that appear prominently in Western civilization. I call this the tertiary or anthropological order of human social life.

Before getting to the elements of the human social order, I emphasize, again, the first and main fact of human social life; namely, the unity of the species. Our species, like every other, is grouped to begin with, and this makes possible all the forms of order we can discover. We can think of this unity, this essential group-ness, as the zero-order of human social life. Much has been made of the fact that human groups of prehistory were of a definite limited size; small bands of 50 to 200 members (Dunbar, 1993; Corporael & Baron, 1997). This much we can infer from archaeological finds. What we cannot so readily infer is the reason for this fact. I begin by supposing only the fact of group life. I leave for another day the question of how group size is determined, though I imagine that it has to do with the sexual forms to which I now turn.

*Primary Order*

I define primary social order as that prevailing at the origin of our species. Any meaningful story of human social life has to begin here, at the least. But as noted at the book's outset, the complete story reaches as far as the imagination—beyond the origins of the species, beyond the origins of life on earth, beyond the formation of the sun and planets, indeed all the way back to the origins of the cosmos. Though we cannot say how, the forms of our social life reflect the forms of life on earth which reflect the forms of the physical universe.

We are clearest about nearest history, about how our social life recapitulates that of our primate and mammal progenitors. From studies of mammals and primates we can identify three elements of primary order in human social life: female care of young, female mate choice, and male competition. These are the most profound elements of social organization—universal, refractory, and conserved by and through millions of years of mammalian and primate evolution. Written into the fiber of our being, these elements unite us with primates and confirm our place on the evolutionary tree. At the same time, and as we shall see, these elements are the bases for specifically human adaptations that distinguish us from other primates and mammals.

*Female Care of Young.* Most important is female care of young. The key to mammalian social life, wrote Wilson (1967), is milk. As simplifications go, this one keeps to truth better than most. Milk ties mother to infant offspring and orients the group to that tie. Among the mammals, primates are the most altricial; their young have the longest and most helpless immaturity requiring the most maternal care and protection. Among the primates, humans are the most altricial of all, and require the most maternal care of all. Milk also encourages females to share care for young. Among chimpanzees, for example, sharing takes the form of sub-adult females offering relief to nursing mothers by acting as temporary "baby-sitters." Or it takes the form of childless adult females playing the role of doting "aunt" to infants (de Waal, 1989). To this, our own species sometimes adds a helpful grandmother. Sharing the burden of infant care does more than make mother's life more bearable, it teaches immature females how to care for infants and provides an outlet for the maternal longings of unproductive or post-productive females. Researchers identify the female-infant group as the most basic and immutable fact of primate social life. Males swirl around and come and go. Females and infants are fixed at the center. Among humans, according to Mead (1949), female care of young is universal. In no known human society are mature males held responsible for care of the young. This is true even of today's Western societies that have gone farthest to question the imperatives of sex roles. In the United States, for example, women shoulder the better part of childcare (Clutton-Brock, 1991; Crano & Aronoff, 1978; Furstenberg & Nord, 1985; West & Konner, 1976; Whiting & Whiting, 1975). And with this added burden women make the greater sacrifices in their lives outside the home for the sake of children (Hochschild, 1989; Lamb, Frodi, Hwang, & Frodi, 1982). These facts appear to be little affected by employment policies in governments and businesses that afford women and men the same opportunities to take time from work to care for children (Hochschild, 1989). It is not clear if men do not care for children because they don't want to take these opportunities or because women don't want to cede these opportunities. Biology suggests it may be a little of both.

*Female Mate Choice.* A second element of primary order in mammalian and primate social life, linked to the first, is female mate choice. For reasons that remain obscure, nature saw fit to invest in females the prerogatives of selecting mates while investing in males a general mate-seeking ambition. As we've seen, this division of female and male responsibility in sexual selection comports with the difference in female and male investment and responsibility for offspring. This has led many to connect the two (Hamilton, 1964; Buss, 1994; Diamond, 1997), reasoning that the risk/reward ratio leads selfish females to choose partners carefully and selfish males to choose partners carelessly. But, this reasoning about separate economic interests of females and males belies the unity of the species and the fact that species adapt as a whole to conditions of existence. If females and males choose mates differently, it is not simply because they have separate interests. They have separate interests because they are parts of a species that evolved a particular solution to the problem of sexual selection. Indeed, the fact that female and male mating interests complement one another is the surest affidavit of species evolution.

It might seem a surprise that the mammal female—usually the smaller and weaker sex—enjoys exclusive power to control reproductively crucial sexual exchanges. This power comes not from the individual female, but from the species. The female group, already organized around offspring, enforces each female's right to choose a mate. A group of females is more than a match for a larger and stronger male. The male group supports this regime by a sexual economy that pits males against one another in competition for females.[1] In the human case, uniquely, female mate choice is occasionally pre-empted by rape. However, the fact that rape is so unusual among mammals suggests that its causes are not biological (as suggested recently by Thornhill & Palmer, 2000), but are instead cultural (see also Chapter 3, note 19).

Female mate choice is plain in the differing bodies, minds, and behaviors of human females and human males. As we saw in chapter 3, the human female has sexual discretion written all over her. She is aroused slowly and reluctantly by a particular male who must prove himself. Mere sight of a naked and aroused male is usually not enough to engage her sexual interest. Moreover her body is oriented to defend her choices. To receive the male she must be sufficiently lubricated and must adopt a particular posture. By contrast, the human male has indiscriminate sexual interest written all over him. He is aroused easily and quickly, not by a particular female but by females in general. Indeed, mere sight of a female— even at considerable distance, or even abstractly in a photograph or video (Symons, 1979)—can do the trick. His body is all urgent unreticent assertion. Female mate choice, like female care of young, is a human universal that remains in force today, again despite politics to the contrary. Women today still set the terms and conditions of sexual relations (their "yes" or "no" still decides the issue). Women today continue to be more chaste and discerning in mate choices than men. Women today still take responsibility for birth control (it seems men are not trusted to plan ahead or think prudently in the moment). And sex crimes of harassment and rape—crimes that subvert mate choice—remain overwhelmingly male crimes upon women.

*Male Competition.* A final element of primary order in mammal and primate social life, linked to the first two, is male competition. Males compete for the opportunity to mate with females. Throughout mammalian life, males compete to show females who has the best genes and/or who is the most promising provider—the one suggested by fighting ability or by impressive feats of strength or daring, the other by success in the hunt and/or by accumulation of resources such as food and shelter. Either way, male competition takes shape in a world defined and run by females who care for offspring and make wise mate choices. Surprising as it may sound to many women today, men strive mainly to prove to women that they ought to be given a chance.

A surprising aspect of male sexual competition, noted in chapter 3, is its moderation. Male contest is not a nasty and brutish war of all against all, but a mannered contest of staged bouts. Mortal combat is rare. Usually there are blustering threats that avert blows when the weaker capitulates to the stronger at the last possible minute. Attacks are measured, aimed to intimidate rather than harm. Male chimpanzees, for example, fight for status without fully using their canine incisors (de Waal, 1989). Male humans invent all kinds of schemes (in hunt, in sport, in politics, in commerce, in conversation) to demonstrate superiority short of hurting one another. Here, again, play appears at the head of social life. From the "frivolous" play fighting of immature males to the "serious" sexual competitions of adult males runs a bold line. Playful male contest is an integral element of mammalian reproduction. It produces a more or less stable hierarchy that all males—both high and low—conspire to maintain.

Together, the three elements of primary social order—*female care of young, female mate choice, and male competition*—comprise the central dynamic of species life. This is the dialectic of sexual opposition and affirmation. On the one hand, female care of young, female sexual choosiness, and male competition divide the sexes according to interest and activity. The sexes stand opposite one another, each having its own business and orientation to the other. On the other hand, female care of young, female sexual choosiness, and male competition unite the sexes in reproductive complementarity. The sexes affirm one another, each needing the other to complete its biological destiny. This push and pull of sex identifies the primary social order as living form, a dance without end.

Finally, we appreciate that as parts of one species life, the three elements of primary social order never appear alone, but always together. We saw some of this in the battle of the sexes and mating games described in chapter 4. Where females care for young, they are bound to choose mates wisely. Where females choose wisely, males are bound to compete openly to show their worth. And where males compete openly, females have a basis to choose wisely and can better bear the burdens of gestation and child rearing. Men and women thus do not act separately, or selfishly as many evolutionary psychologists suppose (e.g., Buss, 1994), but always in concert. We see now how male hierarchy complements female mutuality to protect infant offspring, to promote peace in the group, and to ensure that females are most likely to be fertilized by the most healthy and able males. The three elements of primary social order together establish the foundation of human social life. Upon this foundation, complex and sometimes surprising social structures have been built. We have now to turn to the layered complexities added by secondary and tertiary orders of social life.

*Secondary Order*

I define the secondary or "archaeological" social order as the distinctive human adaptation to Pleistocene life on the African savannah. Lasting millions of years, the Pleistocene period comprises nearly all of our species history, making it the most formative period of our evolution. This is where to look to see how and why we differ from sibling primate and cousin mammal species.

We do not know whether our ancestor's epochal move from the trees to the plains was opportunistic, led perhaps by itinerant male groups pre-adapted by primate social life for adventure and cooperative hunt, or if it was compelled, perhaps by circumstances of climate, disease, or competition within the arboreal niche. We do know, or at least can imagine, what this move meant for the species. From resources and dangers visible to this day we can guess the pressures this move put on the species and the physical and social adaptations that resulted. We can test these guesses by comparing human morphology and social life against those of close relatives, such as the chimpanzee and gorilla, that did not make the same move.

For a primate species already divided between male and female, the move from trees to savannah could not but bring further differentiation and specialization of the sexes. Evolution works with and upon differences. For males the move called for closer and more intensive cooperation, partly to defend a species located more vulnerably in open grasslands and partly to hunt for meat and thereby take nutritional advantage of eating higher on the food chain. This encouraged several mutually reinforcing male adaptations—including an ability to act responsibly in groups; a vocal tract capable of modulated calls and commands in collective action; an ability to imagine and locate objects in space and time; an upright posture to see at a distance and free the hands for uses other than locomotion; a capacity to throw objects accurately over distance; and a larger brain to do all these things. For females, too, the move onto the savannah called for closer and more intensive cooperation, mainly to care and protect young, but also to police and defend female mating prerogatives. This likewise led to a number of mutually reinforcing female adaptations—including an ability to read and respond to feelings in others (men and children); again a vocal tract capable of modulated speech; again an upright posture freeing the hands; and again a larger brain to do these things. The move to the savannah led also to a great increase in female attractiveness to males. As males formed tighter groups oriented to greater adventures farther from females and infants, females needed a firmer hold on male attentions to ensure their return with needed provisions. The species responded with two adaptations that heightened female attractiveness to males: continuous sexual availability and cryptic ovulation. Unique among primates, human females do not advertise when they are fertile and they do not limit their sexual availability to fertile periods. As noted in chapter 3, this makes females a constant interest to males. With the promise of sexual gratification, males do not stay away long; they hurry home.

*Same-Sex Grouping.* The adaptations of male and female to Pleistocene existence produced two distinctively human elements of social order. One is same-sex grouping: a tendency for men to group with men and for women to group with women. Ancient Pleistocene groupings of male and female carry into today, although not with exactly the same activities and responsibilities. On the playground at school, groups of boys and groups of girls choose different activities, while keeping a safe distance so as not to confuse their groups or get "cooties" from one another (Maccoby & Jacklin, 1974). These intrigued separations run into adulthood: onto the college campus, where young men and young women join fraternities and sororities and study different subjects (Willingham & Cole, 1997); into the workplace, where men incline to technical and commercial professions such as science, engineering, and business and women cleave to helping and service professions such as medicine, social work, and education (Browne, 1995; Paglin & Rufolo, 1990); and into domestic life, where most fathers work outside the home while most mothers assume primary responsibility for raising their children (Hochschild, 1989).

Though characteristic of men and women alike, sex grouping figures differently in the lives of each. Compared to women, men are more resolved to group tasks and group goals and are better able to act in close order. To hunt on the open savannah, Pleistocene men moved together quietly to stalk an animal and then to form a closed circle to mob the animal. To ward off threats of a predator or enemy, Pleistocene men collected their efforts to mount a force more impressive than any one man could muster. Men have always created in groups.[2] From different motives come different forms and functions. Compared to women's groups, men's groups are more sharply delineated and their boundaries are more vigorously defended (Lever, 1978). Men are more concerned and clearer about who is in the group and who is not in the group. Men also fight wars in the name of groups, ostensibly to protect or expand their interests, but also to safeguard their boundaries and purity. Compared to women's groups, men's groups are more engaged in questions and controversies about rank (Pratto, 1996). More of what men do is given to status in the group. Compared to women's groups, men's groups are more rule-bound and rule-oriented. Men insist on rules and put rules before play. For men, it is not only whether you win or lose, but also how you play. And compared to women's groups, men's groups are more reluctant to admit members of the opposite sex (Tiger, 1969). As much as men care for women individually, they do not particularly want them in their groups. It is a reluctance with deep roots, for many or most men unconscious, tied perhaps to a vague fear of disorder.

Male grouping is multiply and powerfully determined. It is one part result of female consolidation with offspring. Pushed to the periphery by reproductively central females, males are left to mill and play among themselves. It is one part answer to female mate choice. In a world where females choose partners, males compete to be recognized in a clear status hierarchy. And, in primates and humans especially, it is one part serendipity. With migration of hominid species from trees to open savannah, the hierarchic male group was adapted to the dangers of grassland predation and to opportunities for open-field hunting. Sharply organized around a dominant leader, to which all turned for direction, the male group could effectively coordinate efforts to defeat predators or enemies and to track down, encircle, overcome, and defend animals of prey.

Tiger (1969) notoriously propounded the thesis that human male grouping today recapitulates this archaic heritage of male grouping in hunt and defense. Quoting McLaughlin at length, Tiger agrees that:

> Hunting is the master behavioral pattern of the human species. It is the organizing activity which integrated the morphological, physiological, genetic, and intellectual aspects of the individual organisms and of the populations that compose our single species. Hunting is a way of life, not simply a "subsistence technique," which importantly involves commitments, correlates, and consequences spanning the entire biobehavioral continuum of the individual and of the entire species of which he is a member. Man evolved as a hunter, he spent over ninety-nine percent of his species' history as a hunter, and he spread over the entire habitable area of the world as a hunter. (P. 96)

Male-male bonding, argues Tiger, is a species pattern of comparable evolutionary significance to male-female bonding and female-infant bonding. It is a pattern written in sex differences that augur all-male hunting groups. These sex differences—which include size and strength, locomotive efficiency, tolerance for temperature change, instability of emotional tonus in estrous females, ability to throw things, spatial-geographic ability, and aggressiveness—disadvantage any female who entered the male group and disadvantage any males who permitted females access to the group. Tiger finds this species pattern today in two ready observations. One is that men predominate in areas of social life that demand qualities typical of the hunt, particularly dominance seeking, respect for authority, camaraderie, trust, courage, and valor. This puts men in the middle of wars, politics, commercial enterprises, and competitive sport. Goldberg (1993) builds essentially the same argument from the physiological fact that dominance-seeking is a male speciality. He finds that men predominate wherever there are contests because men are wired to compete and, compared to women, more desperate to succeed.[3] The second observation is that men everywhere form groups that exclude females. They do this, according to Tiger, because they take satisfactions from male-male interactions that they cannot take from male-female interactions. Males more than females are drawn to groups that expressly exclude the other sex, and especially to groups that claim special separateness as "secret societies."

> Males consciously create secret groups for the gregarious and efficacious control of political, religious, and/or economic worlds, and for the enjoyment of male company under emotionally satisfying conditions. Such grouping exhibits the culturally learned and socially mediated manifestation of a broad biological feature of the male life cycle. (P. 140)

From here, Tiger takes a leap to suggest that a great many other and more ordinary social forms, hitherto considered chiefly cultural as opposed to biological, are variations of this biological theme.

> Sports teams, neighborhood gangs, drinking groups, and so on are perhaps fairly evident social-organizational sublimations for the old hominid pattern of ganging, hunting, triumphing, and politicking, set in terms of a very small and local milieu. (P. 155)

Tying these two observations together, Tiger further observes that many male groups involve initiation ceremonies that define and reinforce political and economic hierarchy. As he points out, the punishments and humiliations suffered by candidates for these groups are an impressive catalogue of "ingenious perversities, rigorous ordeals, and bizarre demonstrations of subordination" (p. 14). In many instances, these initiation rituals incorporate images or actualities of nudity, blood, attributions of animal names, and quests of one kind or another that resonate with the male instinct to hunt. Such rites and ceremonies symbolize both practical male concerns for courage and competence as well as hierarchic male concerns for obedience and loyalty. Whether Tiger is correct to find the roots of human male hierarchy in hunting groups of the Pleistocene, there is no doubt that men need and want to form hierarchic groups apart from women. As noted in chapter 4, Mead (1949) identified this need and want in her wide-ranging study of the sexes. To repeat one of her conclusions: "maleness, in fact, has to be underwritten by preventing women from entering some field or performing some feat. Here may be found the relationship between maleness and pride" (p. 160).[4] This is important because men's wish to preserve unisex bonds convenes a sexual division of labor apart from physical and temperamental differences between the sexes.

Sex grouping has different foundations among women. Even before the Pleistocene, women were preoccupied with more personal concerns. Women collaborate to better their reproductive chances in a perilous world, mainly by sharing childcare, food gathering, and homemaking, but also by standing together against unwelcome advances of men. Such collaboration was needed on the Pleistocene savannah where predation was a constant threat, where food sharing was a necessity, and where males left home in groups to hunt. Such collaboration has remained important throughout human history as women continue to rely upon variously reliable men for support. Today, dangerous predators have given way to deadbeat dads in an expensive economy. Thus, women come together in a different way and for different reasons than men. They do not collect to coordinate their efforts for a group goal. Instead, they collect to assist one another in central life tasks of finding a mate, carrying and bearing children, and caring for children until they mature. Where men must act together to make a group, women need only acknowledge their common fate to make a group. Where men care most to accomplish a group goal, women care most to establish relations of mutual support within the group (men care *what* the group is doing, women care *how* the group is doing) (Eibl-Eibesfeldt, 1989; Geary, 1998; Golombok & Fivush, 1994; Willingham & Cole, 1997).[5]

Certainly, to look at women's groups formed around reproductive tasks of childcare and homemaking, there is not the same organization. There is not the same hierarchy, or the same parsing of roles and labor. Rather, there are shifting coalitions of older and younger women and children, grouping and un-grouping as demand or whim dictate. Children take direction from the older women, but authority is wielded loosely, only as occasion demands. There is not the same need to unite and coordinate members in action. Social support is offered and accepted in manifold ways—typically on an ad hoc personal basis. Rarely do such women's groups operate as a unified whole. Interestingly, this pattern appears even in women's groups formed around non-reproductive tasks of modern work, where we might expect social structure to be dictated by economic efficiency. Women organize at work differently than men, typically to form smaller, more intimate, and more egalitarian groups (Acker, 1990; Ferguson, 1984; Farrell, 1994).[6] Whereas hierarchy reigns in groups of men, heterarchy prevails in groups of women. This pattern of female organization can perhaps be attributed to women's preference to support rather than to dominate one another. Put men in a group, they compete. Add their competitions together, you get a hierarchy. Put women in a group, they connect. Add their connections together, you get a flat, more or less coherent, network of personal relations. Compared to men's relationships, women's relationships are less hierarchic, more mutual, more personal, and more idiosyncratic.

*Family.* A second element of secondary social order to evolve with Pleistocene migration to the savannah is family. Family is the most important grouping to come of the species division into male and female—most important because it is the reproducing unit of the species. It consists of a woman with children who is attached more or less exclusively to a man. The woman is almost always the mother of the children, the man is typically but not always the father. Sex between woman and man is usually monogamous (or nearly so), but in some instances it is polygamous as a few powerful men take more than one wife.

The precursors of family appear in the primary order of mammalian and primate social life described earlier. Among our mammal ancestors the hubbub of hierarchy-obsessed males clamoring to impress choosy females produced only brief impersonal matings— flings with no strings. Females mated the highest-ranking males (in some species the alpha male almost exclusively) and, once pregnant, left the sexual stage to care for the young in the female group. Later, females of certain primate species (including the precursors of modern baboon, chimpanzee, and humans), granted sexual favors also to males who consistently helped them with food and children—males that could be described as "friends" (Smuts, 1985). And so was inaugurated a sexual economy in which males were sexually rewarded not only for being dominant, but also for being reliably helpful. This development was crucial because it meant that a great many more males could gain access to females. In principle if not in fact, every male could befriend a female and thereby gain mating chances that otherwise belonged to the dominant male.

It is likely that family evolved as a solution to unique problems of savannah life. Family adapted the species to conditions where men in groups left the village to hunt and to explore and women huddled at home to gather nearby foods and to care for children. Family promised woman a man to return with food, to defend her and her children from attack, and to help with childcare. Family promised man a woman with whom he could mate and from whom he could receive comfort. She gives him sexual outlet and paternal confidence, he gives her resources to raise children, and both give children a fulsome opportunity to grow and develop under parental care. Since the Pleistocene era, family continues to fit and reinforce the pattern of men in groups leaving home to act on the world and women holding back to care for children and home. Thus family appeals to woman and man for different reasons. It consoles woman's concerns for resources in a dangerous world where needy children make her vulnerable. And it consoles man's concerns for mating opportunities and paternal certainty in a world where women could be fertile at any time and are always ready for sex. So congenial is family to human existence that we might wonder if it was a consequence of hominid migration onto the savannah or a factor contributing to this migration. With family to stabilize relations between the sexes, hominid females could cooperate in mutual support with minimal concern for who among them would capture the attention and resources of which males, while hominid males could cooperate for mutual gain in group tasks with likewise minimal concern about which of them would mate which females. Family facilitates cooperation within and between sexes (Fisher, 1982).

It is difficult to overstate the significance of family in the life and reproduction of the species. So central is its reproductive function that failure of a man and woman to produce children can leave their relationship unfulfilled or even undermine it. Success in having children is a force holding couples together. Children give family its reason and organize the motives and relations of man and woman in it. It is difficult also to deny the family as a hard fact of species life. Although founded today upon seemingly abstract ideas of personal commitment and fidelity, family has always been an integral element of our human biology. Family is the element of social order that most directly reconciles the division of the species into male and female to solve reproductive problems of attraction, transportation, selection, and support.

There are two things to say in review of the two elements of secondary social order, *same-sex groups* and *family*. First, we do best to think of these two elements as we think of the three elements of primary social order, as parts of one species life. Again, these elements never appear alone, but always together in a dialectic of opposition and affirmation. In the most robust men's or women's groups there is a hint of family, and likewise in the warmest and coziest domestic scene there is a brooding presence of single-sex groups. One enters a men's or women's group in part to leave family behind and in part to prepare for a return. Men learn to compete fairly with other men so as to be attractive to women. Women learn to make wise choices and to care for young so as to be attractive to men. By the same token, one seeks a family life in part to leave the men's or women's group behind and in part to set the stage for a return. In the family, men and women learn how the other feels, thinks, and acts. Love of other and of children make man and woman whole. But this wholeness comes at the risk of losing one's sexual identity, which must be reclaimed in the same-sex group.

Second, the two elements of secondary social order, *same-sex groups* and *family*, are inextricably tied to the three elements of the primary social order described earlier (that is, female care of young, female mate choice, male competition). Sex groups begin in the battle of the sexes. Men face the mammalian imperative to show themselves in contests so that females can select mates for the good of the species. As men conspire to compete before discerning women, they enact a reproductive scheme that is tens of millions of years old. They do not choose this; they do this because they are mammal and male. What distinguishes men's groups from male groups of other species is the reach of their competitive impulse, which goes far beyond plonking contests of brute strength or hunting prowess. Watch men in groups build a spaceship or a social science and see two of the farther reaches of male competition. For their part, women face the mammalian imperatives to select mates wisely and to nurture young; imperatives that are acute among highly sexed and strongly altricial primates. As women collect to defend their sexual prerogatives and to care for young, they too recap an age-old reproductive scheme. Like the men, they do not choose this; they do this because they are mammal and female. What distinguishes women's groups from female groups of other species is again the reach of these reproductive impulses, which go beyond choosing mates and rearing children. Watch women defend the defenseless, fight for the oppressed, nurse the sick, or support others in modern corporations, and see three of the farther reaches of these aboriginal urges. Humans are mammals like every other, only more so.

The family also begins in the primary social order, and particularly in the mating games played between the sexes. Where sex groups recapitulate the separate male and female parts of the primary social order, family reconciles those parts. Family balances man's concerns about sex (his interest to mate as widely as possible, his anxieties about paternity) with woman's concerns about sex (her interest to find the best genes, her anxieties to find a mate she can count on). The two agree in the family. Man trades a possibility of promiscuous mating for a sure partner and a guarantee of paternity. Woman trades interest in the most impressive man for a lesser but more reliable partner. Family integrates women's concerns within the group for child and home with men's concerns outside the group for hunt and defense. As women mind the children, men worry the group's relations to the wider world. And, family marries women's and men's different concerns for organization—hers for supportive personal relationships, his for hierarchy and group goals. It is more than a stereotype that women think personally about family relationships and that men think formally about those same relationships. She notices and worries that the children are not getting along, or that romance has left the marriage. He thinks the family an organization of rights and duties, with himself the leader and his wife and children the subordinates.

Thus the secondary social order presupposes the primary social order. To be human is not only to stand apart from other animals in uniqueness; it is also to stand with other animals in an evolutionary continuity. *Same-sex groups* and *family* are distinctively human elements of social life, but they could not exist apart from mammalian elements of female care of young, female mate choice, and male competition. The battle of the sexes that separates male and female groups puts them into opposition. The mating game that unites male and female in a reproductive mission gives them reason to work through this opposition. Thus in primary social order we find the original values for human fraternity and for human sorority and the original values for the human family. Design a social life without one of the primary elements of order—without women caring for children, or without women choosing mates wisely, or without men competing for women's attention and favor—and you design a social life without sex groups and without family. Where Tiger (1969) singles out the male hunting group as the backbone of human social life, we see things are more complex.[7]  Male grouping joins female grouping and family to comprise a secondary order that builds upon the primary order of social life described earlier.[8]

*Tertiary Order*

As we've seen, the primary and secondary orders of human social life are universals rooted in biology.  The primary social order is a mammalian trait built into a body plan of reproductively central females and reproductively aspiring males.  The secondary social order is a human trait tied to a suite of hominid adaptations to savannah life, including upright posture, a larger brain, an articulated vocal tract, cryptic ovulation and continuous sexuality.  I now define the tertiary or "anthropological" social order as those elements of social structure that vary from human group to human group.  These are not biological elements rooted in genes, but cultural elements rooted in ideas about how people should live in the group.

Culture is conception.  It is a communal exercise of the human capacity to make and use symbols.  This capacity may have arisen early in group life as our hominid ancestors turned natural communicative signs (e.g., grunts, footfalls, cries) into conceptual symbols (e.g., words, gestures, dances).  Following Langer (1967), I argue elsewhere that the first symbols, and the first elements of culture, were probably visual and auditory images of the group (e.g., choric shouts, communal dances) invented to maintain the integrity of the group amid the isolations of an open and challenging savannah life (Sandelands, 1998).  With an image of the group in mind, people could remain in the group psychologically despite being separated from it physically.  With an image of the group in mind, people could wander farther from the group and operate more autonomously on its behalf.  And with an image of the group in mind, people could coordinate their efforts at a distance, each person knowing his/her place and part in the whole.  A hunting group, for example, could exploit a wider range and capture larger animals.  Culture thus may have arisen as humankind's first technology, its first artifice to take

fuller advantage of its environment. While the capacity for this technology was no doubt a product of biological evolution—arising in a
socially sophisticated animal with a large brain capable of support-
ing symbolic processes—the elaboration and development of this
technology was not primarily a biological process, but cultural process (an evolution of ideas or "memes" rather than bodies or "genes,"
to borrow Dawkins' clever phraseology).

The human capacity for culture inaugurated a social life without
precedent in the animal kingdom. Unlike other animals, people think
about their social lives. People have an idea of the group and an
idea of themselves in the group. People know that they are separate
persons and that they play parts in groups. This small-seeming difference in awareness changes everything about social life. Whereas
other animals have parts in species life (think of castes of social
insects or sexual divisions of labor in mammals), people play parts
in species life.[9] Whereas a worker bee never worries its destiny and
never thinks to throw off the chains that bind it to the hive, people
worry all the time about who they are and about their duties to others. A man is no pigeon in a pecking order, he is a self- and socially
aware member of a group. Hierarchy for him is both a biological
fact and a cultural idea.[10] Places in the hierarchy are "roles" played
by more or less interchangeable group members. With roles come
new dynamics. Roles are decided not by brute contests of fighting
ability, but are won in supplications of the group. And with roles
come new questions. How well does a given member, especially
the leader, perform his role? Can another member perform the role
better? What are the best procedures for fitting persons to roles?
And how can these procedures and/or the roles they assign be
changed? Culture defines a new kind of social order, unlike that of
any other animal, a social order based upon ideas.[11]

A tertiary or cultural social order exists whenever people act toward one another *as members of a group*—that is, when they act in
light of ideas about the group and about their own and others' roles
in the group. We see this order in men's hierarchies as they con-
sciously angle for socially recognized and sanctioned positions of
status and authority. We see this order in mating pairs as man and
woman recognize their bond as a compact to love, honor, and obey
one another and to raise children. We see this order in human organization of all kinds wherever people take recognized places in known

systems of relations.  The places may be branches on a family tree, ranks in a political or military organization, or work roles in a manufacturing organization.  There is a tertiary order everywhere in human social life.

The tertiary social order builds upon the older primary and secondary social orders, typically to preserve and reinforce these orders.  Cultures sanction ideas about social life, and particularly about basic relations between the sexes, to enable people to live together peaceably and in the best interest of the group.  Male chivalry supports respectful competition among men and respectful treatment of women.  Marriage vows sanctify women's mate choice and reinforce monogamy and family.  And criminal laws about rape, sexual harassment, sexual perversion, incest, child abuse, child custody, and child support keep the sexes in balance.  Where culture operates in this typical way to support and reinforce biology it is of modest theoretical interest—a footnote to account for variations in the strength or sharpness of biologically drawn lines.  We can contrast cultures, as did Mead (1949), according to details of how elements of primary and secondary social order are realized—to note a strong family structure here, a weak one there, powerful male groups here, weak and subordinate male groups there, strong monogamy here, mild polygyny there.

Culture is of greater theoretical interest where it appears to be indifferent or even antagonistic to biology, where it calls for social orders that cannot be anticipated from biology.  We find this in Western culture today, in which appear two strongly developed, seemingly anti-biological, elements of social order: the *individual* and the *bureaucracy*.  These two elements of tertiary social order demand a careful look.

*The Individual and the Bureaucracy.*  By definition, the individual stands apart from the group (literally, in-*divid*-ual, "divided from").  The individual is self-contained and self-sufficient—a life unto him/herself, a center of feeling, thought, and action (Langer, 1962).  The individual is neither male nor female.

By definition, the bureaucracy is a logical structure of persons who, within certain bounds, relinquish private interests to take public roles in the group.  The bureaucracy is a rational social system defined by:  (a) rigorous separation of the person from the office he or she holds; (b) delineation of jurisdictions and authority for each office; (c) specification of rights and obligations for each office; (d) specification of qualifications for each office and equitable means of assigning persons to offices and of evaluating their performance in offices; (e) specification of remuneration for official work; (f) specification of a scalar hierarchy of authority; and (g) specification of written rules and procedures to specify how group activities are to be carried out (Weber, 1964).

Individual and bureaucracy are cognate. Flowers upon a single stalk, they balance and confirm one another. Individuals bloom when people can grow and develop apart from the group. Bureaucracy blossoms when people give themselves over to the group to act impersonally. The mutuality of individual and bureaucracy is born of their common root in a particular development of consciousness; namely, awareness of self in the group. With this awareness came thinking and acting for oneself (selfishness), on the one hand, and sacrificing oneself for the group (selflessness), on the other hand. With this awareness came a two-part, two-valued life, one part individual life, one part bureaucratic life.[12]

This two-part tertiary order has been a great boon to Western civilization. The individual is thought to be the key to creativity and to the life of mind (Ghiselin, 1955). Bureaucracy is thought to be the most efficient human organization (Weber, 1964). Where individuals of either sex are available to commit to any bureaucratic role or office, an effective and efficient division of labor can be fit to any task. With these Western elements of tertiary social order, the logic of social life moves from one focused narrowly on sex and reproduction to one allowing broader utilitarian aims. This expands the possibilities of organization to include activities not directly related to the sexual economy of the group. Virtually any domain of interest and activity can be exploited by bureaucratic organization—from great construction projects, mining operations, manufacturing plants, and fast food restaurants, to war-making, prostitution, and art.

This tertiary social order of individual and bureaucracy puts two challenging questions to the theory presented in this book. First, how did these two elements of Western culture evolve from the primary and secondary social orders described above? And second, how do these two elements of Western culture satisfy the book's central claim that social life is sex?

Taking the first question first, there is argument and evidence to suggest that the tertiary order of individual and bureaucracy gained its footing in the written languages of the first Western cultures. Abram (1997) speculates that invention of non-iconic alphabetic languages by ancient Hebrews and ancient Greeks led to a unique individual consciousness. Experiences that were before communicated visually and orally with the help of gestures and sounds that preserved sensuous elements (e.g., in a dance that re-enacts a hunt, or a pantomime about an ancestor), came in the West to be communicated verbally in written texts that preserved fewer of those elements. Ideas began to lose touch with the body and with feeling. Alphabetic writing denotes experiences by strings of arbitrarily defined letters which comprise phonemes which combine to make morphemes which are strung together to comprise utterances. Alphabetic writing relates to its subject by convention rather than by likeness. Text stands apart from subject; it is not *of* the subject, but *about* the subject. Except in some instances of poetry, to speak or write a word or phrase is not literally to have or express an experience, but to denote an experience in a system of symbols (the phrase, "verbal expression," is a metaphor). A reader looks into a text to see not real feelings but *ideas about* feelings. A writer composes a text not to express feelings but to think and talk about them. Reader and writer become self-aware as they realize that the meaning and significance of a text is not in the words, but in the interpretation that they themselves give to the words. Written text invites subjectivity; demands subjectivity.

Although Western subjectivity may have begun in language, further developments brought it into focus and eventually into cultural prominence. Jaynes (1976) finds a crucial development in Greek literature of the seventh century B.C., particularly in Homer, in which epic tales came to include characters with substantial subjectivity. Before this time, story characters appeared "puppet-like" as wooden figures moved about by Gods. At this time, story characters begin to feel, think, and act for themselves, at times even to defy the Gods. Shannahan (1992) brings the account of Western subjectivity forward to note several developments of an ideology of individualism: (1) an early Judaic theology that sponsored a single abstract God apart from and opposed to the natural world; (2) a later Christian theology that identified this God with a person, Christ; (3) Medieval study of religious texts that invited and empowered the reader to interpret the word of God for him/herself; (4) Renaissance developments of visual perspective in painting (which gives priority to the individual perceiver), of personality in art, culture, and politics, and of a personal romantic love ("amour"); (5) Reformation melding of Calvinist Protestantism with economic capitalism, thus to give religious sanction to individual ambition and initiative (the Protestant work ethic); and (6) eighteenth-century philosophical skepticism of Hume and Kant which made individual experience the arbiter of truth, and nineteenth-century romanticism of Nietzsche, Emerson, Wordsworth, and Coleridge which made the individual the center of life and feeling against the murderous distortions of society. According to Shannahan, Western culture is largely the story of the individual.

There were companion developments of Western subjectivity in the rise and proliferation of bureaucratic organization and ideology. As described by Durkheim (1893/1933), bureaucratic organization follows the division of labor. As people migrated into denser social networks of large cities they were engaged in an increasingly fierce economic struggle for existence. To make room for all, people accommodated themselves to one another by taking increasingly specialized roles within increasingly interdependent groups. The "Renaissance man" accomplished in many fields gave way to the practical fellow expert in one. A builder became a carpenter or mason or smith. These density-driven dynamics brought awareness of the self as playing a part in an impersonal bureaucratic structure. And this awareness brought moral value to those who play, or appear to play, their part in the group (Jackall, 1988). Thus the culture elements of individual and bureaucracy sponsor and rest upon the same subjectivity. The self-awareness that gives scope to individual life apart from the group enables a person to put his/her interests aside to be part of an impersonal bureaucratic order. Modern life in the West puts the abiding problem of reconciling these competing demands upon subjectivity. Bureaucracy comes at the expense of individual life (see, Reisman, 1949; Whyte, 1956) as individual life comes at the expense of bureaucracy (see, Bellah et al., 1986; Jackall, 1988).

Turning to the second question of the sexual dimensions of the tertiary order of individual and bureaucracy, it is indeed hard to see the sex in this social life. On first glance, individual and bureaucracy have little to do with sex, much less with reproduction. Individuals have no particular sex—men and women are equally indi-

vidual.  Bureaucracies are rationally impersonal—there are no ambitious men to importune choosy women, no bands of men to hunt
and no clutches of women to care for young, and no families for
man and woman to come home to.  And there is nothing about individuals or bureaucracies to explain how the species meets its reproductive requirements of attraction, transportation, selection, and support.  It seems this tertiary order upsets the central argument of the
book that social order is sexual order.

A closer look at this tertiary social order, however, finds its sexual
elements not far to find.  We notice first that this order is rarely developed to the exclusion or detriment of the primary and secondary
social order.  Indeed, this tertiary social order leaves much about sex
and social life untouched.  The sexes are reconciled as before.  It is
still primarily men who venture from the home to secure a liveli-
hood and win a place in society, and it is still primarily women who
take care of children.  Even where sex differences and sex roles are
downplayed or refused, as they are in certain occupations in the
United States, allowances are nevertheless made for sex.  By day,
men and women may act as sexless individuals in impersonal bureaucracies, but by night they reclaim their sexual identity.  At work
a corporate CEO is coldly exacting and ruthless, at home he is a
devoted  husband and loving father.  At work another corporate CEO
gives no quarter in the clawing contest for position and power, at
leisure she wears lacy lingerie in hopes of attracting a man to love
and protect her.  There is culture *and* there is biology.

We notice further that this tertiary social order is limited by reproductive biology.  People become individual as they abandon their
bodies to think for themselves.  He or she is most individual who is
most detached from bodily feeling and impulse.[13]  And bureaucracy
forms as individuals abandon personal interests to an impersonal
social order.  Bureaucracy stands above concrete persons as an abstract order of relationships among offices.  Just as mind cannot be
sundered from body, culture cannot be sundered from reproductive
biology.  Culture is limited by resolutely sexed bodies commanded
by species needs.  The noblest ideal of individual freedom or of
bureaucratic rationality crumbles when man and woman meet in intercourse.  All sameness disappears, as do all notions of equality.
He commands her, she commands him, both trapped in larger forces.
Cultural possibilities bump up against the hard practicalities of bod-

ies locked in an age-old sexual order. We see the clash between culture and biology, between mind and body, in debates between individual rights and sexual imperatives—for examples in controversies about sexual equality, reproductive choices, and childcare roles (to name a few). The idea that men and women are the same in being individual and therefore are entitled to the same rights, responsibilities, and memberships clashes with the feeling that men and women are different in essence and role and therefore have different rights, responsibilities, and memberships. In Western culture today an uneasy détente between these perspectives is upheld by the distinction between public life, which is individual and bureaucratic, and private life, which is sexual and personal. It is a distinction perhaps more familiar to men whose reproductive biology is tuned to a life in society beyond the home,[14] than to women whose reproductive biology is rooted more firmly in the home and family (see chapter 3).[15] In the end, we find that as no actual person exists only in the mind without body and sex, no actual person is completely individual. And, we find that just as no actual group exists only as a voluntary and rational contract among individuals without any concern for sex, no actual group is completely bureaucratic. Individual and bureaucracy are theoretical constructs, ideal types which lie at the ends of continua upon which real persons and real groups can be arrayed and compared (see Weber, 1964).

So far we have granted little to the tertiary social order of individual and bureaucracy. We found it a partial development of culture that cannot stray far from reproductive biology. But we have yet to say how this social order could arise if it opposes reproductive biology. And more to the point, we have yet to make good the claim of this book that social life everywhere is a play of sex.

The history of Western subjectivity reviewed above begs the question of why individual consciousness and impersonal bureaucratic order at all. The alphabetic language of the Greeks and Hebrews may have been the occasion for self-consciousness, but it could not have been the reason. Just because one *can* take a new perspective does not mean that one *will* take that perspective. I suggest that self-consciousness arose with alphabetic language because the latter provided a new and easier way to reconcile the sexes, a way that did not ask much from the body nor from the group. With self-consciousness, the problem of sexual division no longer required cumbersome joining of male and female bodies and social arrangements of males and females.  It could be solved vicariously, in the head.

In oral cultures, listeners take in stories passively, as they come, with limited personal involvement in fixing their sensuous details and meanings.  In written cultures, such as those of the Greeks and Hebrews in the West, readers take in stories actively, filling in sensuous details and meaning for themselves.  To comprehend a story the reader must invest in its male and female characters.  He or she must take their position and perspective and, in a sense, become them.  Doing so, the reader forms images and ideas of what it is be male and what it is to be female in the society.  These images become internalized as elements of his or her own experience and personality.  I propose that this incorporation and integration of male and female elements in the reader is the cause and basis of individual subjectivity.  Self-consciousness—that is, awareness of oneself as a unique being beyond the body and beyond the group—arises with integration of the sexes within the individual.  Once incomplete and driven to the opposite sex by the body, the person is now complete and self-sufficient in the mind.

The tertiary social order of individual and bureaucracy is thus its own reconciliation of sex, a sexual social form unto itself.  To be an individual in a bureaucracy is not to be a male *or* a female, but to be a male *and* a female.  To look at exemplary individuals in society is to find people remarkable not only for their masculine assertion, competitive zeal, and conceptual power, but also for their feminine acceptance, caring, and emotional perceptiveness.  Christ, Buddha, Mohammed, Schweitzer, Wittgenstein, Einstein, Thoreau, Da Vinci, Tolstoy, Dickinson, King, Gandhi—great artists, philosophers, teachers, scientists, and leaders of every age—draw upon the whole of humanity, upon male and female elements, to make their unique contributions to society.  Genius is not male or female.  Genius is male *and* female.[16]  The individual is thus a prime instance of the cosmic principle of involution, in which the whole is involuted in the part.  The sexual order of the species is involuted in the person.  Jung (1990) describes this involution of sex in the individual as the incorporation of an unconscious image of the female (the *anima*) in the male and as the incorporation of an unconscious image of the male (the *animus*) in the female.  Bureaucracy is no less a making of sex.  It is the extra-personal expression of the intra-personal reconciliation of sex in the individual. A bureaucratic "persona" is what a person becomes when sex no longer needs to be reconciled through others. To reiterate, individual and bureaucracy are cognates originating in the cultural life of the group. As Jung notes, the unconscious individual "anima" and "animus" and the conscious bureaucratic "persona" are alike elements of Western culture that are not found elsewhere in the world (p. 166).[17]

The appearance and success of Western culture is thus explained by the sexual reconciliation afforded by the individual in bureaucracy. Again the social glue is sexual attraction of male and female. Again the energizing dynamic is the play of male and female with and against one another. Sex plays in the individual between the overt sexuality of the body and the covert sexuality of the unconscious mind (anima, animus). The individual is neither male nor female, but androgynous—male *and* female. He/she is sexually complete and sufficient. He/she takes the sexual order of the species into him/herself, thus involuting the whole into the part. Doing so enables the individual to inhabit an impersonal bureaucratic world defined not by sex roles and relations but by rational division of labor.

Thus, the tertiary order of Western culture deals with sex both by leaving it for primary and secondary social orders to reconcile and by involuting these social orders within the individual in bureaucracy. The two possibilities relate as alternatives. As one waxes the other wanes. Both are implicated in the sexual self-sufficiency of the individual and impersonality of bureaucracy. A person can be individual only when freed from the influence of others, and particularly when sex is no more the guiding interest. This can occur when a person distinguishes public life from private life and/or when a person reconciles the sexes in his/her own psyche. How much it will be of one or the other depends on the person and on the circumstances. Likewise, social organization can be bureaucratic only when people make no sexual demands upon one another. This can happen when men and women separate public bureaucratic life from private sexual life and/or when they incorporate sex into themselves to be sexually sufficient individuals. How much it will be of one or the other depends again on the persons and circumstances. Social life in the West today is a confusion of social orders—of men and women relating to each other both as cultured individuals in bureau-

cracies and as biological males and biological females on the reproductive stage.

We complete this section to note interdependencies between the
tertiary social order of individual and bureaucracy and the primary
and secondary social orders described earlier. Again there is continuity. The tertiary social order follows a path of social evolution
begun before the appearance of mammals, altered dramatically by
hominid adaptations to Pleistocene conditions of savannah life, and
brought into a wholly new dynamics with culture. A tertiary social
order of culture arose the moment people became conscious of the
group. Able to think about the group and act on its behalf, people
formed cultures as elaborations of this thinking and acting. That a
tertiary social order would take the particular form of the individual
and bureaucracy, as it has in the West, was inevitable once people
became aware of themselves as persons apart from the group and
gave priority to personal life over group life.

And again there is divergence. The primary and secondary social
orders enacted between males and females trade off against the tertiary social order enacted within individuals and bureaucracies. Body
trades for mind, biology for culture. As we will see in chapter 6, it is
an open question how stable or viable these trades might be. For all
the glory and achievements of individual mind and bureaucratic organization, their inner reconciliation of sex cannot completely take
the place of sexual intercourse. As Freud noted long ago, displacements, sublimations, and projections of sex are only substitutes for
the real thing. They do not bear offspring and coincidentally are not
wholly satisfying. There is a hunger and tension in physical denial
that cannot be met by any flourish of mental development or bureaucratic invention.

The tertiary order of the individual and bureaucracy confirms in a
surprising way the axial principle that social order everywhere is a
play of sexes. The three orders of social life differ in how they reconcile the sexes. The primary social order reconciles the sexes in contacts of males, females, and offspring. The secondary social order
reconciles the sexes in the play of men's, women's, and family groups.
And the tertiary social order reconciles the sexes in androgynous individuals and impersonal bureaucracies. Where primary and secondary social orders preserve species unity in biological forms, the tertiary social order preserves species unity in cultural forms.

## Summary and Conclusion

This chapter describes how the play of the sexes described in chapter 4 engenders social forms. Social order is a primary manifestation of the sexual division of the species. Among humans, the sexes play in three distinct orders of social life—a primary or zoological order shared with mammals that consists of three elements (female care of young, female mate choice, and male competition), a secondary or archaeological order identified with human migration from trees to savannah that consists of two elements (sex grouping and family), and last, a tertiary or anthropological order identified with human culture that in Western civilization consists of individual and bureaucracy (see figure 5.1).

Tertiary Social Order
[individual, bureaucracy]

Secondary Social Order
[male groups, female groups, family]

Primary Social Order
[female nuture, female choice, male competition]

The three orders of human social life are themes within an intricate and dynamic composition.  Behind each is the dialectic of sex: a species unity divided by sex in search of reconciliation.  Each social order reconciles sexual division in its own way by synthesizing the sexes in a working whole.  Between them is a cumulative development that marks the direction of social evolution.  Each order presupposes and builds on its predecessors.  Without female care of young, female mate choice, and male competition, there can be no fraternity, no sorority, and no family.  And without fraternity, sorority, and family, there can be no individual and no bureaucracy.  These contingencies imply continuity and stability.  As a new social order is built upon old social orders, it cannot depart from them too dramatically without undermining itself.  Thus, while we can imagine all kinds of tertiary social orders, we expect to find only those that accord with the biological secondary and primary social orders whence they came.  These contingencies thus imply conservation of social order compatible with reproduction of the species.

The three orders of human social life are more than an evolutionary history, they are present facts in every social life.  In every human group—be it family, church, community service club, military service, business firm, or nation state—go all three orders.  Even the most modern and progressive corporation, which may celebrate an un-sexist individuality and insist upon a rational bureaucracy based on merit, retains elements of the older primary and secondary sexual social order.  We see this in inner strains and conflicts—in self-segregation of males and females into different occupations, in a "glass ceiling" that names the fact that status-driven males push harder and higher into the ranks of corporate leadership than less status-driven females, in disruptions of sexual attraction and sexual harassment in the workplace, and in the institutional sexism that puts women at a career disadvantage because they often shoulder greater burdens of childcare at home (see, e.g., Meyerson & Fletcher, 2000).  These are each conflicts between a tertiary social order of individuals and bureaucracy, in which the sexes are reconciled internally in androgyny, and primary and secondary social orders, in which the sexes are reconciled externally in sex-based groupings (in particular, in same sex groups, in male competition for female interest, in sexual attraction and pair bonds, and in female nurture of offspring).  The universal confluence of the three sexual social orders in every human group means that every theoretical analysis of social life must take each into account.  Recalling our earlier analogy to Arnheim's study of Picasso's painting, *Guernica*, we are reminded how analysis of a complex modern social life is aided by a historical view which reveals how the oldest and most basic sexual themes, rooted in biology, are overlaid with newer and more contingent sexual themes, rooted in culture.

The analogy to Arnheim's study of Picasso's *Guernica* is fortuitous in another respect, for it suggests that our social life expresses some of the same organic values and consequently some of the same beauty as a great work of art.  This is the beauty of that which expresses an entire evolutionary history in a single life.  Picasso's finished painting expresses in one image the complex growth and development of feeling that went into it.  In the same way, our contemporary social life expresses in each of its incarnations the complex growth and development of the species that went into it.  In every human group goes the same unity, the same sexual division, the same play of the sexes, and sexual social order.  Thus, in every human group goes the same three orders of social life.  The group involutes the life of the species.  For that it is a wonder to behold.

Finally, and contrary to the preemptions of most social science which describes the group as a consequence of individuals (see chapter 2), this chapter reverses the equation to describe the individual as a consequence of the group.  Indeed, the individual turns out to be a late and partial achievement of the tertiary social order developed most prominently in the West.  A creature borne of the sexual biology of the group, the human animal must strike out on his/her own to become an independent-minded person.  And this he/she can do with only limited success.[18]  He/she can never outgrow or forsake his/her roots in the species.  Not even the notoriously self-reliant Emerson or misanthropic Nietzsche can deny this connection and indebtedness to the group. Raging against the base estimate of the market, the individualist confirms his tie to it.  He is as fixed in the social milieu as anyone else (indeed, arguably more as he rails to others about it).  The primacy of social order means that the individual grows out of it, as a further manifestation of its sexual origins.  We can see this in Freud's tripartite conception of psyche composed of id, ego, and superego.  The id is of the primary social order.  It is comprised of unconscious instincts, primarily sex, which must be controlled for the sake of social order.  Ego is of the secondary and tertiary social orders.  Part of the ego orients the person to a social world of primary attachments and group affiliations.  This part of ego may be largely unconscious.  Another part of the ego claims a life for itself apart from others and apart from the group.  This part of the ego thinks for itself and is exclusively conscious.  Finally, the superego is of the tertiary social order and corresponds to the impersonal bureaucracy that sets the person in a larger social or cultural system of rules and mores.  In his later writings, Freud came to see individual psychology as coequal and coextensive with group psychology, though he never made much of this insight in his theory.  We now see how profound an insight this was.  Group psychology is older than the individual psychology that comes out of it.  We now see, too, why Freud appeared late in the nineteenth century in urban Western Europe, for then and there the individual (and the bureaucracy) came into prominence.  In the next chapter we will see more about how the social and psychic orders interrelate in social- and psycho- pathologies.  Pathos is more than a window on the sexual dimensions of the individual psyche, as Freud showed.  Even more it is a window on the sexual dimensions of human social life.

# 6

# Pathos

This book tells the story of the sexual basis of our social life. If the story is a good one it should explain both the life of the past and the life of the future. It should be more than a "just so story" about a few conveniently settled facts, it should tell of facts on the move. This chapter asks how we can tell if the story is a good one. In particular, how can we see the effects of sex on a social life that is supposed already to be defined by sex. And, by and by, how can we test whether or not the story is true. We cannot ask less of a scientific theory.

One route to an answer is suggested by the evolutionary fact of conservation. No living thing is created anew. Each is a twist on what came before. A child is a twist of the two knobs of its parents. Modern species are twists of the knobs of ancestral species. Our own species is linked to all other species of the phylum Chordata by a shared strand of nervous tissue, a spinal cord. We have a common ancestor of the Cambrian era. By descent we are tied more closely to the class of mammals and more closely again to the order of primates. The many outward differences of dolphin, tree shrew, prairie dog, polar bear, and person mask remarkable inner similarities of nerve and vascular development, physiology, and chemical blueprint. Through innumerable variations of detail, basic forms are conserved.

This book is about the forms of our social life, forms said to be sexual and dialectical in nature. This dialectic of sex and social life is said to be produced and conserved by biology (through genes) and culture (through ideas about group life). This implies that one way to see the effects of sex on social life is to look for them in times of social unrest or pathos when the dialectic of sex breaks down, that is, when the synthesis of the sexes is lost and a new or reclaimed synthesis of the sexes is sought. During these times, when social life is imperiled by misaligned sexes (perhaps due to economic or technological factors), we should expect changes to bring them back into line. We should expect men and women to seek ways of life to bring sex back into play to reproduce the species.

No doubt many of the biological and cultural dynamics that fix sex in social life are beyond our ken. As psychoanalysts never tire of pointing out, sex moves us in ways we mostly don't understand. We become aware of sex when its checks and balances surprise or chagrin. We may be surprised or put off by a custom such as female circumcision in the sub-Sahara, or a religious teaching that carnal pleasure outside procreation is a sin, or a bureaucratic rule that prohibits sex within military ranks. Or we may resist new ideas such as birth control, the Equal Rights Amendment in the U.S., reproductive choice, or feminism. A close look at such customs and resistance finds the commonality that all work, in their time and place, to hold safe the primary species dynamic of men competing for access to discerning women. All are "answers" to fearful threats that women will "awaken" sexually to pursue men indiscriminately and/or that men will lose heart and shrink from energetic and fair contest for women.[1] We also become aware of sex when we find ourselves drawn to new ways of life that promise better sexual relations or at least a surcease from sexual antagonism. For an example to which we will return shortly, the feminist movement of the 1960s attracted many women (and a few men) to a new life of greater and more satisfying contact between women and men. For another example to which we will return shortly, Internet pornography today attracts many men (and a few women) to a vicarious sex life beyond that of their daily existence. Cultures change as people are attracted to more vital sexual and social lives.

In theory, there are two circumstances in which the living dialectic of sex can break down. One occurs when differences between the sexes become so large as to preclude the sexes from working together on behalf of the species. The sexes require common ground upon which to mate and to raise offspring. The other occurs when differences between the sexes become so small as to fail to interest each sex in the other. The sexes must differ to attract one another and to contribute positively to one another's life. The first is a breakdown of ability.  The second is a breakdown of will.  In this chapter, I consider both circumstances in order to see if sex affects social life as we suppose.  I consider these circumstances in connection with two "moments" of sexual and social unrest in the recent history of the United States.  Comprised roughly of the postwar period of the 1950s and early 1960s and the recent period of the late 1980s and 1990s, these "moments" are periods of change in sexual relations that have had, and are presently having, visible effects on social life.

## Worlds Apart

The sexes differ too much if they lack the common ground necessary to work together for the good of the species.  To make a living dialectic, it is not enough that the sexes differ.  They must have a basis and means to work through their differences to reproduce.  Sex loses hold of social life when the sexes are too far apart; when they are physically too much separated in time and space, when their cares do not complement one another, and when the contacts between them are too few or too impoverished.

Such an unhealthy separation of the sexes became evident in the United States in the 1950s and early 1960s when, after the disruptions of two world wars and the Great Depression, a booming economy brought to a head social and material changes that had been transfiguring the sexes for decades, indeed for centuries.  Pivotal among these changes was migration of families from farms in rural towns to manufacturing organizations in cities and suburbs.  This migration was ushered by gains in the productivity of the American farm, gains that enabled a growing population to be fed by fewer farmers.  With this migration came changes in social life.  Movement from the rural town to the city broke up extended families in favor of nuclear families consisting of husband, wife, and children.  Movement from the farm to the factory brought changes in work.  For one, it brought a decline in the number of self-employed entrepreneurs.  According to figures cited by Mills (1951), at the beginning of the nineteenth century nearly 80 percent of the population was self-employed.  By 1940 this number had declined to barely 20 percent of the population.  For another, it brought increases in division of labor and introduction of labor-saving machines, thus engaging people in narrower tasks more remote from the whole.  Work became increasingly alien to human aims and needs.  And for a third, it separated the sexes. Men left home to work in factories and office buildings and women stayed home to tend children and house or apartment.

Distinguished as never before in time, place, and interest, the ground between the sexes was swallowed up in a wave of techno- logical and economic "progress." Whereas life had before centered upon a family farm or business that both husband and wife might have worked to support, life for men centered upon the corporation and life for women centered upon domesticities of childcare and housewifery. For the better part of his waking hours, a man allied his efforts, not to his fellows on behalf of a concrete family or com- munity, but to an impersonal order on behalf of an abstract corpora- tion or profession. For the better part of her waking hours, a woman poured her energies and talents into domestic tasks made mundane and socially isolating by labor-saving technologies. She and he were no longer directly connected in their activities.

A key to understanding the myriad changes leading up to the sexual crisis of the 1950s is a much older social innovation—money. Money made possible two revolutions in human organization, revo- lutions well described by Riesman (1948) and Fromm (1955), from which this account borrows. Before money, in the barter economies of antiquity, social activity centered about production and exchange of useful goods and services. To accept the risk of depending on others for necessities, one's stock in trade had to be equally neces- sary. This kept society rooted in traditional folkways of subsistence, including the sex roles of primary and secondary social order de- scribed in chapter 5. Riesman called this type of society "tradition directed," guided as it was by ancient traditions of social behavior and interaction. Fromm emphasized how stable and self-sufficient this type of society was. Thus, in the England of the Middle Ages, the basic rounds of life and relations between the sexes were guided by pagan and Christian teachings and rituals dating hundreds if not thousands of years (see also Lacey & Danziger, 1999). To get along in this society, a person did not have to find a place or learn to play a part; places and parts were given by tradition according to sex.

The first great change in the character of society in the West came well before British colonization of the New World with expansion of money economy from the period of the Renaissance, through the Protestant Reformation, and into the industrial age of the nineteenth century.  As money came to pervade economic activity, its physical and social characteristics became more important in economic development.  Money is not like the bartered goods of a hunt, or harvest, or even the spoils of war.  Money is abstract.  Its value is not intrinsic.  It cannot be eaten or slept upon or worn for protection from the elements.  It becomes useful and valuable only as people of a society accept it as tender for real objects of value.  And money is quantitative.  It is a metric to measure and compare.  Its abstract denominations make it possible to price and exchange goods and services in an impersonal market, thus making money the lifeblood of economic exchange.

With greater use of money came new forms of social activity oriented to commercial capitalism.  With money to keep score, men fashioned new contests for themselves—contests for profit, contests of accumulation.  By the close of the nineteenth century, with the industrial revolution in full flower, men's activity had evolved from mild-mannered collaborations and sharing of perishable returns to all-out competitions to make and keep as much money as possible (Fromm, 1955).  And with money to equate goods and services came a multiplication of the things men could do to make a profit.  The range and complexity of economic activity mushroomed creating, for men especially, new opportunities and challenges to find and take a part in the economy.  Ancient traditions were no longer adequate guides to social activity.  The need now was for men of initiative who by hard work and thrift could find a place for themselves in the burgeoning economy.  The need now was for what Riesman called "inner-directed" people who were self-starting, self-defining, self-reliant, and who had the ambition and work ethic to succeed in a competitive marketplace.  And by accumulating money and monopolizing the means of making it, men took on a new relationship to women.  With greater means of income and less dependence on their wives to earn it, men took on greater power in the relationship with women.  Women needed men in a new way.  Social power and prestige concentrated in the men's realm of commerce, leaving women to feel left out, left behind, second-class citizens.

The second great change in the character of society in the West came lately and pointedly in the U.S. as a result of economic success.  An economy that produces more than its people need must find ways to consume more than its people need.  For example, the postwar United States of the late 1940s and 1950s needed a steady market for automobiles to absorb Detroit car makers' capacity to supply them. Detroit needed to stay busy to take up Pittsburgh's capacity to supply steel. And Pittsburgh needed to stay busy to keep coal mines in West Virginia and iron mines in Pennsylvania and the Midwest humming. It was often said and true that what was good for General Motors was good for the nation. Plenitude produced a new economic era oriented to consumption. Advertisers and marketers arrived to stimulate consumer demand beyond need.[2] New model cars came out every year, women's fashions changed with the winds, and appliances were invented to produce every ease and luxury (think of the electric carving knife and the electric toothbrush). People responded with a new psychology of abundance to replace the old psychology of scarcity. Impulsive spending took the place of long-term saving. What the economy needed, and got, was not the self-starting and thrifty "inner-directed" men and women of early capitalism, but obedient and spend-thrifty consumers. Riesman called these new men and women, who became numerous in the period of the 1950s and early 1960s, "other directed," to mark their sensitivity to the expectations and preferences of others. These were the socially anxious "organization men," open to the impersonal demands of bureaucracy, who sought mainly to be accepted by the corporation. And these were the socially anxious "housewives," open to the advertiser's pitch, who sought mainly to make the best possible home for her children, her husband, and herself. These were the men and women needed to make a mass production economy work, to produce more than necessary and then consume the surplus.

Although too slow, too broad, and too deep to be understood, the economic changes of this period were nevertheless felt. Despite unprecedented gains of material wealth and ease, men and women alike grew uneasy and troubled. Men felt put off from life. Many occupied factory or office jobs obscurely related to the business of the whole. No more did they team up as fellows to hunt, fish, or farm to support the family or group. No more did they band together as comrades to defend the group against enemies and elements. Now they herded as cattle from suburban homes onto crowded commuter trains to mass in large impersonal organizations to make obscure contributions toward dubious goals. Here is Whyte's (1956) alienated "organization man" and here is Hollywood's cynical "man in the grey flannel suit." Euphemisms of the "corporate jungle" aside, men had taken several steps from nature and from the exigencies of family and community life that once granted them a secure place in the life of the group. Now they turned screws on assembly lines or pushed paper in bureaucratic warrens; their contribution to family or group a ledger entry on a weekly payroll. Goodman (1960) estimated that by 1956, less than 10 percent of men were engaged in subsistence activities of producing necessary food and shelter. A far greater percentage were enlisted in jobs to make goods and services not unquestionably useful. Goodman concluded that the dominant organized system of U.S. society crippled men by limiting opportunities for growth of excellence and manliness in worthwhile work. Young boys could not grow up to be men, because this system does not want men (real men are not safe and do not suit). "[T]he young men who conform to the dominant society," writes Goodman, "become for the most part apathetic, disappointed, cynical, and wasted" (p. 12).[3] As we saw earlier, Mead found American men at this time in the quandary of having too few opportunities to exercise the old heroism that brought meaning and attracted women.[4]

Women felt no better. To begin, they were married to men married to corporations, and corporations were viciously thorough competitors for their husbands' attention.[5] No maternal skill, homemaking, or sexual favor could compete with the demands of the corporation. But, in addition, women had issues of their own. They, too, felt small and put off from life. Raised in the same economic and cultural milieu as men, women acquired many of the same bureaucratic sensibilities and consumer tastes, but without the same opportunities to pursue those sensibilities and tastes. Sartre's better half, de Beauvoir (1952), famously pronounced women the "second sex" because they are denied opportunities in the wider world of society by a body that mires them in menstruation, pregnancy, nursing, and childcare. Looking past an immutable biology, Friedan (1963) lays blame for women's plight at the feet of an American culture whose false consciousness, which Friedan called the "feminine mystique," confines women to shallow lives of motherhood and domesticity:

The feminine mystique says that the highest value and the only commitment for women is the fulfillment of their own femininity. It says that the great mistake of Western culture, through most of its history, has been the undervaluation of this femininity. It says this femininity is so mysterious and intuitive and close to the creation and origin of life that man-made science may never be able to understand it. But however special and different, it is in no way inferior to the nature of man; it may even in certain respects be superior. (P. 43)

As Friedan describes, this idea of femininity, perhaps fit for women of an earlier age of more desperate subsistence and reproduction, was not fit for American women of the 1950s and 1960s who had grown larger, more educated, and more ambitious than ever before in history.[6]  Friedan marshals evidence from scientific surveys, expert opinion, magazine articles, and personal interviews to find few women fulfilled in the role of housewife and mother.  Instead, she finds dispirited women unable to use their talents—unchallenged, bored, and depressed.   These women compensate their inner emptiness by tyrannizing their husbands with insatiable sexual demands, by living through children they smother into neurosis, by obsessing over housework, and by chasing fugitive pleasures of adultery, shopping, tranquilizers, and alcohol.

Looking at the sexes together in the light of economic history we can suggest that many men and women were alienated and isolated. The "problem that had no name" (to borrow Friedan's phrase) in the 1950s and 1960s, shared by women and men alike, was that they had become strangers.  Taking their cues from others, many men and women came to distrust each other and themselves.  Men lost some of their inner sense of what it was to be men.  They moved from the family to the corporation to become "organization men." They took their cues from a boss at work.  Manliness became a bureaucratic persona or a Hollywood caricature.  He was to be Clark Gable or Humphrey Bogart.  Along the way, men lost some of their manly virtues of adventure, fraternity, and independence.  Clutching the apron strings of the corporation, they returned to childishness, unready for mature self-hood or constructive relations with women.  Meanwhile, and despite their commanding biology, women likewise lost some of their inner sense of what it was to be women. They retreated into suburban houses to become "housewives."  They took their cues from a husband (who was himself lost) or from an advertising pitchman who told them what blender to use to make the kids' milkshake and what shampoo to use to repair their split ends. Womanliness became a man's fantasy image or again a Hollywood caricature.  She was to be Audrey Hepburn or Marilyn Monroe. Along

the way, women lost some of their womanly virtues of resourcefulness, sorority, and joie de vivre.   Beholden to childish husbands,
they too returned to childishness, unready for mature self-hood or
constructive relations with men.   Each sex thus began to see itself
apart from the other.   Each sex began to view the other strange, with
some of the fear of an unknown enemy.

The problem of the sexes being too far apart showed in the sexuality of the times.   Ironically, there was no trouble having children.
This period saw the highest birthrate in the nation's history—a veri-
table "baby boom."   Women threw themselves into being mothers,
as if finding in motherhood the one true thing.   And men took relief
in providing for their families, believing it made their monkey-bar
scramble in the corporation worthwhile.   The trouble was more in-
sidious.   In a consumer economy overwhelmed by surpluses, there
were few real urgencies left but to have and provide for children.
This made sex an increasingly frantic activity on the one hand, and
an increasingly distorting activity on the other hand.   Some of the
frenzy and distortion showed up in a popular culture increasingly
preoccupied with sex—particularly with its nitty gritty details about
sexual organs, techniques, and mechanics, and perversion.    Ellis
(1962) compared the number of types of references to sex in American mass media (newspapers, magazines, television, radio, music,
plays, novels, and non-fiction books) in 1950 and in 1960.   The
number of references to sex increased over 250 percent over this
period.   And among these, more than half were judged explicit in
content.   This same ten-year period also saw, among other things,
introduction of mass circulation men's magazines, such as *Playboy,*
that featured female nudity, increased consumption by women of
lascivious novels and periodical fiction, and new magazines expressly oriented to homosexuality.   Friedan (1963) reported a preoc-
cupation with sex in women's magazines in the thin disguise of
"health" features such as "Making Marriage Work," "Can this Marriage be Saved," and "Tell Me, Doctor."   The increase in sexual hunger was not limited to interest in media images or fantasy.    Kinsey
(1953) found among American wives that most reported greater
sexual desire than their husbands could satisfy and that one out of
four engaged in some extramarital sex.   Kinsey (1948) found among
American husbands that the majority of their sexual outlets were not
in relations with their wives and that after the fifteenth year of mar-

riage, one out of two was engaged in extramarital sex. Even in marriage, sex was becoming the only thing between men and women. Friedan (1963) discussed the dramatic decrease in the age of marriage during this period—a figure which reached below twenty years by the end of the decade—not as an indication of increased maturity, but rather as its opposite, an indication of immaturity as men and women rushed into marriage and family to evade adult responsibilities. Women, Friedan concluded, sought marriage to "solve" their looming identity crisis. By marrying, a woman relieved herself the burden of making her own life. She was Mr. X's wife or Mary's mother. Men, Friedan believed, acceded to marriage, not to solve a problem of identity, but to recover a mother figure on whom they could depend. By marrying, a man returned himself to the care of a woman. He was also promised a regular partner for sex. How often these young people, many barely seventeen years of age, did not realize the bargain they struck until entanglements made it difficult to reverse.

* * *

If this book is correct on key points about sex and social life—about the unity of the species, about the division and play of sex, about social order arising as a synthesis of sex, and about the conservation of sex and social life—we would expect that the sexual conditions of the 1950s and early 1960s could not continue. We would expect compensating changes in social life as men and women move to establish closer and more vital relations. These expectations are born out by movements in American culture, commencing during this period, that attracted interest, in part, because they brought the sexes closer together.

American culture invented at least three "answers" to the sexual alienation and separation of the 1950s and early 1960s. One of these came in efforts to transcend the culture by loosely organized youth movements such as the "Hipsters " in the late 1940s, "Beats" in the 1950s, and "Hippies" in the 1960s and 1970s. These movements shared an epochal idea that the ways and means of industrial capitalism, particularly technology and large-scale bureaucracy, keep people in (comfortable) chains that deny their full humanity (see Roszak, 1969). Although none of these movements attracted a large or sustained following, all evoked strong and mostly angry reactions from the cultural mainstream, giving them influence beyond their numbers. These movements are epitomized by the "Beat Generation" that emerged in New York City's Greenwich Village in the late 1950s, reached to the West Coast and especially San Francisco, and later gave rise to the Hippie movement of the 1960s and 1970s. Drawing on earlier protests against the industrial age by the likes of Emerson, Thoreau, and Whitman, leading figures of the Beat movement such as Burroughs, Corso, Ginsburg, and Kerouac celebrated a transcendent individuality beyond oppressing social conventions (Foster, 1992).[7] Theirs was what Kerouac described as a "wild self-believing individuality" (in Donaldson, 1979). They modeled this quest on traditional mysticisms that sought universal enlightenment through heightened personal experiences. Such experiences, or "kicks" or "highs" as they were called, were to be had in expressionist art, particularly poetry, in drug states, in music, particularly jazz, and in sex. But unlike traditional mysticisms, which demand self-denying discipline and community support to attain enlightenment, these "kicks" were more personal. And for all the talk about brotherhood, they were selfish. The Beats of course did not believe this about their practice, but believed instead that personal pursuit of pure experience led necessarily and inevitably to connection with others.[8]

The failure of the Beat movement, and of its echoes in the Hippie movements of the 1960s, ultimately came in the fact they did not build a viable community or accomplish anything of value. The Beats balked for good reason at the hollow roles and vacuous consumerism of the modern "rat race," but offered no mandate or program to put a better society in its place. Indeed, the Beats were notoriously apolitical. They inveighed for no cause, signed no petitions, and organized no voters. Indeed, they withdrew from the greater society thinking there was no alternative to it. In this respect they resembled the bourgeois middle class they despised—a middle class that likewise accepted the existing social order as brute and unchangeable (Goodman, 1960, compared them wittily to "griping soldiers who do not intend to mutiny"). But even more damaging to the Beat movement's posterity was its unworkable plan for sex. It made sex un-biological and unproductive. The Beats, and later the Hippies, were notorious (and no doubt envied by many) for an easy sexuality uncomplicated by commitments of marriage and family. They sought to raise sex from the messy burdensome realm of nature and body—of pain, menstruation, pregnancy, nursing, and parenting—to the lighter realm of spirit and mind. Sex was a chance for heightened experience, an opportunity for yet another "kick" or "high." This sex was not to reproduce the body but to transcend the body. And truth be told, this sex was more for men, who were glad for the license to sow their oats widely, than it was for women, who were concerned as ever to choose their mates wisely. Viewed sociologically, the Beat generation was a men's club, its activities an exercise of male protest and prerogative. As Foster (1992) observes, the traditional concerns of women have little place in Beat writing. Corso's poems attack marriage and depict women, especially mothers, as grotesque. Ginsburg (1977) notes in an early journal that "[t]he social organization which is most true of itself to the artist is the boy gang, not society's perfum'd marriage." Kerouac writes as a misogynist when he admits in his "Visions of Cody" (1972) that "[as] far as young women are concerned, I can't look at them unless I tear off their clothes one by one." And Burroughs' novels choose a sexuality unencumbered by illusion or sentiment such as romantic love (which he imagined to be a fraud perpetrated on men by women). In an essay entitled "Women: A Biological Mistake?" (reprinted in 1986) he argues for an androgyny that fuses the sexes in a single organism. For the Beats, sex is an individual (and mostly male) affair, aimed for transcendence rather than reproduction, and ideally realized by incorporating male and female elements within the individual. The Beat solution to the sexual crisis of the 1950s was to tear it from its moorings in the biology of primary and secondary social order, and reserve it for the tertiary social order of the individual. But this narrow prospect opposed human nature and could bring no happiness to the person and no children to the group.

From the buds of the Beat generation grew a second answer to the sexual alienation and isolation of the 1950s that aimed to create community groups in opposition to the larger society. With varying degrees of intention (see Zicklin, 1983) and success (see Roberts, 1971), a few groups in the 1960s put word to deed to create alternative communities—communes—intended to be friendlier to human nature and friendlier to the environment. Varying in size, formality, doctrine, and militancy, these efforts generally consisted of back-to-

nature movements to reclaim an older and simpler life of subsistence—a life on the farm before economic capitalism, before large-
scale bureaucracy, before blind consumerism, and before brutaliz-
ing production technologies.    In 1970, the *New York Times* estimated there were more than 2000 communes in the United States
(Fairfield, 1972).  Most were founded to refuse or at least minimize
what were felt to be the worst elements of economic capitalism by
creating a smaller and more intimate social world in which one's
actions and social relations would contribute directly to securing
basic needs.  Roberts (1971) described the urge to communal life as
the urge to reclaim the satisfactions of a primitive "re-tribalized"
existence.

Back to nature meant, among other things, back to the body and
back to sex.  An important aspect of the simpler commune life was
that it put the sexes back in touch with themselves and with each
other.  Whereas the Hipsters and Beats of an earlier day sought sex
as a rarefied experience and means of transcendence, communalists
regarded sex an expression of animality, to be sought and enjoyed
without social convention or philosophical pretense.  In their pursuit
of naturalism, they shed many of the isolating conventions of comportment and dress of the larger society to find a more expansive
common ground.  Men matched women in growing their hair long,
in wearing colorful offbeat clothes, and in adorning themselves in
beads.  Women joined men in taking off their bras, in refusing to
shave, and in forsaking hairdos and cosmetics.  And except for a
few notorious experiments in group marriage and free love,[9] the
majority of communes kept to nature's sex roles and behaviors.
Despite egalitarian ideals that reached across old lines of status, class,
and race, communes sought the old grooves of sex difference and
complementarity.  Men and women reproduced a rough division of
labor; men in groups took on heavier tasks outside the home, women
in groups tended children and household chores.  Sex, marriage,
and family were wilder in the middle-class suburb than on the communal farm.  As Berger (1971, p. 18) noted:

> The women's liberation movement would probably not approve of the position of
> women in most communes. ... Women tend to do traditional women's work: most of
> the cooking and cleaning (they are more concerned with tidiness than most men), and in
> the rural communes much of the traditional female farm roles in addition ... They are
> ideologically less forceful then men and express themselves with generally less author-
> ity.

Wagner (1982) came to the same conclusion in his study of larger corporate communes:

> When I encountered the strongly patriarchal ideology of the "Haran" commune, ... I concluded at first that the commune, which was founded prior to and independently of the "Sixties," was an anachronistic "exception." This conclusion was abandoned quickly in the face of contrary evidence. Not only are the leaders of modern corporate communes usually male, but also the communes frequently manifest strict sex-role divisions which in many respects parallel those of Haran.

With varying success, the commune movement of the 1960s relieved the alienation and isolation of the sexes plaguing the wider culture. Its means was the psychologically astute one of turning back the clock of economic progress to a time in which men and women enjoyed meaningful lives that fit their nature and complemented one another. In this crucial respect, the movement was more reactionary than revolutionary. At the same time it defied established cultural precepts of economic organization it emphasized established cultural precepts about sexual organization.[10]

As matters went, the 1960s era communes did not prove to be stable and sustainable organizations. As Roberts (1971) notes, few survived into a second year and, of these, few survived beyond a second year. The reasons for failure were many. A few communes were attacked and undermined by outsiders who could not abide their values and unconventional ways, or who could not bear the loss of property values around the commune. Other communes failed for reasons that groups of all kinds fail—for want of effective leadership, for want of a compelling ideology or purpose, for want of means to handle internal conflicts, for reasons of economic inefficiency. No doubt drugs and experiments with sexuality contributed to some failures, as drug-addled members withdrew into hazy isolation, or as resentments of sexually jealous members wormed their worms. Perhaps the only safe generalization to make about the failure of the communes is that they were always too far out on the margin of the wider culture and too out of step with the times to succeed. No matter how astute their social psychology, their efforts of nostalgia were too little too late. Economic man had long ago abandoned the family farm for a high rise uptown condominium. Except for a few youth, accustomed to university crash pads and urban Bohemias, alienated by modern life, and idealistic enough to believe they could do better, most members of modern society could not imagine an alternative social life, much less reclaim the senses and skills to live it.

Although the Beat and the later commune movements did not answer the sexual alienation and isolation of the 1950s and early 1960s, they were important in setting the stage for the more practical-minded and impactful women's movement. This movement, which drew strength from the contemporaneous civil rights movement, sought to make industrial society more hospitable to women and by so doing improve relations between the sexes. The idea, in essence, was to put the sexes on the same footing by opening to women the opportunities in society enjoyed by men. Women could become more like men and, in time, men could become more like women, thus closing the distance between the two. Behind the march for equality was an ideology of individualism reminiscent of the earlier Beat generation. Feminists joined the Beats in conceiving of human nature as individual nature, as reaching beyond body and sex to flourish in adventures outside the home. And feminists believed, with the Beats, that happiness comes with personal growth and development. Thus, Friedan (1963, pp. 310-311), for example, based her feminism upon humanist claims for self-development:

> Scientists of human behavior have become increasingly interested in the basic human need to grow, man's will to be all that is in him to be. Thinkers in many fields—from Bergson to Kurt Goldstein, Heinz Hartmann, Allport, Rogers, Jung, Adler, Rank, Horney, Angyal, Fromm, May, Maslow, Bettlelheim, Tillich and the existentialists—all postulate some positive growth tendency within the organism, which, from within, drives it to fuller development, to self-realization. This "will to power," "self-assertion," "dominance," or "autonomy," as it is variously called, does not imply aggression or competitive striving in the usual sense; it is the individual affirming his existence and his potentialities as a being in his own right; it is "the courage to be an individual." ... In this new psychological thinking, which seeks to understand what makes men human, and defines neurosis in terms of that which destroys man's capacity to fulfill his own being, the significant tense is the future. It is not enough for an individual to be loved and accepted by others, to be "adjusted" to his culture. He must take his existence seriously enough to make his own commitment to life, and to the future; he forfeits his existence by failing to fulfill his entire being.

Unlike the Beats who rejected the economic opportunities of the larger society as life-denying and alienating, feminists believed the road to self-development for women ran through those very opportunities. Men and women could get along in the new era only by becoming full partners in the society. This meant, above all, that women must be given the same opportunity and encouragement to extend themselves in the larger world beyond the home. Women must be allowed and encouraged to grow beyond the maternal role. Again, from Friedan (1963):

> What happens if the environment frowns on that courage and strength—sometimes virtually forbids, and seldom actually encourages that growth in the child who is a girl? What happens if human growth is considered antagonistic to femininity, to fulfillment as a woman, to woman's sexuality? The feminine mystique implies a choice between "being a woman" or risking the pains of human growth. Thousands of women, reduced to biological living by their environment, lulled into a false sense of anonymous security in their comfortable concentration camps, have made a wrong choice. The irony of their mistaken choice is this: the mystique holds out "feminine fulfillment" as the prize for being only a wife and mother. But it is no accident that thousands of suburban housewives have not found that prize. The simple truth would seem to be that women will never know sexual fulfillment and the peak experience of human love until they are allowed and encouraged to grow to their full strength as human beings. For according to the new psychological theorists, self-realization, far from preventing the highest sexual fulfillment, is inextricably linked to it. (P. 317)

Friedan was hardly the only feminist theorist of this period, but she was the most influential in igniting a resurgent women's movement beginning in the middle 1960s, and she is generally credited with having clearly analyzed the "problem that has no name" among suburban housewives. With Friedan, the feminist answer to sexual alienation and isolation came in the belief that women have the same needs as men to grow and develop. By encouraging and satisfying this need in women through economic opportunity it would be easier for women and men to understand one another and to work together for the commonweal. This hopeful belief was abetted by the idea noted above that individual life unfolds in a realm of mind beyond the body and beyond male and female biological imperatives. Sharing an interest to grow, particularly in that most human and open realm of mind, women and men would no longer be separated by incomprehensible differences. Neither would they defer or submit to the other; each would play an equal part in the life of the species, be this in the realm of work or the realm of family. Both would take ungrudging pride in the accomplishments of the other, no matter what the arena, and no matter who may have been outshone in the process. And most delicious of all, sexual relations would have a new more relaxed basis, plagued with fewer frustrations and capable of greater heights. Here Friedan (1963, pp. 322-323) cites Maslow (1954) approvingly:

> In self-actualizing people, the orgasm is simultaneously more important and less important than in average people. It is often a profound and almost mystical experience, and

yet the absence of sexuality is more easily tolerated by these people. ... Loving at a higher need level makes the lower needs and their frustrations and satisfactions less important, less central, more easily neglected. But it also makes them more wholeheartedly enjoyed when gratified. ... Food is simultaneously enjoyed and yet regarded as relatively unimportant in the total scheme of life. ... Sex can be wholeheartedly enjoyed, enjoyed far beyond the possibility of the average person, even at the same time that it does not play a central role in the philosophy of life. It is something to be enjoyed, something to be taken for granted, something to build upon, something that is very basically important like water or food, and that can be enjoyed as much as these; but gratification should be taken for granted.

The women's movement encountered problems, of course. One was and is today that the men's world of economic organization is no place to grow as an individual (about this the Beats were right). Perhaps for this reason the aim of personal growth was sacrificed to the narrower aim of economic independence from men—an aim that per force separates the sexes. Another was that despite its humane intent to liberate both women and men, the women's movement succumbed to an identity politics that made enemies not only of many men but of many women as well. What Friedan envisaged as a mutual interest of the sexes became a contention between them. Battle lines were quickly and thickly drawn. Some animosity came as resistance to any compromise of the sexual division of labor between work and home (the "feminine mystique" was then and is today yet a powerful idea). Who could doubt women's biological destiny to bear and nurture children and man's biological destiny to venture from the home to support the family? And some animosity came as frustration with this resistance, which many feminists no doubt regarded as incomprehensible and out of touch with the times. Who in this United States today could question or deny the individual right to grow and develop to the full? The battle matched traditionalist chauvinism with feminist militancy and had the unintended effect of defeating some of the cooperation hoped for between the sexes. At its sniping worst, feminism became a view that men are irrelevant in women's lives. With the megaphone of *Ms. Magazine*, publisher Gloria Steinhem told an incredulous world that "A woman needs a man like a fish needs a bicycle" and, reflecting on women's progress, noted with some pride that "We [women] are becoming the men we intended to marry." But self-esteem purchased at the expense of men was purchased also at the expense of cooperation with men. Deserved or not, feminism became identified with male-bashing and man-hating, leading many who might once have marched behind its banner to leave its ranks.[11]

Although of varying popularity over the years and over its several incarnations (cf., Mitchell & Oakley, 1986), the women's movement, unlike the back-to-nature and Beat movements before it, can be identified with real changes in sexual relations. Laws changed to ensure equal opportunity for women in the workplace and to protect women from sexual intimidation and harassment. Barriers to education and economic achievement fell, so completely that women now outnumber and outpace men in school and women are gaining parity with men in the workplace. And values changed. No longer are women expected to forsake a working career to be mother and housewife (though many still do). No longer is the feminine mystique promoted as natural law and common sense (though it still has spokespersons on the political and religious right). No longer are men expected to be the sole or even the primary breadwinner in the family (though many still are). And no longer are men ridiculed for making less money than their wives, for putting their wives' career ahead of their own, or even for staying home to mind the kids while their wives work (though people still talk privately).

In sum, our theory of sex and social life leads us to expect that the sexual crisis of the 1950s and early 1960s would invite compensating changes in sexual and social relations in the years that followed. Though vaguely stated and tested only against the broadest of cultural trends, I believe this expectation is largely confirmed. In the 1950s men and women stood in an untenable relation—alienated from themselves and isolated from one another. Today they stand together more or less as equals at work and in the home. In the 1950s men and women had little in common save a frantic urge for sex and reproduction. Today they share entire lives. No more are they the strangers they once were. No more do they fail to connect and understand as they once did. The sexes and social life have evolved together. The critical question is whether the many changes wrought in U.S. society since the 1950s have returned the sexes and social life to health. It is to this question that we presently turn.

## Mystery Lost

The sexes differ too little if they do not want to work together for the good of the species. Common ground alone does not make a living dialectic. There must be motive and reason to work together.

There is more to sexual attraction than the organ lust we remember in high school. Woman attracts man with a rounded figure and special organs, but her allure depends on how she carries herself, on her femininity. Man attracts woman with a muscled figure and special organs, but his allure, too, depends on how he carries himself, on his masculinity. Ordinarily, body and behavior run together and sexual attraction unfolds smoothly. However, where body and behavior clash, where males want for masculinity or females want for femininity, sexual attraction is lost. Where there is little sexual attraction, there is little sex, and little chance for the species to reproduce. The living dialectic of sex thus loses hold of social life when the sexes do not differ enough and in the right ways to attract one another. Male antithesis must oppose female thesis to make a constructive synthesis.

Arguably such a loss of sexual attraction is happening today at the turn of the millennium in the U.S. and much of Europe. A burgeoning post-industrial information and service economy is taking women outside the home into the economy in numbers and stature to rival men. In the process, age-old sexual divisions and social orders are being undermined and effaced. There are losses particularly of secondary social order. Going are the men's groups of adventure beyond the home (of hunt, war, exploration) and women's groups of home and childcare. Today, men and women leave home together to work indistinguishable jobs in indistinguishable bureaucracies. And they leave their children in the care of a third bureaucracy of day care or school. Going, too, is the nuclear family made of husband and wife with children—a victim in the U.S. of both a marriage rate that has dropped 43 percent from 87.5 marriages per 1,000 unmarried women in 1960 to an all time low of 49.7 marriages per 1000 unmarried women in 1996, and a divorce rate that has soared 30 percent since 1970 to hover at nearly 50 percent today.[12] Family life is shrinking to ever-smaller dimensions. Never mind "quality-time" with the kids, there is homework for all, and then some time alone together "vegetating" before a television or computer screen. For many people the family is no longer the center of social life. Its functions of social and emotional support have been usurped by the corporation. As Hochschild (1997) observed in her study of middle-class workers in one large corporation, people talk increasingly of their workplace as home and of their co-workers as family and talk increasingly of their home as a workplace and their spouse and children as co-workers.

More alarming because more dangerous for the species are losses of primary social order. Going, too, are the most basic sexual elements of social life: female care of young, female mate choice, and male competition for the female. Having left home for the wider world of work, women ceded much of their involvement in their children's lives. This has been more than a shift in time and attention, but more subtly and importantly a shift in sensibility as work has called from women ambitions, competitive passions, and specific intellectual skills at the expense of the sympathy, adaptive flexibility, and practical intuition demanded of childcare. Furthermore, in adopting an aggressive and mannish bearing in their work relations with men, women have adopted a more aggressive and mannish bearing in their sexual relations with men. In the United States today, as never before, women join men in pursuing sex for sensual pleasure rather than procreation and nurture. Freed by easy birth control and justified by a women's movement that brought attention to women's sexual response, women share in the "sexual revolution" begun in the late 1960s and 1970s that continues to this day. Demanding greater sexual satisfaction they have become more promiscuous. According to a 1999 study by the Rutgers University National Marriage Project, whereas 90 percent of women born between 1933 and 1942 were either virgins when they married or had premarital sex only with their eventual husbands, today over half of teenage girls have sexual intercourse by age seventeen, and on average they are sexually active for seven to eight years before getting married. And demanding greater sexual satisfaction, women have become more critical of men's sexual performance, much to the latter's chagrin.

Along with these changes in women, men have withdrawn from women and from the chase for success to win her favor. Between the late 1960s and early 1980s, public opinion pollster, Yankelovich, recorded changes in men's beliefs and interests in economic success. Among college men in the middle 1960s, roughly seven of ten believed that hard work led to success. Among college men in the early 1970s, nearly two-thirds no longer believed this. By the 1980s, a majority of men said they no longer seek or are satisfied by conventional job success. Only 20 percent say work means more to

them than leisure. And more than 50 percent say work is no longer
their major source of satisfaction. For men, writes Yankelovich, "self-
fulfillment has become severed from success. Men have come to
feel that success on the job is not enough to satisfy their yearnings
for self-fulfillment, and they are reaching out for something more
and for something different. ... Somehow the conventional systems
no longer satisfy their deepest psychological needs nor nourish their
self-esteem, nor fulfill their cravings for the 'full rich life'" (quoted
in Friedan, 1981, pp. 133-134). This loss of interest in success has
continued into today. In 1996, the British magazine, the *Economist*,
published a cover story entitled "The Trouble with Men" that described the decline of male achievement in school and at work in
Britain, Europe, and the United States. Throughout the European
Union, boys graduated from secondary schools at a rate barely 80
percent that of girls. In the United States, boys are more likely than
girls to be held back a grade and are twice as likely to drop out of
school. At the same time, men's participation in the labor market
has decreased while women's has increased. In part, this is because
whereas women have been eager to take blue-collar and white-col-
lar jobs held by men, men have not been eager to take clerical and
pink-collar jobs held by women, despite the fact these are the fastest
growing jobs in the new information and service-based economy.[13]
Echoing the *Economist's* findings on men and education, a recent
*New York Times* report finds that college campuses in the U.S. that
were for decades dominated by men are becoming dominated by
women. Although there are slightly more college-age men than
women, according to Department of Education statistics, there were
8.4 million women and only 6.7 million men enrolled in college in
1996. According to the reporter, Lewin, "[g]iven the widening income gap between high school graduates and those with advanced
degrees, ... many education experts worry that men's failure to pursue higher education will seriously limit their life choices."[14] Writing in 1981, Friedan interpreted trends in men's orientations to
achievement hopefully to suggest that men today are at last finding
meaning in pursuits outside work, in the family and in the home.
But a stronger case can be made that men today are not so much
seeking a broader life as they are discouraged from the only life
they know and understand as the family breadwinner. Such a case
has been recently made by Fukuyama (1999) and Tiger (1999) who

find that women's new economic independence, together with her nearly flawless control over fertility, has fundamentally changed the bargain between men and women. As women no longer need men to provide for their offspring, men feel less responsible for their families and more inclined to abandon them. Feeling less responsible, men lose the ambition to succeed.

Lending credence to this new picture of the sexes are collateral reports of a crisis of manhood in response to the ascendance of feminism. In 1981, *New York Times* art critic, John Russell, wrote in wonder of "The Retreat of Manhood as Mirrored in the Arts." In plays, movies, painting, sculpture, and opera, Russell traced a hundred-year decline of man from powerful hero to whining baby. Not coincidentally, this decline came with the emergence of a triumphal, freestanding woman. Fifteen years later one finds in the *Times* a more regular wonder at the loss of virility in the American male. Columnist Maureen Dowd, in particular, turns her biting wit on, among other things, the "pink think" of male politicians and media moguls who save no masculine scruple to curry women's favor, and the desperation of middle-aged men seeking lost potency in testosterone patches and the latest erection springing drug.[15] And writing in 1998, *Harper's Magazine* columnist, Fay Weldon, bemoans the feminization of Great Britain's men, particularly those in politics:

> This is the Age of the Anima. Male voters searched for it in themselves and found it. Here in Britain, Tony Blair's New Labour Party presents itself as female, using the language of compassion, forgiveness, apology, understanding, and nurturing—qualities conventionally attributed to women. ... I write, you must understand, more of patterns of thinking and speaking than of anything so vulgar and simple as generative parts. If women can wear trousers and still be female, men can wear trousers and be women in spirit. In New Britain, see woman-think and woman-speak. The marginalization of the intellectual is registered under the heading "seeking a feeling society"; a pathological fear of elitism, under "fairness to others"; the brushing aside of civil liberties, under "sensitivity to the people's needs." The frightening descent into populism becomes merely a "responsiveness to the voter's wants." (Pp. 65-66)

> The personal became the political, and political personal, and lo! that person was a female, and victorious. The gender switch was thrown and women turned into the oppressors of men, and men, as victims will, retaliated by taking on the role of those who oppressed them. The first step that women took in the emancipation was to adopt traditional male roles: to insist on their right to wear trousers, not to placate, not to smile, not to be decorative. The first step men have taken in their self-defense is to adopt the language of Therapism: a profoundly female notion—that all things can be cured by talk.[16] (P. 66)

Looking at women and men together we no longer find a picture of responsible sexuality. Sex roles are being inverted, the gender switch thrown, as women venture from economic dependence upon men to assume a more active or even dominant posture toward men and as men shrink from economic ambition into a more passive and deferential posture toward women. With these changes, the most basic acts of sexual reproduction—of attraction, transportation, selection, and support—are going unassigned and unmet.

The dynamics creating the sexual crisis of the 1990s are not new, but continue those that created the earlier sexual crisis of the 1950s and early 1960s. Again the base cause is economic, the continued rapid development and success of industrial capitalism. However, whereas in the 1950s capitalism separated men from women, making "organizational men" of the one and lonely "housewives" of the other, in the 1990s capitalism joins men, women, and now children in one alienating bureaucratic society. Through the 1950s, the woman's world of home was set against the man's world of organization, as a last, and in the event frail, bastion of the old sexual social order. As long as women cleaved to the old roles of wife and mother, men returned home at the end of the day to reclaim some of the male identity he lost at work. But as women succumbed to capitalism's siren call, there was no one to keep interests in others ahead of interests in self, no one to find the value in a life beyond its economic return, and no one to keep greedy materialistic impulses from being mistaken for real needs. Anticipating this trend by some fifty years in Great Britain, Kenealy (1920, p. 190) writes:

> The chief cause of latter-day conjugal unrest and disaffection is to be found—not in the natural state of marriage, but in a decline of those personal traits which make for happiness therein. Girls brought up as now, without home-interests or training, but, on the contrary, with mainly self-realising and self-absorbing aims and pursuits, are deficient not only in domestic aptitudes but lamentably also in emotional qualities. ... So keenly self-centred the majority of women have become, so bent upon their hobbies and careers, as to have lost nearly all of that sympathetic adaptiveness natural to woman, which enables her to forget—and forget with pleasure—her own in the personality and interests of others.

The "feminine mystique," decried by de Beauvoir, and lampooned by Friedan, proved to be the last gasp of a dying way of life. De Beauvoir, Friedan, and others did not destroy the feminine mystique, they were avatars of a social order beyond biology made inevitable by capitalism's conquest of women.

The power of capitalism to remake society yet again and precipitate a new sexual crisis comes in its denial of sex. Its twin developments of bureaucracy and consumerism join men and women in an encompassing economic order apart from nature and apart from male and female sensibilities. Bureaucracy orders men and women around like robots. Before factories, on the farm, they were man and woman. In the factory, they became sexless "personnel" to be administered by a new class of bureaucrat. Today they are sexless and soulless "human resources" to be managed like any other factor of production, like steel or hydroelectric power. There are jobs to be done in certain ways according to a set schedule, by men or women it does not matter. Consumerism likewise de-sexes the person by barraging the senses with products to stimulate and then satisfy spurious "needs" having little or no connection to the body or to sex. Worries about whether one's car is sleeker more powerful than the neighbor's, about which of thirty-seven varieties of vinegar should go in the salad, or about whether this or that article of clothing is in style this season, may be cleverly tied to sex by an advertiser's pitch, but the tie is an artifice that over time and repetition alienates the person from their body and from the opposite sex. Having learned to rely on others for direction, men and women lose sight of who they are and what they need. Facing substantially the same consumer environment they come to resemble one another as never before. They look, dress, and act the same, work the same jobs for the same organizations, juggle the same demands of family, and have the same material wants and the same shallow satisfactions. This sameness, together with the norm of sexual equality that grows up around it, militates against sex-typed division of tasks and responsibilities. With kids and dinners and rented movies to pick up, baby sitters and laundry and parcel post to drop off, play dates and soccer rides and vacations to schedule, and no time for emergencies, there is a lot to negotiate. The product of it all: men and women relate in a new way, not as complements, but as harried antagonists, equally authorized and equally responsible. Even when married, they are more competitors than teammates. Sex is no more the main factor deciding their lives. At night, naked in bed, they may recall a primitive complementarity and attraction, but all the livelong day they meet as vendors in a marketplace.

The sexlessness of the current age should not be confused with the ideal of individuality argued by essayists such Emerson, Thoreau, and Nietzsche, given emotive resonance by poets such as Whitman, Ginzburg, and Corso, and made into therapy by psychologists such as Goldstein, Rogers, and Maslow.  To be an individual is to be a life unto oneself, self-contained, and apart from the group.  Far from this ideal, to which he/she relates as a degenerate case, today's man or woman is neurotically insecure, conformist, and dependent upon others for approval and direction.  Lasch (1979) labels this personality type "narcissistic" and describes it, after Freud, in terms of a strong dependence on others for vicarious warmth, a strong fear of dependence, a sense of inner emptiness, repressed rage, and unsatisfied oral cravings.  Whereas the individual stands serenely apart from the group and acts with perfect spontaneity and sweetness amidst its carking hubbub, today's man or woman obsesses with the opinions of others and anxiously presents him- or herself before their good judgments and graces.[17]  Separating the narcissist from the individual ideal is an oppressive self-consciousness.  In a capitalist economy that separates price from value, style from substance, form from content, and want from need, people think of themselves as actors not persons.  All the world's a stage, wrote Shakespeare presciently, and each has his or her parts to play.  A bureaucrat takes an impersonal office or role.  He or she is not a leader, or a manager, or a clerk, or an assembly worker, but plays as such, taking marks and reading lines as directed.  A consumer compares an advertiser's image of a richer, fuller, and better-looking life against his or her own sadder reality.  If the disparity between the real and the hoped-for is great enough, the advertiser can hope the consumer's self-loathing will motivate a purchase.  The advertiser makes a sale and the consumer takes another step down the road of self-consciousness.  Eventually and inexorably, the self-consciousness of economic capitalism infects and transforms sex.  The person no longer thinks of himself as male or female, or even as a male doctor or female lawyer, but simply as a person in the role of business executive, professor, garbage collector.  Forgetting that as a male or female he/she has a definite and inalienable part in the life of the species, he/she is subtly encouraged to believe that to be a man or a woman is to affect one more culturally prescribed role.[18]  This confuses sex, which is of the body and God-given, with "gender," which is of the mind and culturally prescribed. This is a way of being at odds with oneself. And this is a way of being lost.

Narcissism cripples social life by putting a ponderous self-consciousness ahead of free-flowing and finely calibrated instinct. Awkwardness and doubt result. This is nowhere more true than in relations between the sexes. The problem is put wittily by Thurber and White (1929), who decades earlier found in self-consciousness a relationship-destroying bafflement. Here they write of that peculiar uncertainty that can shake the comfort of an embrace:

There is no more disturbing experience in the rich gamut of life than when a young man discovers, in the midst of an embrace, that he is taking the episode quite calmly and is taking the kiss for what it is worth. His doubts and fears start from this point and there is no end to them. He doesn't know whether it's love or passion. In fact, in the confusion of the moment he's not quite sure it isn't something else, like forgery. He certainly doesn't see how it can be love.

Let us examine this incident. He has been sitting, we'll say, on a porch with his beloved. They have been talking of this and that, with the quiet intimacy of lovers. After a bit he takes her in his arms and kisses her—not once, but several times. It is not a new experience to him; he has had other girls, and he has had plenty of other kisses from this one. This time, however, something happens. The young man, instead of losing himself in the kiss, finds himself in it. What's more the girl to him loses her identity— she becomes just anyone on whom he is imposing his masculinity. Instead of his soul being full of the ecstasy which is traditionally associated with love's expression, his soul is just fiddling around. The young man is thinking to himself:

"Say, this is pretty nice now!"

Well, that scares him. Up to this point in the affair he has been satisfied that his feeling was that of love. Now he doesn't know what to think. In all his life he has never come across a character in a book or a movie who, embracing his beloved, was heard to say, "This is pretty nice," unless that character was a villain. He becomes a mass of conflicting emotions, and is so thoroughly skeptical and worried about the state of his heart that he will probably take to reading sociological books to find out if it's O.K. to go ahead, or whether, as a gentleman, it's his duty to step out before he further defames a sweet girl and soils her womanhood. (Pp. 72-76)

The authors advise that if you're not sure of the difference between love and passion it is best either to give them both up or quit trying to split hairs! This story is funny because it speaks a truth about the unconscious spontaneity that is natural to male-female relations. But it is also a truth made unfunny by its epidemic absence today. Left to worm its worms, self-consciousness makes the sex act, the most natural act in the world, a trial. "Meanings" are rarely so sure as instincts. The man who plays at sexual initiative, or the woman who plays at sexual submission, must not let on that they are just playing, or else the act can not come off satisfactorily. This is perhaps easier to see in the man, whose sexual physiology, in addition to being more obvious, is more fragile and liable to upset. When a woman self-consciously holds herself apart from the act, apart from a free and easy submission to the man, he is apt to lose his nerve and initiative. He must believe the submission in order to function properly. Though less obvious, the same holds for the woman. When a man self-consciously plays at sexual initiative without confidence or conviction, she is unable to greet his overtures with the sensitivity needed for arousal. With too much self-consciousness the sex act becomes an absurd and ridiculous spectacle, unnatural as can be.[19]

And so it is in sexual relations particularly that we see the current crisis of the sexes being too much alike. Sex today is an increasingly superficial and unserious, market transaction, based on light attractions. As noted, genuine sexual attraction is a subtle business that rests as much on how men and women comport themselves as it does on overt differences of body. Insofar as the sexes share the same sexless self-consciousness and act out the same narcissistic sensibilities and impulses, they have only body differences between them. Although we lack the longitudinal data needed to compare the present era with past eras, sex today is plainly burdened by self-consciousness. According to the 1992 National Health and Social Life Survey (Laumann, Gagnon, Michael, and Michaels, 1994), the most common sexual problems reported by men today are climaxing too early (reported by 28.5 percent of men), anxiety about performance (reported by 17 percent of men), and lack of interest in sex (reported by 15.8 percent of men), while the most common sexual problems reported by women today are lack of interest in sex (reported by 33.4 percent of women), inability to orgasm (reported by 24.1 percent of women), and sex not pleasurable (reported by 21.2 percent of women).[20] These are problems of being too self-conscious about sex. With the sexual revolution of the 1960s, and particularly with the advent of hormonal birth control and the sexual consciousness-raising of the women's movement, the focus of sex has changed from one that included reproductive aims and concerns to one that centers more exclusively on physical pleasure. Increasingly, men and women seek sex's physical pleasures without its old dimensions of love and marriage. And increasingly, men and women seek sex's physical pleasures in non-coital intercourse, particularly oral intercourse, that does not involve face to face interaction or even substantial cooperation and mutuality. Laumann et al. (1994) report a revolution in sexual technique between the birth cohorts of 1933-1942 and 1951-1960, with dramatic increases in lifetime experiences of oral sex from 62 percent to 90 percent respectively. [21] Thus, where the hyper-sexuality of the 1950s led to early marriages and a baby boom, the hyper-sexuality of the 1990s leads into the self. Men and women marry later than in the past, if they marry at all. And today's birth rate of 2.1 children per woman is nearly 40 percent lower than the birth rate in 1960.[22] As these basic elements of primary and secondary social order (of sexual discernment by women, nurture by women, competition among men, fraternity, sorority, and family) deteriorate, sex loses its grip on social life. Sex has been torn from its moorings of male-female love and made an object unto itself, a commodity. [23]    We are an animal at odds with itself, losing the ability to satisfy the most basic reproductive functions of attraction, transportation, selection, and nurture.

Perhaps more revealing of the sexual crisis today are confusions of sexual identities. The same narcissism that leads to shallow sensation seeking and promiscuity leads, as well, to sexual ambivalence and pan-sexualism. With less to distinguish man and woman there is less to recommend one or the other for a particular role or even for a sexual partner. Confusion about sexual identity appears most generally in controversies about sex roles, rights, and responsibilities. Today's debates about who has the right to make which reproductive choices (of birth control, abortion, sex selection, genetic engineering, and child-custody), about who should take which responsibilities in the family, about whether women should participate with men in military combat, about barriers to equal opportunity in education and work, about parameters of sex in the workplace, about the definition of sexual harassment, and about funding of men and women's sports in college athletics, are significant mostly for existing at all. What were once matters of natural fact are now questions about how a sexless egalitarian society should operate. So familiar are these issues today that it is difficult to appreciate how far we have come in raising them. After all, it was not so long ago that democracy's most basic civil right of suffrage was granted to women, over strenuous objections at the time. Confusion about sexual identity today is perhaps even more obvious in questions about sexual orientation. Whether or not reports of increased homosexuality can be trusted, there is no doubt that public attitudes about homosexuality have changed dramatically in favor of greater openness and tolerance (Koch & Weiss, 1998). One need not go far to find books, newspapers, magazines, films, university courses, and parades to celebrate gay and lesbian lives. Sexual orientation is regarded by many today as a lifestyle to be chosen and countenanced like that of a religion or political party.[24] Today there is no more debate about homosexuality itself, but about whether children's school textbooks in New York City should include images of alternative sexual lifestyles and whether they should speak at all of a heterosexual ideal.

* * *

Once again, if this book is correct on key points about sex and social life—that is, about the unity of the species, about the division and play of sex, about social order arising as a synthesis of sex, and about conservation of sex and social life—then we would expect counter-trends opposing today's sexual crisis. We would expect people to be drawn to ideas and folkways that relieve the pain and loss of sexes too much alike. However, and unlike the sexual crisis of the 1950s, we do not today enjoy the benefit of hindsight. We are in the midst of social trends that are still forming and we cannot yet tell which of these will be still born or die young and which of these will prevail over a longer term. Indeed, we cannot yet tell whether there can or will be *any* final solution to today's sexual crisis.

Nevertheless we can again identify three kinds of answers to the dilemma of too much sameness between the sexes. There are, first, efforts to reclaim the lost difference and complementary relation between the sexes. One has been the so-called "backlash" (Faludi, 1991) against the difference-defying precepts of feminism; particularly its demands for equal outcomes as well as for equal opportunity, its demands for a comprehensively sex-neutral speech, and its refusal of any sexual difference or priority. While appreciating many of the changes to society feminism has provoked, many women and

men today have come to see feminism as a tyrannical political correctness. Of these women and men, fewer are ready to identify themselves as "feminists" (Friedan, 1981). Another effort to reclaim lost
difference and complementarity has come from the "religious right"
in American politics, a large and growing constituency built upon
commitments to heterosexuality, monogamous marriage, and family. Among this group we find, for example, Southern Baptists, who
at a recent convention amended their essential statement of beliefs
to include a declaration that a woman should "submit herself gra-
ciously" to her husband's leadership, and that a husband should
"provide for, protect and lead his family."[25]

Such efforts to reclaim sexual differences and complementarity
reflect a more general trend in the culture. A look at any magazine
rack tells the tale. Among women, there is renewed interest in old-
line magazines such as *Good Housekeeping*, the *Ladies Home Journal,* and *Family Circle* that purvey advice about marriage, childcare,
cooking, and housekeeping. *Good Housekeeping* advertises itself
today as the magazine for women who are the "new traditionalists."
*Martha Stewart Living* is a popular new magazine that tends in the
same direction. There is also continuing interest in health and beauty
magazines such as *Shape, Health, Vogue, Elle, Cosmopolitan, Self,*
and *Mademoiselle* that retail advice mainly about attracting and keeping men. Less prominent today than twenty years ago are magazines such as *Working Woman, New Woman,* and the recently re-
vived *Ms. Magazine,* expressly oriented to women's social and economic rights and opportunities. Among men, old-line magazines
such as *Esquire, Gentleman's Quarterly* and even *Playboy* have returned from a twenty-year acquiescence to feminism to join a new
wave of militantly masculine magazines such as *Maxim* and *Men's
Health* that celebrate men's distinctive values and potency. Thus, in
1996 *Esquire Magazine* ran a cover story by Michael Segell entitled
"The Second-Coming of the Alpha Male" which identifies today's
sexual crisis for the modern male and emphasizes the need for a
new manifesto for male coping:

> The vexing issue for all men—whether pro-feminist or Promise Keeper, mytho-poet or
> Million Man Marcher—is still with us: how to affirm the time-honored virtues of alpha
> manhood in a culture that, for the past two decades, has been conducting the most
> sweeping gender experiment since simians scrambled up on two legs.

The fact is that men who are effective in the world are the products of hardwired instincts and schoolyard socialization that have often put them painfully at odds with the new and politically correct expectations of a gender-equal society. What's needed is a handbook for the Second Coming of the Alpha Male, a guide to blending the best of traditional male behavior with the fresh emotional insight—call it psychological potency—that enables a man to win the love of a modern woman with whom he can form a true and lasting bond. (P. 76)

For better and worse men's magazines now play more narrowly to male concerns for dominance, social status, wealth, and the sexual adventures to which the former are thought to lead.[26]

And such images of the sexes as we now find on the magazine rack crowd the mind with those offered by other media. On television, long running popular shows such as *Friends*, *Cheers*, and *Seinfeld*, deal ironically and endlessly in the battle of the sexes. While nodding at today's new man and woman, these shows nevertheless rely on the tension created by older sexual complementarities. Newer shows such as *Men Behaving Badly* and the popular *The Man Show* are even more blatant about their sexist claims. At the same time, big-budget Hollywood movies have returned to safe, time- and focus-group-tested plot lines of traditional sexuality. The era of the antihero is over. Dashing males again endure arduous trials and surmount impossible odds to win the discerning hearts of fair ladies in distress. Turning to nightclubs, today's comics make a living mulling incomprehensible differences between the sexes. Audiences laugh, exclaiming to one another "isn't that so true?!" And right around the corner, bookstores peddle best-selling titles such as *Men are from Mars and Women are from Venus* and *You Just Don't Understand* that set the record straight on how men and women differ and show how valuable and exciting these differences can be. One controversial best seller entitled *The Rules: Time-Tested Secrets for Capturing the Heart of Mr. Right* instructs today's young women in the quaint virtues of chastity, careful discernment, and earnest commitment. Linking all of these efforts, from the backlash to feminism to the declarations of the Southern Baptist to fulminations of popular culture, is a fond wish to dance the old dance of complementary sexes.

As noted, it is too early to tell whether such efforts to reclaim sexual difference can succeed. There is reason for doubt as these efforts oppose powerful economic and social forces that have not changed. The fact these efforts exist at all suggests a lost cause—

people secure in their sexuality give it no thought.  And, indeed, there is a hint of fancy in these efforts, a concession that the old sex differences can be had today only in stolen moments of comedy or dream.  It is one thing to prate about the return of the alpha male in a men's magazine, or to laugh at a television sitcom or with a comedian about sexual follies, but it is another thing again to turn against the hard contingencies of modern economy.  This harder reality shows up in cynicism that mocks even the most earnest efforts to reclaim old sexual identities.  The self-consciousness of the age turns every plaint into a posture or pose.  By its light, there are no real men or real women in the world, only pretenses in quotation marks—"real men" or "real women."  Thus, liberal newspapers across the land were quick to derogate the Southern Baptists' declaration of male and female responsibilities as insensitive, mistaken, and arrogant.  Martha Stewart, eponymous publisher of the women's magazine, *Martha Stewart Living*, takes her lumps in comedy skits, on television shows such as *Saturday Night Live*, that poke fun at her womanly grace, aesthetic sensibility, and homemaking prowess.  Macho men's magazine, *Maxim*, got its comeuppance from *New York Times* columnist, Maureen Dowd, who described its embrace of "simple-minded gender stereotypes" as a reaction against the women's movement by "guys who really want to be 14 again."  "Viva la difference," she grants, "but this is ridiculous."  And, best-selling dating guide for women, *The Rules*, met its match on the "Shouts and Murmurs" page of the *New Yorker*, wherein humorist Christopher Buckley offered to men the "Counter Rules: Time Tested Techniques for Attracting Ms. Right While Avoiding Ms. Commitment."  " RULE 1: THE MOST IMPORTANT THING IN ANY RELATIONSHIP IS GETTING TO "YES! YES! OH GOD, YES!""

A second answer to the dilemma of too much sameness between the sexes is one we've seen before—for persons to reconcile male and female elements within themselves in androgynous, self-sufficing individuality.  With sex out of the way, men and women can relate equally and without prejudice as individuals.  This answer is a turn upon the original course of feminism which sought an individual life for women as a means of independence and as a means of bringing them closer and into better relations with men.  That course failed, not because women became more individual, but because women joined men in the same alienated submission to bureaucracy and consumerism. This answer is a return to the ideal of Emerson and Thoreau that sought individuality as an end in itself. By developing and incorporating both male and female elements in one psyche, a person becomes a more complete and self-sufficient human being, less commanded by sexual instincts.

Although this answer to the problem of sex is rare in our self-conscious narcissistic age—few today thrill to Emerson and fewer still challenge themselves to live as individuals—it survives in contemporary feminism and perhaps a few other cults of humanistic psychology. In 1981, at a time when women felt severely pinched between demands of work and family, and when women began to wonder if feminism had sold them a bill of goods, Friedan called for a "second wave" of the women's movement to include men as full partners in resolving the problems family life in the modern economy. Indeed, for Friedan, it was men who would have to change the most for progress to continue. As women developed their masculine side by entering the male realm of work, men would have to develop their feminine side by joining the female realm of home and childcare. Doing so would enrich men's lives by putting them in touch with the joys of childcare and homemaking and would ease their relations with their wives by relieving them of some of the stress of reconciling demands of work and home by themselves. Friedan believes this assimilation and integration of male and female roles within individual men and women is in no way antithetical to healthy and happy relations between the sexes. To the contrary, she believes that relations between the sexes are enriched and strengthened when they share equally in working outside the home to provide for the family and in working inside the home to raise the family. The more the sexes share, the better they understand one another and the deeper and more lasting their bond.

Unlike the first answer to today's sexual crisis of too much sameness between the sexes, an answer whose prospects are too near to judge in perspective, we can be sure this second answer of taking flight into individual life cannot succeed. Its fatal flaw is that it cannot create and sustain a human community. This was the lesson learned from the Beats in the 1950s. Feminism, like Marxism before it, may not have been given a fair historical test, but that does not make it any less at odds with human nature. As individuals take species life into themselves by taking the sexes into themselves, they cut themselves off from that life and no longer participate in its re-production. They stand alone, as islands to apart from the main-land. Thoreau lived unto himself admirably at Walden Pond, but while there he did not serve the species and did not reproduce. In-deed, Walden was but a two-year experiment, with breaks. More interesting would be to know what he thought about the individual life after ten or perhaps twenty years alone. How would his then over-developed sensibilities and skills for getting along alone serve him when it came time to get along with others?    The individual ideal fails for the most fundamental of reasons; it divorces mind from body. The individual exists as a life of mind, not as a life of the body. The body has sex and participates in species life according to that sex. Its attitude and behavior are elicited and conditioned by sexual instincts that do not belong to it, but belong to the species. The body has no future unless and until it reproduces in conjunction with its opposite sex. In contrast, the individual mind does not have a sex. As we saw in chapter 3, and again in chapter 5, the individual human mind is both sexes together, reconciled. Individual life be-gins as a person takes leave of the confinements and importuning of a sexed body by separating out for itself a realm of mind apart from the body. A person lives as an individual to the degree he or she succeeds in this separation.[27]    But with this success, the person qua individual cannot reproduce. Having assimilated both male and fe-male to itself, and having left the body behind, the individual has neither the will nor the way to reproduce. Individual life may be a personal answer to problem of too much similarity between the sexes, but it is no answer for the species.

A third and final answer to the dilemma of too much sameness between the sexes comes in the form of denial, and specifically in the form of unconscious psychic mechanisms of repression, projec-tion, and sublimation. As Freud showed, one way to deal with a crisis is to act as if it does not exist, either by denying it outright, or by pretending it is something other than what it is, or by putting one's anxiety about it into the service of some other activity or aim. It is often said about Americans today that while their culture is over-run with the sights and sounds of sex—in advertising, in movies, on television, on the radio, in the press, on the Internet—Americans themselves are uptight and prudish about sex. It is as if the imagery of sex—particularly of sexual difference, attraction, and intercourse—takes the place of the real thing. Perhaps if their sexual relations were more satisfying, they could let go of this imagery. At least they might give up their eager and hypocritical sanctimony about every new sex scandal that hits the papers. I suspect this insight about Americans reaches to the core of the problem of sexual sameness. Today's economic order of consumer capitalism, which is most developed in the United States, puts people at odds with themselves. While nature made man and woman different and by this means attracted one to the other, today's economy recognizes no such difference and no such attraction. Indeed, sex is dangerous to the economy because it augurs a social order oriented to reproduction rather than consumption. Sex is thus something to be ignored in the economy, and if it cannot be ignored, something to be denied by the economy. As consumer capitalism has undermined sex by effacing the differences that attract male and female, it was left to the psyche to conserve sex by forcing its differences and attractions underground, either to remain under the tension of repression, or to be projected into other, non-sexual realms, or to be sublimated in one creative act or another.

Repression is an anxiety process. Freud's image was of a hydraulic process by which the ego, under the watchful eye of the superego, held down wayward sexual impulses arising from the id. A significant feature of this process, according to Freud, is the certain occurrence of occasional faults or breaks in repression at which anxious sexual impulses erupt into behavior and consciousness—the return of the repressed. In the U.S. today, we see the repression of sex in telltale anxieties. For some, anxiety appears as prudishness or lost interest in sex. It is not that sex has actually lost its appeal but that its repressed elements of difference and attraction have become too fearful to contemplate or act upon. For others, anxiety appears in guilty fears about sexually transmitted diseases such as herpes, syphilis, and AIDS—fears that by irrational inflation give spurious reason for abstinence. For others, men particularly, anxiety appears in exaggerated worries about sexual performance, about whether he can satisfy this dangerously strange woman who might want something more or different than he can offer. For others still, women particularly, anxiety shows in exaggerated fears of men as raping brutes that given half a chance will force themselves on them in parking lots, in the woods, on the street at night, at fraternity parties

(Paglia, 1994). We see the repression of sex also in its unconscious eruptions and returns. The repressed returns in annual rituals of sexual license such as the Mardi Gras in New Orleans, the Burning Man festival in Nevada, and pilgrimages of hormone-drunk college students on spring break. The repressed returns in fantasy images of exaggerated sex differences and lusty attractions. In the movies, male actors become more improbably muscled while female actors become more impossibly buxom. In a recent animated movie for children, the Disney company bulked up its leading male, Tarzan, almost beyond human recognition. Disney's Tarzan joins a new GI Joe doll for boys and the ever-surreal Barbie doll for girls in a parade of superabundantly sexed physiques. And these are the tamer displays of public prurience. Witness the lewd spectacle of the hearings in confirmation of Judge Thomas's nomination to the U.S. Supreme Court or the tragicomic sex scandal leading up to the spectacular impeachment of the President Clinton by the U.S. House of Representatives. Behind these and innumerable other returns of the repressed in public are daily returns of the repressed in private, particularly in the growing appetite for sex on the phone, on the Internet, on cable television, in magazines, and in rentals of videotapes.[28] For all of the fear and reluctance about sex, there is a lot of it being watched these days, most of it un-progressive in its portrait of sex differences and sex roles.[29]

Repression is but one form of denial. Where sex differences and attractions are not repressed, they can be projected into other realms or sublimated in art or some other creative enterprise. One projection, common among today's culture critics, has been to confuse sex with the social relations it produces. A dominant position is said to be male, a subordinate position is said to be female, and any exercise of power between them is said to be intercourse. Brown (1966) identifies the leader as phallus and the group as womb.[30] Ferguson (1984) condemns hierarchy as male oppression of female. And feminists interpret men's sexual overtures toward women at work and in school as power plays, often as sexual assault and harassment (Schwartz, 1997). One sublimation, on the scene for many years now, is the music of youth. Always sexually charged, this music is distinguished today by its themes of sexual difference and opposition. Male "rappers" define urban macho while denigrating women as sex-hungry whores. Female folk-singers commune in concerts

for women, wondering "where all the cowboys have gone?" Where
the rock and roll of the 1950s was shocking for its precocious sexuality, today's rap is shocking for its sexual and social animus.

Thanks to denial in all its forms—repression, projection, and sublimation—the most natural relation of  life, sex between man and
woman, has become a terror—fearful, awkward, misplaced, and transcended.  Unlike the first two answers to the problem of sexual
sameness, whose efficacy we found reason to doubt, it appears this
third answer continues to work.  Yet it remains an unsteady and
somewhat unhappy solution to the problem, coming as it does at the
expense of natural desires and needs.  We give up the better part of
our humanity in exchange for the comforts of a prolific consumer
economy.  It may be a Faustian bargain.  There are signs of decay
and failure as our society loses the interest and will to reproduce.
No society can be long for this world when its men are discouraged
from ambition and contest for women and when its women are dis-
tracted by the economy's rewards and blandishments from having
and nurturing children.   In time, those societies best able to reproduce triumph over those least able to reproduce.

Lastly, we note that this third answer to today's sexual crisis may
shed light on a few mysteries left open by the first answer which
seeks the return of old sexual complementaries.   One is the irrational vigor of efforts to reclaim sex roles that are long and perhaps
irretrievably gone.  What's the use in pretending the sexes differ
when the overwhelming logic of the economy insists they be the
same?  Another is the fancy of these efforts.  Why should claims of
sexual difference come mainly in stolen moments of comedy and
fantasy?  These mysteries lift as we see that the efforts to reclaim lost
sexual identities are unconsciously motivated.  They are instances
of wishful thinking in the face of denial.  And like most instances of
wishful thinking, they make life a little more bearable even while
having no chance of coming true.

Again to summarize, our theory of sex and social life leads us to
expect the current sexual crisis in the U.S. and Europe to bring compensating changes in sexual and social relations.  Again, although
vaguely stated and tested against broad cultural trends, which are
only now coming into focus, I find this expectation largely confirmed.  As men and women today stare blankly at one another in
diffident sameness, increasingly unwilling and uninterested to col-

laborate for the good of the species, they seek sexual difference and attraction to restore the vital dialectic between them. It remains to see whether a return to sexual difference and attraction will come by real changes in behavior or, as seems more likely, by fantastic projections of repressed impulses.

## Conservation Again

Nature rewards not particular roles of the sexes, but a constructive and reproductive relationship between the sexes. Natural selection has adapted the sexes to the environment, to be sure, but it has adapted the sexes to each other even more. Each sex is the other sex's most significant factor of selection. Each sex is thus tuned to the other and evolved to adapt itself to the other. Buried in this chapter's ruminations over fifty years of sexual and social movements and counter-movements in the United States are assumptions about how nature has contrived and rewarded the relationship between the sexes. While we may speak of conservation abstractly as an evolutionary process of neutral value, as soon as we try to say what relationship between the sexes is conserved, we feel our own anxieties and hopes rise and risk losing sight of the difference between the way life is and the way we would like it to be. Mindful of this folly, of which no writer seems immune, I disinter these buried assumptions about the natural relationship between the sexes so they can be examined in the light of day.

People have different ideas about what is natural and proper between the sexes, and therefore different ideas about what is or is not conserved by the evolution of the species. On the one hand, there are those such as Kenealy (1920) and Mead (1949) who join me in believing that sexual polarity—intimate complementary relation between male and female—is essential in human life. Kenealy, whose views closely match my own puts the matter plainly: "It cannot be doubted that human perfection reaches its climax in the accentuation of the differences between the sex characteristics, physical and mental, of the one sex from those of the other" (p. 26). And, in what is practically a restatement the two evolutionary principles emphasized in this book—namely, growth by differentiation of parts, and involution of the whole in parts—Kenealy finds that species grow by the sexes playing together as parts of a whole: "the ever increasing complexity of organization and faculty which has characterized

Evolutionary Progress, has had for aim, as it has had for method, the ever further differentiation and more perfect segregation, but, nevertheless, the ever closer and more intricate association of the contrary factors of Maleness and Femaleness" (p. 44). Mead (1949) echoes the point, finding that humanity thrives only as the natural differences between the sexes are kept alive and in play:

> Our tendency at present is to minimize all these differences in learning, in rhythm, in type and timing of rewards, and at most to try to obliterate particular differences that are seen as handicaps on one sex. If boys are harder to train, train them harder; if girls grow faster than boys, separate them, so the boys won't be damaged; if women have a little less strength than men, invent machines so that they can still do the same work. But every adjustment that minimizes a difference, a vulnerability, in one sex, a differential strength in the other, diminishes their possibility of complementing each other, and corresponds—symbolically—to sealing off the constructive receptivity of the female and the vigorous outgoing constructive activity of the male, muting them both in the end to a duller version of human life, in which each is denied the fullness of humanity that each might have had. Guard each sex in its vulnerable moments we must, protect and cherish them through the crises that at some times are so much harder for one sex than for the other. But as we guard, we may also keep the differences. Simply compensating for differences is in the end a form of denial. (P. 372)

For sexual polarity to be the aim and method of evolution, and for each sex to realize sex membership fully, each sex must be a whole human being. Again, both Kenealy and Mead join me in emphasizing that it is not enough that the sexes complement one another, they must also understand one another well enough to make productive use of their differences. In my terms, as part of the whole, each sex must involute the whole. Thus, while claiming identity as a man, each man must be part woman, and while claiming identity as a woman, each woman must be part man. "Man is at his best," writes Kenealy, "when the woman in him is dominated by his natural virile traits. Woman is at her best when the man in her is sheathed within her native womanliness. This way, each is a highly evolved and a finely specialized creation" (p. 28).

> [S]uch possession in latency, of the qualities of the other, not only enhances for members of both sexes the potence of their own, inspiring and enriching these, but it engenders more perfect sympathy and understanding between them. The woman in man endues him with intuitive apprehension of the Woman-nature; of its needs and modes, its disabilities, its sufferings and aspirations. The man in woman informs her of the intrinsic values of his sterner calibre, and thus lends her patience with his impatiences, moves her tenderness and care for him in his rougher, more arduous lot, wins her admiration of his enterprises and ambitions. Moreover, the man in her strengthens and intelligises her mental fibre, stiffens and renders more stable and effective her more pliant will and softer, more delicate aptitudes (pp. 28-29).

On the other hand, there are those such as Friedan (1981), who question whether there is *any* natural or proper relationship between the sexes, and who doubt in particular that this relationship must be one of polarity. According to Friedan, far from being the basis of social life, sexual polarity causes endless misunderstanding, conflict, and, in men particularly, homosexuality and violence. Citing anthropologist Bateson, Friedan contends that the more polarized the roles of men and women, the more alienated are men and women from each other. In societies, such as those where women are shrouded in veil or chador and are walled in sexual ghettos, human sexual needs for intimacy are alienated and violence breeds. Citing psychoanalyst Reich's work on fascism, Friedan goes on to point out that "[i]n war, the seclusion of men from intimate daily relations with women as a virtual condition of the necessary violence has been taken for granted through history, as well as the prevalence, and condoning of rape among warriors" (p. 311). And citing Slater's study of men and women in ancient Greece, Friedan joins in the inference that polarization of the sexes through inequality led men to look for intimacy with other men and to seek women merely to contract for children to continue the race (p. 311). According to Friedan, sexual polarity is the root of social evil. Never mind that not one of these cases is an example of a true sexual polarity. Not one describes a complementary sexual relationship built upon mutual understanding. Each presents the opposite of polarity. In each, one sex shuns the other or seeks the other on such narrow grounds as to make a vital relation impossible. Nevertheless, Friedan (1981) leaps from this platform to conclude: "Thus, sex-role polarization and inequality lead to and are reinforced by sexual obsession-revulsion, which leads to and is reinforced by sexual dehumanization and alienation from the core of generative, authentic human love and life—and this feeds violence" (p. 312). Generative, authentic love, she goes on to argue, can transpire between a man and a woman only when both are equally able to grow as individuals to their full and equal humanity. Refreshing the point she first made in *The Feminine Mystique*, self-actualization is the key to a vital and loving society. The need, she argues, is for a second "feminist" movement in which men join women in creating true mutuality at work, in the home, and in care of children. Summarizing Friedan, there is no cause or place for polarity. Collaboration between the sexes occurs as they share activity and it is blocked as they keep activity to themselves.  In the end, Friedan does believe there is a natural and proper relationship between the sexes, and that is equality and sameness in all things.

Obviously these opposing views of the importance of sexual polarity in social life lead in different directions when it comes time to leave theory for practice.  Friedan wants to make society safe for individuals by making sex an irrelevance.  Kenealy and Mead want to make society safe by protecting its heart and soul of sex.  I join the latter, believing they see more deeply into subterranean play of the sexes that creates both society and the individual who grows from it.  The irony and fundamental flaw in Friedan's position is that it does not appreciate how the admirable quest for self-actualization presupposes the very sexual distinctions and polarities said to be its enemy.  If not for the social order created by sex, there would be no individual thinkers of Friedan's caliber and no cause or place for them to build their theories and mobilize their movements.  In Mead (1949) I find the most trenchant and historically accurate analysis of how concerns for the individual arise from but do not vitiate older and more basic concerns for society based on complementary sexes. I quote her at length here because I believe she offers a sympathetic and satisfying integration of the two views of polarity:

As matters now stand and have stood through history. ... From each sex, society has asked that they so live that others may be born, that they cherish their masculinity and femininity, discipline it to the demands of parenthood, and leave new lives behind them when they die.  This has meant that men had to be willing to choose, win, and keep women as lovers, protect and provide for them as husbands, and protect and provide for their children as fathers.  It has meant that women have had to be willing to accept men as lovers, live with them as wives, and conceive, bear, feed, and cherish their children. Any society disappears which fails to make these demands on its members and to receive this much from them.

But from men, society has also asked and received something more than this.  For thousands of generations men have been asked to do something more than be good lovers and husbands and fathers, even with all that involved of husbandry and organization and protection against attack.  They have been asked to develop and elaborate, each in terms of his own ability, the structure within which the children are reared, to build higher towers, or wider roads, to dream new dreams and see new visions, to penetrate ever farther into the secrets of nature, to learn new ways of making life more human and more rewarding.  And within the whole adventure there has been a silent subtle division of labor, which had its roots perhaps in a period of history when the creativeness of bearing children outweighed in splendour every act that men performed, however they danced and pantomimed their pretense that the novices were really their children after all. In this division of labour, there was the assumption that bearing children is enough for the women, and in the rest of the task all the elaborations belong to men. This assumption becomes the less tenable the more men succeed in those elaborations which they have taken on themselves. As a civilization becomes complex, human life is defined in individual terms as well as in the service of the race, and the greater structures of law and government, religion and art and science, become something highly valued for themselves.

Reviewing the changes in sex and social life in the United States over these last fifty years, we see that modern life under prolific economic capitalism, per Mead's historical analysis, has thrown the sexes into new alignments with which we continue to struggle for balance and rest and happiness. Given Mead's assessment of 1949, and given the demographic dislocations and even more the proliferation of self-consciousness of the last fifty years, we may have to admit the gloomy possibility that there is no prospect of a stable and relaxed alignment of the sexes. Recalling the three sexual orders of social life described in chapter 5, we now see how decisive is the break between the first two "biological" social orders and the third "cultural" social order. Although all three of these social orders are produced by sex, the third involutes the sexes within an androgynous individual and impersonal bureaucracy. Thus, in the third social order, the polarity of the sexes no longer plays between biological males and females toward reproductive ends, but plays within un-biological individuals and bureaucracies toward their own ends. The individual draws upon the sexes in selfish acts of creativity and ideation. The bureaucracy draws upon the sexes in selfish acts of economic capitalism. With the third social order, sex jumped its tracks from biology to culture. It is no wonder that Friedan and others could maintain today that the individual is and should be beyond biology and beyond sex. Their mistake comes not in their assessment of the individual, but in not seeing the individual as but the tip of a larger iceberg in which sex plays the preponderating part. With the third social order came a new problem of reconciling biological imperatives of sex with cultural imperatives of economy and politics. The last fifty years of U.S. history are a story of struggle between economy and sex for social life.

We have yet to settle the question of whether the ascendance of economy over sex during the last fifty years, and ascendance of tertiary sexual order over primary and secondary sexual orders, can serve the species in the long run. A mere generation and a half of experience is a slender stalk upon which to graft prognostications. There are indications in the economically advanced West that the social center cannot hold.  In the United States, the world's richest nation and the nation best able to shoulder the costs of reproduction, the birth rate has declined precipitously.  In place of reproductive sex we have put decadent sex—inverted, perverted, and increasingly bodiless.  As parents, 1950s baby boomers kid themselves in self-congratulations for defusing the ballyhooed "population bomb" of the 1960s and 1970s with a zero-population growth rate, unwilling to admit the terrible truth behind their "restraint," that they are not much interested in having and raising kids.[31]  As Lasch (1979) noted, narcissism in parents today comes with a discouraging unconcern for their children's future.  Spiritually and morally empty themselves, they feel they have little to pass on to the next generation.  And in any case, they have little wish to sacrifice their own self-fulfillment to do so.  Yet, there is no getting around species biology or the fact that sex must have its day.  Sex will certainly assert itself in the superior reproductive fitness of groups and cultures that keep men and women constructively related.  The winning groups will be those that give priority to sex roles and relations compatible with reproductive biology.  Although fearful to contemplate, sex could assert itself in some catastrophe of climate, disease, war, or economy that reclaims the urgencies of a subsistence existence.  Pious debates about sex roles and relations are a luxury enjoyed only by societies bloated by material surplus and leisure.  Short of wishing a cure worse than the disease, perhaps the best hope for a self-conscious West is to keep up the bitter rivalry between cultural and biological influences on society, thus to let people grow as individuals and at the same time to leave room and reason for people to come together as man and woman to do the species' business.  Eternal bickering between feminist and traditionalist may not be a future of dream, but it is better than no future at all.

# 7

# Conclusion

I wrote this book to answer a philosophical challenge—namely, to provide a framework of ideas to think about how sex organizes human social life. As I noted at the outset, this is a challenge for good reasons. Not least, the story of sex and social life is much older than we are. A primary fact of biology, sex has organized social life from nearly the beginning of life. We learn little about sex from evolutionary comparisons among primate or mammalian species that appeared too late to illuminate its world changing effects. In our own human lives, sex is so matter of fact that we cannot see it as the factor it is. But there is more to the philosophical challenge of sex and social life than the age and obviousness of sex. There is a problem with the way sex is usually thought about within social science. Today, sex is too often regarded inaptly as an attribute or interaction of persons instead of as a fundamental dynamic of the species. Sex is not, as many psychologists believe, an incidental feature of the individual, like hair color or skin pigmentation. Rather it is a part played in the life of the species. It is not something a person *has,* but something a person *is.* And sex is not, as other psychologists believe, a relationship between individuals like a friendship or political affiliation. Rather, it is a dynamism of species life manifest in the coordinated movements of complementary males and females. The bias to see sex in terms of the individual, a bias that runs pervasively through today's theories of evolutionary biology and social complexity, has kept social science from seeing clearly how sex figures in the social life of the species.

I believe this book contributes to our understanding of social life by insisting that the sexes be seen as *parts of the species whole.* By dividing a unitary species into opposed male and female parts, sex compels play and integration of those parts. The most basic forms of social life—female care of young, female choice of mates, male competition, fraternal hierarchy, sororal support, family, bureaucracy, and individual—are species solutions to problems of division and specifically to problems of reproduction created by division (i.e., attraction, transportation, selection, and nurture). These social forms are not made by selfishly motivated individuals; they express the ongoing life of the species. Social life enacts a holistic dialectical logic; male antithesis greets female thesis to compel a social synthesis.

For the purposes of analysis and exposition, I describe the sexual basis of social life in terms of four "moments": unity, division, play, and order. These are not so much points in a temporal sequence as they are ways of looking at species life. The species is an organism, a unity in which divided parts play within a discernible order. Each moment of social life interleaves with its three companions. There is no order without play, division, and unity. There is no play without order, division, and unity. There is no division without unity, order, and play. And there is no unity without division, play, and order. Looking at social life these several ways we see how each moment fits into the explanation of the others.

I describe social life as an evolution beginning with the zero order of the species group, moving through a primary or "zoological" order of males and females in which females select males to mate and care for offspring and males compete for access to females, moving again through a secondary or "archaeological" order of fraternity, sorority, and family, and ending with a tertiary or "anthropological" order of individual and bureaucracy. I picture this evolution, treelike, in figure 5.1 as a branching development of the species from a germ of unity to an elaborated structure. This development follows from the two master principles of evolution described at the outset: growth by differentiation of parts and involution of the whole in the parts. Thus, the most developed forms of social life, visible today in the West as individual and bureaucracy, developed from precursor social forms of fraternity, sorority, and family, which in turn developed from precursor social forms of female mate selection, female nurture of offspring, and male competition for access to females.

Finally, I examine these ideas about sex and social life in the light of powerful upheavals of sexual relations in the United States over the last fifty years.  Based on the evolutionary principle of conservation, according to which evolved forms preserve aspects and elements of the forms from which they came, I suggest and find that the sexes react to changes in their relations in ways that reclaim and preserve the reproductively necessary tension between them.  Looking at the period of the 1950s and early 1960s I find the sexes too separate and too distinct to work together constructively.  Looking later I see changes in society aimed to reduce the distance between the sexes and to find common ground upon which the sexes could work together on behalf of the species.  Looking at the period of the late 1980s and today I find the sexes too similar and too indistinct to work together constructively.  This appears to be leading to changes in social life aimed to increase the distance between the sexes so that they once again attract one another to work together on behalf of the species.  Not only did sex organize the species way back when; it organizes and reorganizes the species today in response to new conditions of social life.  Sex is the living dialectic of the species, a female thesis and male antithesis ever in need of synthesis.

Having reached the book's end, it remains to tie together a few of its loose ends.  We now have an answer to the so-called "dark matter mystery" posed in chapter 2.  The integrity and coherence of human social life is no mystery, but simply an expression of the abiding unity of the species.  Human society is no composition of selfishly motivated individuals, but a finely differentiated unity in which every person is connected to every other person.  Parts do not explain the whole, nor does the whole explain the parts.  Both develop at once with the growth of the species.  This restates our two master principles of evolution: The whole grows as a differentiation of parts and parts connect by involuting the whole.  The whole of human society grows as a differentiation of male and female parts and these connect by involuting the whole of human society.

To the question, "What holds the human community together?" we can now give the confident answer, "sex."  That which divides the species keeps it together.  The word sex is both a noun and a verb.  It refers both to a division and to an integration.  This book brings a fresh appraisal of Freud's master concept of "libido," which we now see is more than a psychic force, but and more profoundly, a species force.  Freud was correct to think that love, and particularly sexual love, is the force that keeps us together.  But he was too much the psychologist and not enough the sociologist to see that love is not a personal motive but a species motive. As Aristophanes reminded us in chapter 1, a species that divides male and female must contrive to attract and unite the two to reproduce. The couple, the family, the men's group, the women's group, the bureaucracy, and even the individual, are social elements of sexual reconciliation. This is true even of the lover's knot. John loves Mary, and Mary loves John, not only because she is charming, bright, and pretty, and he is dashing, intelligent, and handsome, but mainly and more profoundly because he is male and she is female. People have the love needs they do because they are parts of a sexual species.

It is no idle curiosity that of all the animals we are the sexiest—we are most intrigued by sex differences, we make the most of sex differences (finding in them subtle nuances lost on other animals), and we are the most occupied with sexual attraction and sexual relations. We bring more energy and resourceful inventiveness to mating than any other species. As noted in chapters 4 and 5, this fact is key to our unparalleled playfulness and thereby to our unrivaled social organization. Sex makes for play and play makes for organization. Indeed, it may be that our species is best distinguished, not by its capacity for reason, as *Homo sapiens*, nor by its capacity for play, as *Homo ludens*, but by its capacity for sex, as *Homo sexus*. To be sure, reason is a distinctively developed human faculty. And certainly, as Huizinga (1950) points out, play lies at the core of human intellectual and cultural life. But, sex is behind both and responsible for both. As any novelist can confirm, it is the play of sex, above all, that makes our social life so interesting.

Human sexiness brings a uniquely human problem. Sex in humans is more than biological instinct; it is tied up with all kinds of cultural conventions and mores. For the most part there is little difficulty in this as cultures arise to support reproductive biology. Occasionally, however, cultures arise that do not support and may even oppose reproductive biology. We see this in Western cultures today, such as in the United States, where the division and play of female and male has ramified and folded back on itself to produce sexually undifferentiated individuals and sexless bureaucracies. As noted in chapter 5, these late developments of Western culture are "answers" to the sexual division of the species. But, as shown in chapter 6, they reconcile male and female unproductively. Marriage rates and birth rates decline as individuals and bureaucracies flourish. With the appearance of an individual and bureaucratic life to rival the communal life of male and female have come new tensions and problems. Today, as never before, a person must reconcile an individual life that stands apart from the group with a group life that insists that he or she play a definite part. Today, as never before, a person must reconcile an androgynous individual life with a definitely sexed male or female life. And today, as never before, a person must reconcile the reasonable social value for individual equality with the reasonable social value for male and female prerogatives. Sex is, paradoxically, our most animal quality *and* our most human problem.

Many commentators on the scene today (e.g., Bellah et al., 1986; Etzioni, 1999; Putnam, 1993) attribute problems of modern life to a lack of feeling for society, to a lack of care and concern for the community. Selfish interests, we are told, are the bane of social life. Writes Adler (1938), "the great mistakes in life—war, capital punishment, race-hatred, hatred of other peoples, not to speak of neurosis, suicide, crime, drunkenness—spring from a lack of social feeling and are to be looked upon as inferiority complexes, as pernicious attempts to deal with a situation in a way that is inadmissible and unsuitable" (p. 55). Humankind is said to depend on the cooperative efforts and social feelings of all. Its main tasks, to which each individual must contribute his/her share, are love (leading to reproduction), work, and community. This outlook is often invoked as moral precept and authority, as Adler does:

> A movement of the individual or of the mass can only be counted worthy if it creates values for eternity, for the higher development of the whole of humanity (p. 279). ... When we speak of virtue we mean that a person plays his part; when we speak of vice we mean that he interferes with co-operation. ... all that constitutes a failure is so because it obstructs social feeling, whether children, neurotics, criminals, or suicides are in question. (P. 283)

Taking issue neither with the want of social feeling revealed in most social ills, nor with the immorality of its denial or usurpation, we should note that the idea of social feeling is too vague to guide right conduct. To know the good and bad in action and relation one must know how our actions and relations contribute to or detract from social feeling. This means understanding the inner workings of social life and feeling. Thus it is important to know that sex, more than any other characteristic of our species, comprises social feeling. Differences between male and female may try the patience with misunderstandings and compromise. But these are the differences that incite the passions to complete ourselves by joining with others. Sex is the basis and means for human cooperation.

A basic problem for all sexual species, especially our own, is to reconcile the sexes while maintaining their differences. This calls for mutual respect and cooperation in dealing with natural conflicts. In a word, the need is for play, for that mode of cooperative antagonism that makes the most of respective differences, that realizes the strengths of diversity. This suggests the error of those agitating for war between sexes, who spare no misogynistic or man-hating tactic to mobilize their group against the other. This suggests, too, the error of those seeking to abridge sex differences by legislating sameness of activity and outcome. Unity follows from working with and through differences, not from either cherishing or denying those differences.

It is a measure of the gracelessness of our age that so many leading thinkers believe sex is not a gift of nature but a problem to be overcome. We see this in the ambition of many efforts of psychosocial re-engineering. This is particularly true of modern feminism, which, as Hrdy (1981) points out, has courageously pushed for sweeping reforms in the face of terrible odds:

> The female with "equal rights" never evolved; she was invented, and fought for consciously with intelligence, stubbornness, and courage. But the advances made by feminists rest on a precarious framework built upon a unique foundation of historical conditions, values, economic opportunities, heroism on the part of women who fought for suffrage, and perhaps especially technological developments which led to birth control and labor-saving devices and hence minimized physical differences between the sexes. This structure is fragile. Should it collapse, it is far from certain that the scaffolding needed to surmount oppressive natural and cultural barriers could ever be pieced together again. ... Injustices remain; there are abundant new problems; yet, never before—not in seventy million years—have females been so nearly free to pursue their own destinies. (P. 191)

The presumption of this brave new world is staggering—nature is the oppressor; females have been denied their true destinies for 70 million years, and thanks to today's feminists, women are at long last free. It is a wonder that anyone could be smart enough to better nature's design for our species, or powerful enough to abridge the basic rules written into our nature. As we have seen, the story of sex and social life is the story of a life bigger than our own; a story of profound but barely glimpsed unities; a story of a biologic division hundreds of millions of years old; a story of an all-powerful organic dialectic that holds the sexes in tension and keeps the species alive. Into this very long story wanders the human animal, the first species in which evolution has become conscious of itself, the first species selfishly occupied with meaning and posterity, and the first species audacious enough to believe that the story of evolution up till now has been for its benefit and can be changed for its purposes. One is reminded of Mark Twain's admonishment of our egotism about history. In the expanse of history, he wrote, we are but the topmost layer of paint at the very tip of the Eiffel Tower, yet we think the tower was built for our benefit and that we are its master.

To close, I offer some grandiosity of my own by lending an ear to idea that has been whispering to us from the beginning of the book. In chapter 1, I claimed, without explaining myself, that sex and social life are better described by the lively works of artists such as Plato, James Brown, and Thurber and White, than by the dry theories and speculations of social scientists. In chapter 2, I asserted, without explaining myself, that among the indicators of our species unity some of the best are art symbols of the group, such as song, dance, and myth. In chapter 3, I showed, without explaining myself, how the division and play of sex appear in artistic images such as the T'ai-chi tu, Greek poetry, and American folk dance. In chapter 5, I suggested, without explaining myself, that the problem of understanding social life compares to the art critic's problem of understanding a work of art. And in chapter 6, I noted, without explaining myself, how problems of sex and social life in the United States appear in Beat poetry, magazines, television, film, and video and Internet pornography. It is time for explanation, or at least an attempt at one. Why is art so persistently identified with sex and social life? I believe the answer is that art shares with these the fundamental quality of living form. Art is alive in the same way that sex and social life are alive. For this reason, art is our natural and preferred means of thinking and communicating about sex and social life. Sex and social life are represented by art with a fidelity that cannot be duplicated any other way, least of all perhaps by a literal and discursively organized language of science.

Thus, I believe that social scientists, whose occupation requires them to express what they know in words, must find ways to draw upon art in the study of sex and social life. In an earlier work (see Sandelands, 1998), I argued that human societies are living forms known intuitively as feelings of the whole rather than as discretely perceived persons in interaction. These feelings, which are personal and subjective, are made public and objective by the uniquely human capacity for artistic abstraction. Through art, people turn invisible feelings and forms of social life, including those of sex described in this book, into visible objects and performances that can be shared and studied scientifically. After writing this book, I am more convinced of the affinities between art and social life and of the need for a critical science to use each as a window on the other. Art is not, as many on local school boards or national endowments seem to believe, simply a recreation or means of emotional release or enjoyment. It is a primary (perhaps *the primary*) mode of abstraction by which we understand and master ourselves and the world around us. It is our tough luck that artistic abstractions do not fit neatly the categories and structure of language, but we should not take sides against understanding because we have trouble finding the words for it. From art, we have everything to learn about sex and social life.

Thus, too, I believe when social scientists turn to moral questions of policy, they must apply aesthetic as well as rational criteria to evaluate sexual and social arrangements and to suggest reforms of these arrangements. As a case in point, consider today's sexual crisis, described in chapter 6, of sexes grown too similar as men and women alike have become wrapped up in their own individual and bureaucratic lives. I described this problem in dialectical terms as a failure of men and women to attract and interest one another enough to reproduce the species. More illuminating, I think, is to describe this problem aesthetically as a failure of proportion and balance. To see sex and social life through art is to appreciate the beauty and value in sexual relations and social orders that are well-proportioned and well-balanced.

Figure 5.1, of chapter 5 (reproduced here as figure 7.1a) is a picture of balance and harmony—beautiful in its own right. It depicts the sexual organization of human social life as a growth upward from an old and thick thrust of primary social order made of

**Figure 7.1a**

**Figure 7.1b**

female nurture, female male choice, and male competition, through a newer and thinner branching of secondary social order made of sex groups and family, to a recent flowering of tertiary social order made of individuals and bureaucracy. By comparison, today's sexual crisis appears, as in figure 7.1b, as a misshapen and unnatural development. Today the elements of the tertiary cultural order—of individual and bureaucracy—are overdeveloped in relation to the elements of the primary and secondary biological orders from which they came. Our social life is top heavy, distorted—in a word, ugly. The problem for the species is not the fact of a tertiary social order of individual and bureaucracy. In proper measure and proportion, this order is a positive development that enhances adaptation to diverse and changing environments.  The problem, rather, is the overdevelopment of this order *in relation to* the primary and secondary social orders that make it possible and give it strength.  Culture has run away from biology, at the expense of both, and at the expense of the species.  Likewise, the problem for the person is not the fact of being an individual or the fact of being fixed in the bureaucratic grid.  In their proper measure and proportion these, too, are positive developments that enhance adaptation to diverse and changing environments.  The problem, rather, is narcissistic over-development of individuality and bureaucratic office-taking *in relation to* the biological roles and relationships of male and female.  The individual mind has run away from the social body, at the expense of both, and again at the expense of the species.  The issues of proportion and balance that perplex species and individuals alike are aesthetic as well as rational.  They are issues for which we must have a feel as well as reasons.  They are issues of beauty—of human lives well and truly lived.

# Notes

## Preface

1.  Abram (1997) has made much of these lapses, finding that development of alphabetic language in Greece emancipated symbols from sensuous experience. This enabled human thinking to turn back upon itself in abstract thought but it came at the expense of direct contact with the life and mind in all things. Contrasting the sensibility of late written cultures with that of traditional oral cultures Abram finds the latter unaware of breaks between matter and life and between life and mind. For the latter, all the world lives and thinks.
2.  This kind of criticism often takes the form of lengthy accounts of a few exceptions (see, e.g., Hrdy, 1981). This makes it harder to see how or even that the exceptions prove the rule. Indeed, it begins to seem that the exceptions are the rule.
3.  Goldberg (1993) gives the example of the hypothesis of universal patriarchy which was notoriously unseated by Margaret Mead's erroneous conclusions about the Tchambuli of New Guinea. Mead's subsequent qualification of her own work in 1973 reads as follows "It is true ... that all the claims so glibly made about societies ruled by women are nonsense. We have no reason to believe that they ever existed. ... men everywhere have been in charge of running the show. .... men have been the leaders in public affairs and the final authorities at home." (Quoted in Goldberg, 1993, p. 35).

## Chapter 1

1.  Plato recounts Aristophanes' descriptions as follows:

    First of all I must explain the real nature of man, and the change which it has undergone—for in the beginning we were nothing like we are now. For one thing, the race was divided into three; that is to say, besides the two sexes, male and female, which we have at present, there was s third which partook of the nature of both, and for which we still have a name, though the creature itself is forgotten. For though 'hermaphrodite' is only used nowadays as a term of contempt, there really was a man-woman in those days, a being which was half male and half female.

    And secondly, gentlemen, each of these beings was globular in shape, with rounded back and sides, four arms and four legs, and two faces, both the same, on a cylindrical neck, and one head, with one face one side and one the other, and four ears, and two lots of privates, and all the other parts to match. They walked erect, as we do ourselves, backward or forward, whichever they pleased, but when they broke into a run they simply stuck their legs straight out and went whirling round and round like a clown turning cartwheels. And since they had eight legs, if you count their arms as well, you can imagine that they went bowing along at a pretty good speed.

The three sexes, I may say, arose as follows. The males were descended from the Sun, the females from the Earth, and the hermaphrodites from the Moon, which partakes of either sex, and they were round and they went round, because they took after their parents. And such, gentlemen, were their strengths and energy, and such their arrogance, that they actually tried—like Ephialtes and Otus in Homer—to scale the heights of heaven and set upon the gods.

At this Zeus took counsel with the other gods as to what was to be done. They found themselves in rather an awkward position; they didn't want to blast them out of existence with thunderbolts as they did the giants, because that would be saying good-by to all their offerings and devotions, but at the same time they couldn't let them get altogether out of hand. At last, however, after racking his brains, Zeus offered a solution.

I think I can see my way, he said, to put an end to this disturbance by weakening these people without destroying them. What I propose to do is to cut them all in half, thus killing two thirds with one stone, for each one will be only half as strong, and there'll be twice as many of them, which will suit us very nicely. They can walk about, upright, on their two legs, and if, said Zeus, I have any more trouble with them, I shall split them up again, and they'll have to hop about on one.

So saying, he cut them all in half just as you or I might chop up sorb apples for pickling, or slice and egg with a hair. And when each half was ready he told Apollo to turn its face, with the half-neck that was left, toward the side that was cut away—thinking that the sight of such a gash might frighten it into keeping quiet—and then to heal the whole thing up. So Apollo turned their faces back to front, and pulling in the skin all the way round, he stretched it over what we now call the belly—like those bags you pull together with a string—and tied up the one remaining opening so as to form what we call the navel. As for the creases that were left, he smoothed most of them away, finishing off the chest with the sort of tool a cobbler uses to smooth down the leather on the last, but he left a few puckers round about the belly and the navel, to remind us of what we suffered long ago.

Now, when the work of bisection was complete it left each half with a desperate yearning for the other, and they ran together and flung their arms around each other's necks, and asked for nothing better than to be rolled into one. So much so, that they began to die of hunger and general inertia, for neither would do anything without the other. And whenever one half was left alone by the death of its mate, it wandered about questing and clasping in the hope of finding a spare half-woman—or a whole woman, as we should call her nowadays—or half a man. And so the race was dying out.

Fortunately, however, Zeus felt so sorry for them that he devised another scheme. He moved their privates round to the front, for of course they had originally been on the outside—which was now the back—and they had begotten and conceived

not upon each other, but, like the grasshoppers, upon the earth. So no'
say, he moved their members round to the front and made them propagate
among themselves, the male begetting upon the female—the idea being that if,
in all these clippings and claspings, a man should chance upon a woman,
conception would take place and the race would be continued, while if the man
should conjugate with man, he might at least obtain such satisfaction as would
allow him to turn his attention and his energies to the ever reintegrate our
former nature, to make two into one, and to bridge the gulf between one human
being and another.

2. These comparisons are illuminating, not because we expect another animal society
to be a model of human society, but because the abstract principles common across
them are easier to see, and to talk about, in animals.

3. Povinelli (1993) has suggested that among the higher primates mature Chimpanzees
may share this capacity for role taking in social life. However, whereas we have
developed this capacity to the height of great civilizations, among chimps this capacity remains primitive.

4. This book is *not* about gender, which is the meaning cultures give to the sexes. The
idea of gender relativizes sex by emphasizing local meanings over universal meanings. Yes, cultures deal somewhat differently with the sexes, but I want to understand how cultures themselves are rooted in sex. Thus, I choose to focus on sex and
not gender in order to see certain things and not others. In particular, I want to see
across cultures to what they share in common. I want to see into human nature. I
make this choice in good faith, with eyes and mind open. Even if it is true as some
say that all talk about humanity is politics, I want to take my stand with what is true,
whether or not it is what I want or think should be.

## Chapter 2

1. Against this are occasional voices for the idea that social life is a unity of some kind.
A feeling comes—call it a "social sense" (Langer, 1962), or a "consciousness of
kind" (Giddens, 1979; McDougall, 1909), or a "sense of society" (Sandelands,
1994), or "natural pity" (Rousseau, 1762/1950) that seems to encompass persons in
a larger social whole. But these vague ephemera of feeling fall short of the facts
demanded by a rigorous empirical science. Allport (1927) ridicules such feelings
with demands for proof. What, he asks, is there to see of a group but individual
behavior? And Geertz (1965, p. 100) mocks these feelings by pointing out that such
claims have been "present in some form or another in all ages and climes. It is one
of those ideas that occurs to almost anyone sooner or later." Thus many in social
science reasonably choose not to focus on social unities but instead on clearly
visible chart-able persons.

2. It is in some ways ironic that social science makes the individual the focus of study.
When Darwin broke onto the scene, species and instincts were all the rage. Tarde
proposed a herd instinct to explain why people gather in groups. Trotter saw this
same herd instinct in man as a continuation of a fundamental biological principle of
multi-cellularity. Others such as Spencer and Le Bon spoke freely of the human
race. But somehow talk about the species or races or groups became talk about
persons. Thus, Freud (1922) spoke of the *person's* "instinctive libido," McDougall
(1909) of the *person's* "gregariousness"; Maslow (1954) of the *person's* "need to
affiliate," and recently, Baumeister (1991) of the *person's* "need to belong." Such
ideas make the group personal, an individual want.

3.     It is interesting to note that although Hamilton (1964) first proposed his theory of inclusive genetic fitness as an alternative to group selection, he later came to see it as an example of group selection (see Hamilton, 1975). This accords with E.O. Wilson's (1975) observation that kin selection is not everywhere distinct from group or demic selection. The two run into one another as kin groups function as vehicles of selection.

4.     Indeed, it now seems but a historical accident that natural selection has been conceived to operate almost exclusively upon individuals. Perhaps this is because Darwin wrote about evolution with examples drawn from animal husbandry where breeders modify species by mating some individuals and not others. Or perhaps this is because Darwin did not yet know about genes, or because he never defined groups in terms clear enough to compete with individuals (see his concepts of "species" and "varieties" which are notoriously vague).

5.     It is profitable to ask how selfishness became part of evolutionary reasoning. I believe it is a projection of our own selfishness into life around us. First, we imagine that life itself has the same goals that we selfish individuals have. As we long for immortality, we imagine reproduction to be the goal of life (we say that the goal of life is life itself). And second, we imagine that success in reproduction (immortality) goes to actors that selfishly make that their priority (be these actors individual genes elbowing for a ride into the next generation, or males and females angling for sexual intercourse, or nations warring over ideologies and resources). This reasoning seems to us so intuitive that we do not see how it depends upon the dubious premises that life has a goal, that the goal is immortality through reproduction, and that things such as genes, and persons, and groups, make this goal their own.

6.     Waddington remarks on the near tautology of the theory and its silence about processes: "[with selection] you come to what is, in effect, a vacuous statement. Natural selection is that some things leave more offspring than others; and you ask, which leave more offspring than others: and it is those that leave more offspring; and there is nothing more to it than that. The whole guts of evolution—which is, how do you come to have horses and tigers and things—is outside the mathematical theory" (1962, p. 82).

7.     What is most impressive about this cooperation is that it emerges under abjectly antithetical conditions. Biological connection trumps the cultured hates of nationalism. There is room for the comforting thought that it takes some effort to get people to kill one another. The group is first in social life and the first group is the species itself.

8.     Most agent-based models of group behavior guarantee the integrity of the group by the whole-defining mathematics used to describe them. Michael Cohen (personal communication) has pointed out geometric representations of complex systems can make them self-closing. Structure emerges only in the proximities of a fixed landscape. Even a random walk in one dimension has an expected return to its origin of infinity. A random walk in two dimensions has an expected return to its origin of 1. By contrast, a random walk in three dimensions has an expected return to its origin of 0, which may be why models of complex systems are rarely posed and modeled in 3 dimensions.

9.     Durkheim's maxim that the social cannot be derived from the individual is not universally accepted. Moscovici (1997), for one, presents a spirited defense of an individual-centered conception of society, finding (mistakenly I believe) that Durkheim and others unwittingly smuggle ideas of individual psychology into their accounts of society. Moscovici errs in thinking that society is made by the feelings and ideas

by which we know it (i.e., that society *is* what we know and feel, and nothing else). On this account there can be no society but for a psychology that comprises it.

10.  It is ironic that even though, and indeed because, we are the most individuated animal, we have the most vital and developed societies. Whereas other animals relate to one another in stereotyped ways, as if commanded by genes, we relate to one another more flexibly and creatively, as if emancipated by thought. We are capable of a wide range of groups, from ad hoc teams in disaster relief to families to bowling leagues to multi-national corporations. If we are not the most groupy animal, we are certainly the most elaborately and resolutely group-centered animal. We devote more time, energy, and thought to being with others than any other animal. We think of one another constantly and scheme endlessly to uphold the group.

11.  The unity of matter prefigures the unity of life and the unity of mind. Looking across the phases of matter, from solid through liquid and gas to plasma, there is a bond that energy transforms but does not break. Unities prevail as well in organisms, minds, and societies. That which thinks is alive and that which is alive is a material whole. All life is integral, bounded, dynamic, growing, evolving, and yet to be resolved. This unity defies explanation. Analyze it as we may, slice it this way or that, no story of parts conveys the living whole. To paraphrase Wordsworth, when we dissect we murder.

12.  Writing elsewhere of love, Freud (1930/1961) points particularly to its transcendence beyond the selfish ego:

> Normally there is nothing of which we are more certain than the feeling of our self, of our own ego. This ego appears to us as something autonomous and unitary, marked off distinctly from everything else. ... There is only one state — admittedly an unusual state, but not one that can be stigmatized as pathological— in which it does not do this. At the height of being in love the boundary between ego and object threatens to melt away. Against all the evidences of his senses, a man who is in love declares that 'I' and 'you' are one, and is prepared to behave as if it were a fact. (Pp. 12-13)

13.  See, e.g., Plomin, Owen & McGuffin, 1994; Bouchard, Lykken & McGue, 1990. To this we can add the recent suggestion that single born persons can retain a feeling of and for a twin lost in gestation or birth. A few of these people go through life haunted by a sense that they were not born alone, that a part of them is missing, that they took a guilty part in some grievous offense.

14.  See, e.g., Gross, Bender & Rocha-Miranda, 1969; Rolls, 1995; Perrett, Heitanen, Ocam & Benson, 1992).

15.  For examples, see Koolhaus et al. 1990; Ferris and Delville 1994; Argiolas and Gessa, 1991; Uvnas-Moberg, 1994; Carter et al. 1995.

16.  Elsewhere Brown notes: "The truth, the healing truth, the wholesome truth, the truth that will make us whole, is not in individual psychology, nor in the currently so fashionable ego psychology, but in what the later Freud called "mass psychology." This is "the psychology of mankind as a whole, as one mass, or one body" (p. 85).

17.  Anticipating this point, Haldane (1932) sees the mistake in the idea that animal societies are agglomerations of individuals. He argues that animal groups, including our own, are not creations of individual animals, but species facts, there from the beginning. Groups do not and can not originate from individuals because there are no individuals to make them. Individual life and character is always and everywhere already determined in and by the group.

# Chapter 3

1.  Ovid minced no words in the telling. In Hughes' (1997) translation, here is Salmacis after spying Hermaphroditus swimming naked in the pool:

> "I've won!" shrieked Salmacis. "He's mine!"
> She could not help herself.
> "He's mine!" she laughed, and with a couple of
> bounds
> Hit the pool stark naked
> In a rocking crash and thump of water—
> The slips of her raiment settling wherever
> They happened to fall.  Then out of the upheaval
> Her arms reach and wind round him,
> And slippery as the roots of big lilies
> But far stronger, her legs below wind round him.
> He flounders and goes under.  All his strength
> Fighting to get back up through a cloud of bubbles
> Leaving him helpless to her burrowing kisses.
> Burning for air, he can do nothing
> As her hands hunt over him, and as her body
> Knots itself every way around him
> Like a sinewy otter
> Hunting some kind of fish
> That flees hither and thither inside him,
> And as she flings and locks her coils
> Around him like a snake
> Around the neck and legs and wings of an eagle
> That is trying fly off with it,
> And like ivy which first binds the branches
> In its meshes, then pulls the whole tree down,
> And as the octopus—
> A tangle of constrictors, nippled with suckers,
> That drags towards a maw—
> Embraces its prey.

2.  In the play of these forms we see the feelings of moving between men's club or women's kaffeklatch and domestic partnership.  Perhaps there is wisdom in this image for our gender-bending age—for men and women to meet happily, they must come from, and occasionally return to, groups of their own kind.

3.  Though the imagery of sex in folk dance may strain credulity today, it did not a few generations ago.  Here is the jealous lover, Falkland, in Sheridan's *The Rivals*, distressed to learn that his sweetheart, Julia, has been dancing in his absence:

> A minuet I could have forgiven—I should not have minded that—but country dances!—Z–gds!  Had she made one in a cotillion I believe I could have forgiven even that—but to be monkey-led for a night!—to run the gauntlet through a string of amorous palming puppies!—to show paces like a managed filly!—O

Jack, there never can be but one man in the world whom a truly modest and delicate woman ought to pair with in a country dance; and even then, the rest of the couples should be her great uncles and aunts!

4.    Although widely separated in time and complexity, these three moments of evolution are linked—nucleated life made sex possible by locating the genome and providing infrastructure and resources for genetic transfer and mixing; and sexual life made symbolic thinking possible by differentiating the species and enabling rapid adaptations to circumstances.

5.    Wagner, Elejabarrieta & Lahnsteiner (1995) found that a sample of 169 European adults drew strong parallels between the social behavior of males and females and the reproductive biology of sperm and egg. However, they presume the parallel is spurious and argue that people mistakenly impute to sex cells (about which they know little) commonplace characteristics of the sexes (about which they know a lot). Among these characteristics are activity, dominance, and speed. This they say is an error of reading moral content into observations that even scientists are liable to make. I suggest that the widely recognized parallel between sex cells and fully formed sexes is more than spurious inference but evidence of anisogamy.

6.    The biology of attraction is fundamentally a biology of division—it is not simply that opposites attract, but that elements formerly united and now complementary attract. "Libido" thus is the name for the biological force released when organic wholes are divided and parts separated—be it a colony of bees, flock of birds, or human family. This can happen either by physical separations of members from the group, or by differentiation of members from one another so that they no longer related to each other as before.

7.    Freud ascribes libido to persons, even while he acknowledges its species typicality. It is more accurate to ascribe libido to relationships between and among persons. It is an interstitial force akin to gravity or to magnetism. It exists wherever people are together and it appears as a uniting force opposed to separation.

8.    Most discussions of sex, human or otherwise (e.g., Symons, 1979; Hrdy, 1982; Williams, 1975) emphasize the different interests of the sexes apart from the interests of the whole they together comprise. This reflects a bias in evolutionary theory for reductive accounts of natural selection focused on individuals, rather than on social units such as couples, groups, or entire species. Thus, males and females are supposed to have evolved differently because of the different demands life has made upon them (Buss, 1994). This is a grave misconception because it denies the main fact of sex which is that it an attribute of the species, not of its individual members. Sex is a solution to the species problem of reproduction. Its details of sexual difference and sexual intercourse are about how this problem is worked out. Species that survived are the species that solved this problem best. Thus, to understand the meaning of sex we must see male and female as interdependent parts of a larger whole. Male and female are dynamically opposed in the life of the species. There is no use or meaning in talking of one without the other. Thus the meaning of sex is in how its differences work together to further the interests of the species.

9.    This is a frequent theme of feminist utopian and dystopian novels.

10.   This is why no culture celebrates female wantonness and why every culture reproves female promiscuity. Wantonness and promiscuity are an affront to female identity because they are abdications of judgment. They also undermine male hierarchy by diminishing its value in mating.

11.   There is comedy and pathos in this, to be sure. Paglia (1990) compares us wittily to birds:

Pigeons on the grass, alas: in such park side rituals we may savor the comic pathos of sex. How often one spots a male pigeon making desperate, self-inflating sallies toward the female, as again and again she turns her back on him and nonchalantly marches away. But by concentration and persistence he may carry the day. Nature has blessed him with obliviousness to his own absurdity. His purposiveness is both a gift and a burden.

12.  But "decide" she does. Thornhill & Gangestad (1995) report that females orgasm during copulation more frequently with bilaterally symmetrical males. Baker & Bellis (1994) find that females orgasm more frequently with lovers other than their regular partner. In this the female may be unconsciously giving reproductive advantage to the better genes of a lover.

13.  A strong affidavit to this appears in the mating preferences of wealthy females who have surplus resources for having and raising children. Even more than their less advantaged counterparts, these women demand wealthy resourceful mates (Symons, 1979). Of particular interest, it appears that these women seek men who are not just wealthy and resourceful in absolute terms, but who are more wealthy and more resource than they (Buss, 1994; Wieder & Allgeier, 1992). If an overbold inference might be permitted, it is as if the female seeks a mate with a superior position in the society. This could make evolutionary sense if, as suggested earlier, female mate preferences were based on comparisons rather than absolute assessments. Minimally, the female should seek a partner better off than she. Ideally, she should seek a partner better off than any rival.

14.  Whereas Gilligan and Chodorow attach greater significance to the role of the mother than Freud, it is not clear how their feminist story differs from his masculinist story of the Oedipal complex. Where Freud emphasizes the body difference of a penis to explain why men and women relate differently to mother and father, Gilligan and Chodorow do not say why men and women relate differently to mother and father. For their purposes of explaining sexual inequality it is enough to note only that there is a difference that makes a difference.

15.  Something of this melancholy is captured in this poem about mother and daughter by Sharon Olds:

Brushing out my daughter's dark
silken hair before the mirror
I see the grey gleaming on my head,
the silver-haired servant behind her. Why is it
just as we begin to go
they begin to arrive, the fold in my neck
clarifying as the fine bones of her
hips sharpen? As my skin shows
its dry pitting, she opens like a small
pale flower in the tip of a cactus;
as my last chances to bear a child
Are falling through my body, the duds among them,
her purse full of eggs, round and
firm as hard-boiled yolks, is about
to snap its clasp. I brush her tangled
fragrant hair at bedtime. It's an old
story—the oldest we have on our planet—
the story of replacement.

16.  That no male quite achieves this ambition does not make it less powerful a motivation. A few males manage to achieve substantial mating prerogatives. That these Don Juans are widely and luridly celebrated shows the ambition unconsciously at work. For most males in most societies this ambition is consoled by the monogamous mating pair and the social institution of marriage. He makes his home his castle and is rewarded with privileged (if not always exclusive) access to the female who is his wife. She of course gets a reliable husband and father for her children.

17.  Horney (1967) describes the male plight clearly:

> Now one of the exigencies of the biological differences between the sexes is this—that the man is actually obliged to go on proving his manhood to the woman. There is no analogous necessity for her; even if she is frigid, she can engage in sexual intercourse and conceive and bear a child. She performs her part by merely being, without any doing—a fact that has always filled men with admiration and resentment. The man, on the other hand, has to do something in order to fulfill himself. (P. 145)

This contingency of male development and difficulties males have in meeting it is reflected in the higher rate of gender identity and personality disorders among males (Eme & Kavanaugh, 1995).

18.  To be sure, the male does not entirely cooperate with his fate. He seeks in various ways to resist or co-opt female choices of mates—e.g., through social institutions of matchmaking and marriage by which he asserts legal claim on the female, or through economic exploitation by which he controls resources she needs to survive, or through countervailing ideas of female beauty by which he imposes an insecurity upon her, or through exertions of personal power in sexual harassment, abuse, and rape. Such resistances, which are more or less effective, and which are more or less acceptable to male and female (albeit often for different reasons), underline the point that for all his freedom of movement in the outer world the male answers the female. Aside from rare and universally repugnant instances of rape, he doesn't take her, she takes him.

19.  Failure to abide by female choice defines the criminal act of rape, an act that appears to be uniquely human. Rape is not an act of animal impulse, but a human act of meaning. Rape is not explained by the superior size and strength of the male, though that is certainly an enabling condition. Sex differences of size and strength are much greater in primate species close to ours, such as the chimpanzee, baboon, gorilla, and orangutan, where rape is practically unknown. Rather, rape is explained by the human male's consuming need for meaning—a need that can impels him to put his will ahead of her biological prerogatives. The rapist above all wants a female (any female) to acknowledge and validate his power. It is not the sex act per se that drives him, but his need for female cowering and submission and humiliation. Rape is the last refuge of meaning for the man who cannot make his own. Rape threatens the natural order, which is why it is universally sanctioned, even among criminals. In the male game for female favor, whereas the ordinary man plays fairly and the criminal cheats, the rapist mocks the game altogether by taking the female for himself. That is the most egregious transgression that no male can abide.

20.  Chimpanzees make an interesting comparison on this point. After fighting, male chimps waste little time making amends through the quiet and familiar ritual of grooming (de Waal, 1989 describes them as attracted as magnets). Female chimps, on the other hand, are slower to make up and can harbor grudges for much longer

periods. In this way male chimps establish a pattern of winners and losers that can be recognized by females, even as they prepare behind the scenes for a new round of contests and perhaps a new round of winners and losers.

21.   This sensibility is epitomized in this speech by the revered football coach Vince Lombardi:

> Winning is not a sometime thing; it's an all the time thing. You don't win once in a while; you don't do things right once in a while; you do them right all the time. Winning is a habit. Unfortunately, so is losing.
>
> There is no room for second place. There is only one place in my game, and that's first place. I have finished second twice in my time at Green Bay, and I don't ever want to finish second again. There is a second place bowl game, but it is a game of losers played by losers. It is and always has been an American zeal to be first in anything we do, and to win, and to win, and to win. . . .
>
> . . . It is a reality of life that men are competitive and the most competitive games draw the most competitive men. That's why they are there—to compete. To know the rules and objectives when they get in the game. The object is to win fairly, squarely, by the rules—but to win.
>
> And in truth, I've never known a man worth his salt who in the long run, deep down in his heart, didn't appreciate the grind, the discipline. There is something in good men that really yearns for discipline and the harsh reality of head to head combat.
>
> I don't say these things because I believe in the "brute" nature of man or that men must be brutalized to be combative. I believe in God, and I believe in human decency. But I firmly believe that any man's finest hour, the greatest fulfillment of all that he holds dear, is that moment when he has worked his heart out in a good cause and lies exhausted on the field of battle—victorious.

22.   This is perhaps mainly because male hierarchy is recognized and respected and reinforced by all. Indeed a striking feature of male hierarchies is that they are maintained as much by low-ranking members as by high-ranking members. When an unfit or impertinent male challenges a ranking male, it is often other low-ranking males who conspire to bring down the challenge, often without intercession by the challenged leader (Whyte, 1943).

23.   This perfect and unique fit of male to female genitalia is a primary argument for the naturalness of heterosexual coitus and the unnaturalness of oral and anal intercourse, be it heterosexual or homosexual. There is no getting around the fact that penis and vagina fit together in a way that other organ-orifice combinations do not. These organs share a common development and evolved to work together.

24.   Delayed orgasm may also have an evolutionary function in fostering sexual frustration in females. Where one male does not satisfy the female she will be impelled to seek satisfaction elsewhere, presumably from males better able to do so. This may explain the finding that married females report a higher incidence of orgasm with sexual partners outside the marriage (Buss, 1994; Baker & Bellis, 1994).

25.   These differences are harder to see today because standard I.Q. tests hide differences between sexes to equalize their scores (either by discarding items that favor one sex or by balancing items that shade toward one sex with items that shade

toward the other sex). Nevertheless, females score better on items relating to esthetics (e.g., matching colors and shapes, discriminating between pictures), language (e.g., speech, word choice, vocabulary), hand skills, and social perception. Males score better on items relating to mechanical ability, mathematical reasoning, and logic (Geary, 1998).

26.    H.L. Mencken (1918), in a wise and witty book, *In Defense of Women*, amplifies this point, observing that great intelligence in men is found only if they do not think like men but add a substantial feminine sensibility:

> Find me an obviously intelligent man, a man free from sentimentality and illusion, a man hard to deceive, a man of the first class, and I'll show you a man with a wide streak of woman in him. Bonaparte had it; Goethe had it; Schopenhauer had it; Bismarck and Lincoln had it; in Shakespeare, if the Freudians are to be believed, it amounted to downright homosexuality. (P. 7)

A few paragraphs later he gives theoretical expression to the point:

> The truth is that neither sex, without some fertilization by the complementary characters of the other, is capable of the highest reaches of human endeavor. Man, without a saving touch of woman in him, is too doltish, too naive and romantic, too easily deluded and lulled to sleep by his imagination to be anything above a cavalryman, a theologian or a bank director. And woman, without some trace of that divine innocence which is masculine, is too harshly the realist for those vast projections of the fancy which lie at the heart of what we call genius. Here, as elsewhere in the universe, the best effects are obtained by a mingling of elements. The whole manly man lacks the wit necessary to give objective form to his soaring and secret dreams, and the wholly womanly woman is apt to be too cynical a creature to dream at all. (Pp. 8-9)

27.    There is the abiding question of how mind arose from body. Almost certainly it came as a social and sexual development, probably along different lines for females and males. For females, thought may have developed around a maternal role which rewarded females who were emotionally open and sensitive to the myriad needs of their children. Such females would have been more likely to pass their genes on to succeeding generations. For males thought may have been refined in group activities of hunt and defense. Life on the open savannah no doubt made great demands on male groups to develop and coordinate their senses to maximum advantage. Now dispersed over distance in the open plain, group members needed an internal image of the group and its leader to hold their place and role in its activity. Jaynes (1976) suggests that this internalized leader presented itself to group members as an "inner voice," appearing as a kind of hallucination when the leader was not physically present. That these demands of savannah life led to distinctive female and male minds is suggested by differences in male and female brains visible today. The male brain is larger and more specialized than the female brain (Blum, 1997). In particular it comes with greater cerebral mass and with a sharper break in function between the right hemisphere, where spatial abilities are centered, and the left hemisphere where language and self-awareness are centered. Jaynes (1976) cites this very hemispheric specialization of the male brain for language and speech as evidence for his idea that the male incorporated the inner voice of the leader. There is an intriguing parallel here as well to the finding in psychoanalysis that males tend to have a more well-developed ego and especially a more well-developed superego than fe-

males. According to Freud, ego and superego arise with introjection of idealized figures into the psyche. In more common parlance, we internalize the voices of our parents, especially perhaps that of our fathers. If the male is more concerned to establish his place in the ranks of society, it would make sense that his brain is structured to facilitate this process.

28.     In discussing sex differences it is easy to trip on the question of whether they are biological or cultural in origin. To those put off by the idea that sex differences are given in nature there is comfort and hope in the idea that sex differences are cultivated and therefore malleable. Are they truly important, or are they made important by cultures that turn trivial differences into great inequalities of social, economic, and political power (Eagly, 1995)?

I find the debate about the nature and nurture of sex differences unhelpful. No doubt culture shapes the feelings, thoughts, and behaviors of males and females. We are born to a social world already made, a world that comprehensively and relentlessly defines different parts for males and females to play. We do not choose this world, it is true, and for that we might feel put upon or perhaps even oppressed. But at the same time we must recognize that cultures do not form and develop in a vacuum. Cultures are made by real people with and upon their real lives. They arise as males and females repeat and normalize the lives that best suit them and the group. The question of nature versus nurture is unhelpful because it cannot be answered. Insofar as culture articulates biology there is no parsing the two to say where biology ends and where culture begins.

More serious, I find the debate about the nature and nurture of sex differences misleading. First, the debate pits culture against biology, as if culture generally calls for behavior that biology does not. I accept that a culture could mislead us to act against our nature for a time, but probably not for long, and not about something so basic as sex. To maintain otherwise (e.g., Millett, 1970; Hrdy, 1981) is to imagine a species deluded from its beginning and for its entire history. Moreover, if culture is opposed to biology as the debate implies, there is no explaining how the capacity for culture evolved in the first place. What advantage could our apish ancestors derive from such an un-biological capacity? Second, the debate makes culture a monolith that acts upon us from outside. We become poor innocents coerced into alien feelings, thoughts, and behaviors. This would be more terrifying if it did not demonize that which is essentially us. Culture is not outside. It is something that we make, that we are. Its restless dynamics are our own. Its values are our own. Those who blame a monolithic culture for their troubles are a bit like those in a democracy who blame government for poor leadership. The solace in blaming an enemy is paid at a heavy price of personal responsibility and self-understanding.

29.     This is why misogyny doesn't have a complement in females, and why boys resent being called a "girl" or a "mama's boy" far more than girls resent being called a "tomboy" or "daddy's little girl." Females have no identity to disavow. They are free to just be. Males have to overcome their beginnings in the custody and care of females. They are not male until they have done so.

# Chapter 4

1.     This pattern is confirmed by a few rule-proving exceptions. A few species of bird and fish reverse the pattern of parental investment and leave to males greater responsibility for offspring. Substantial male investment in offspring is made possible in birds by external gestation of the fertilized ovum, and in fish by external fertilization and gestation of the ovum. Ever resourceful, nature invents various ways to satisfy

reproductive imperatives of attraction, transportation, selection, and support.

2.    It should be asked why this contest between the sexes is about who gets stuck caring for children rather than about who has priority in this critical aspect of reproduction. By her central place in reproduction, the female controls the destiny of the species. The male, ill-equipped and standing on the outside, is left to hope things go well.

3.    The anisogamy of sex cells is dramatic. A mature human egg has roughly one million times the mass of the sperm that fertilizes it. A mature Kiwi bird egg has roughly one million billion times the mass of the sperm that fertilizes it (Diamond, 1997).

4.    This significance of this small-seeming point should not be underestimated. As Mead (p. 57) notes:

> Living in the modern world, clothed and muffled, forced to convey our sense of our bodies in terms of remote symbols like walking sticks and umbrellas and hand-bags, it is easy to lose sight of the immediacy of the human body plan. But when one lives among primitive peoples, where women wear only a pair of little grass aprons , and may discard even these to insult each other or to bathe in a group, and men wear only a very lightly fastened G-string of beaten bark, or— once they have killed their man—a flying-fox skin that is a fine homicidal decoration, but very un-concealing, and small babies wear nothing at all, the basic communications between infant, child, and adult that are conducted between bodies become very real.

5.    Fox extended this idea in a parenthesis that may come closer to the truth about our profoundly social nature. This is to say instead or in addition that the male is "the female kin group's way of making another female kin group." (p. 13).

6.    A possibility that Mead herself acknowledges:

> In our current Western theorizing, it has been too often ignored that envy of the male role can come as much from an undervaluation of the role of the wife and mother as from an overvaluation of public aspects of achievement that have been reserved for man. (P. 92)

7.    Some of these variations may be idiosyncratic, others may be tied to resources. Where times are tough and where resources are tight, such as among the Arapesh described by Mead, the battle of the sexes may keep closer to the universal outline— if only because this is the most efficient way to meet the reproductive needs of the group. Where times are good and resources plentiful, such as among the Samoans or Balinese described by Mead, the battle of the sexes may diverge from the universal form. Cultures play upon patterns established biologically with a freedom left to them by circumstances. Under benign circumstances sex roles can vary more freely—in some instances to exaggerate biological patterns and in other instances to mitigate biological patterns. Putting a moral spin on it, good times can be decadent.

8.    Paglia goes on to remark ironically about how human culture feeds on this difference between the sexes, taking from it ever new energies and dynamics:

> Hence the sexes are caught in a comedy of historical indebtedness. Man, repelled by his debt to a physical mother, created an alternative reality, a heterocosm to give him the illusion of freedom. Woman, at first content to accept man's protections but now inflamed with desire for her own illusory freedom, invades

man's systems and suppresses her indebtedness to him as she steals them. (P. 9)

One can only smile in wonder about how this latest turn in the war of the sexes will turn out. Man now finds himself more tightly bound to mother and woman, without a place to retreat and find his own identity and meaning. Presumably he will react in some new (and perhaps more terrible) way to preserve his prerogatives.

9.    Reik (1957) confirms that men and women experience and participate in the battle of the sexes differently. Having a more powerful ego ideal born of greater hierarchical concern, the man falls harder in love, and is more devastated by it. He puts the woman in place of his well-formed ego-ideal (to compensate for disappointments he has in it). He wants somebody to complete himself. Thus he idealizes the woman, blind to her failings. He goes at love full speed ahead, damn the torpedoes, in frantic and desperate pursuit. By contrast, the woman in tune with nature has less concern for ego and ego ideal. Her love takes a different shape because she puts the male in place of a less developed and less importuning ego-ideal. She is not so concerned to find somebody to complete herself, she is already complete. Her concerns are more pragmatic. How much life is in him? What can he offer me? Will he stick around to help with the kids? It is perhaps for this reason that women are attracted to power; almost without regard for its morality. Good girls like bad boys, not because they are bad but because they are powerful. Morality is at best a secondary concern—secondary because power is more important and secondary because the ego-ideal is less a prominent factor in the female. Power for the female also trumps beauty, which as fairy tales such as Beauty and the Beast remind, do not always run together. Compare this to the male who cares more for beauty in a woman because he sees her as a reflection upon his more fragile ego.

10.   For example, human males are on the average 12 percent larger than human females, whereas chimpanzee males are on the average 25 percent larger than chimpanzee females. Of course, there are other numerous less obvious differences as well, including those of sex organs, hormones, physiology, and brain development.

11.   If there is any significance to the smaller size difference between human males and females, it may be that it makes the human battle of the sexes less brutal and more open to negotiation and play. Compared to a male gorilla or chimpanzee, a man cannot so easily bully a woman (though of course it still happens). Thus, while our battle of the sexes may be more intense because there is more to fight about, it may be physically less violent. Our battle of the sexes is more open to idiosyncracies, provisional arrangements, shifting truces, adaptations. This may give our species an advantage in adapting socially to a diversity of circumstances.

12.   Mead (1949) questions the value of looking at sex differences with political and/or practical aims. "The more we ask questions about sex differences only so that we can get rid of them, or exploit them quantitatively, the more likely we are to find ways of eliminating them, both as bases of inequality and waste in the world, and also as bases of diversification of and contribution to the world" (p. 15).

13.   Perhaps the strongest and most surprising affidavit for the givenness and value of sex roles and relations comes in homosexual relations where they appear against all biological and cultural odds. Homosexual couples are made of recognizably male and female parts (Singh, Vidaurri, Zambarano, & Dabbs, 1999). Personal advertisements in gay and lesbian magazines clearly indicate whether a person is masculine (top) or feminine (bottom) in orientation and assume interest of one in the other. The effeminate gay male and mannish lesbian female in particular invert heterosexual attraction, preserving its form while reversing its polarity. It remains an open

question how this inversion takes place (see, e.g., Bem, 1997).

14. Female infidelity in humans may be a vestige of a primate past that continues to have adaptive value for the species. Infidelity enables her to attract the genes of a more desirable mate while enjoying the benefits of support by a regular partner. Her infidelity is a reason for male sexual jealousy and so motivates abiding male attention and support. And, her infidelity feeds male status striving by keeping alive the contest for her favor.

15. Still we can question the choice available to the human female. Her sexual desire is enigmatic. If she is taken in by the power of a dominant male, do we call this "a choice," or do we ascribe it to unconscious forces beyond her control? We may not be able to trust her own explanations for her attentions.

16. A few readers perhaps may doubt this formulation in their own experience. A woman may wonder about the choices she is supposed to have had, seeing little choice in the one or few men that came her way. And a man may smile at the idea he had to decide whether to play the field or devote himself to one woman. But rare is the woman who learns how many consorts she could have enticed to mate. And rare too is the man who can or cares to remember the women he did not call back for a second date or the entrapping relationships he unwittingly sabotaged. Mate choices and dilemmas are largely unconscious. Furthermore, we should distinguish between choices and markets. Although both Russian and American consumers make choices at the market, the former envies the many more choices that the latter hardly notices.

17. This is not to say that sexual selection does not also operate on females, but to say that it operates in a different and more indirect way. Females who mate with the most fit and best providing males are most likely to have children who will survive to reproduce and thus are most likely to have their genes selected into later generations. In so far as the most fit and best providing males are choosy about their mates, then female characteristics that recruit these males will tend to be selected.

18. Thus women misunderstand men's contests, seeing in them affront and bitterness that is not there. Men can be furious rivals in marketplace or courtroom in the morning and drinking or golf partners in the afternoon. More than women, men separate the public sphere of contest and the private sphere of relationship.

19. This difference between men and women recalls the observation in chapter 3 that male aggression toward female and toward other males is modulated whereas that of females is not. This difference shows up also in primate comparisons. De Waal (1989), for example, found among chimpanzees at the Arnhem colony that male chimpanzees fight without using their dangerous incisors, while female chimpanzees fight without this scruple in bloodier battles.

20. The only commemoration of fertility is the monthly bleeding of the menses which occurs only after the fact. That this is an ineffective and probably inoperative signal of fertility to males is suggested by anthropological reports of cultures that fail to note connections between menses, fertility, and sexual intercourse.

21. There are, it should be noted, many who think ideas of "sexual play" and "social life" are too big or too vague for a sober social science. Psychologists diminish "play" as a serious item of study (cf. Sandelands, Ashford & Dutton, 1983). They see play a lazy catchall for unserious activities pursued in moments of leisure or mirth. Or they see play as a function rather than an activity, as a move to develop life skills (of hunt, fight, nurture, and association) under conditions of calm and safety. Or they subsume play in the broad category of intrinsically motivating activity (Berlyne, 1960). They do not see play as a category of activity to study in its own right (see Csikszentmihalyi, 1975). In much the same way, biologists regard life a

useful fiction—like the ether of nineteenth-century physics or the phlogiston of nineteenth-century chemistry. They think it a figure of speech, perhaps necessary in the breach, but to drop as soon as possible. Says Dawkins (1989), "Human suffering has been caused because too many of us cannot grasp that words are only tools for our use, and that the mere presence in the dictionary of a word like 'living' does not mean it necessarily has to refer to something definite in the real world" (p. 18). And observes von Bertanlanffy, "The history of biology is the refutation of vitalism" (in Barlow, 1991, p. 110). Such doubts about the scientific value of ideas of play and life are perhaps connected. Both are regarded as remote and vague abstractions rather than as concrete realities—and this while common sense finds nothing so sure as play or so real as life. Disparaging both we do not see the links between them. If we do not see play we cannot see its vitality. If we do not see life we cannot see its interior play of divisions. In a perverse twist on the empirical foundations of science we come to think our models of intrinsic motivation more real than the play they describe and our models of bio-physical and bio-chemical mechanisms more real than the life they describe. We forget that models are not reality, but hopeful abstractions of reality. We forget that models purposely ignore complicating dynamics and nuances of play and life.

# Chapter 5

1.   This explains the particular horror of male gang rape that radically overthrows nature's balance of female and male interests and female and male social organization. Its criminality is intuitive and biological. It defies species interest for males to undermine sexual selection in this way.

2.   Stand before the pre-historic Stonehenge, or the pyramids of ancient Egypt, or the medieval Cathedral at Chartres, or the skyscrapers of New York City today and see the single-mindedness and coordinated muscle of groups of men over the ages. Discount men's bias in the telling and human history is still a tale of men's groups venturing forth to do things: to build, to explore, to conquer, to know. Impressed by the size and extent of men's constructive and destructive enterprises, some complain that it is now a man's world, that there is little scope or place for woman. But this is to forget men in groups act on the world on behalf of the species. This is also to ignore the possibility that the world that now alienates some women alienates some men as well. And this is to miss the irony, noted by Paglia (1990) that it is the very luxuries and conveniences of the modern world that allow people, women and men, the time and means to complain about it:

> We could make an epic catalog of male achievements, from paved roads, indoor plumbing, and washing machines to eyeglasses, antibiotics, and disposable diapers. We enjoy fresh, safe milk and meat, and vegetables and tropical fruits heaped in snowbound cities. When I cross the George Washington Bridge or any of America's great bridges, I *think* men have done this. Construction is a sublime male poetry. When I see a giant crane passing on a flatbed truck, I pause in awe and reverence, as one would for a church procession. What power of conception, what grandiosity: these cranes tie us to ancient Egypt, where monumental architecture was first imagined and achieved. If civilization had been left in female hands, we would still be living in grass huts. A contemporary women clapping on a hard hat merely enters a conceptual system invented by men. It is hypocritical for feminists and intellectuals to enjoy the pleasures and conveniences of capitalism while sneering at it. Even Thoreau's Walden

was just a two-year experiment. Everyone born into capitalism has incurred a debt to it. Give Caesar his due. (Pp. 37-38)

3.  Goldberg (1993, p. 68) epitomizes his argument this way:

> ... the central argument presented in this book, is that differences in the male and female neuro-endocrinological systems are such that the environmental stimulus of hierarchy, status, or a member of the other sex elicits from the male a stronger tendency to give up whatever must be given up—time, pleasure, health, physical safety, affection, relaxation—for the attainment of a higher hierarchical position, for a social role which is rewarded by greater status, and for dominance in male-female relationships. This differentiation of tendency, and a population's observation of the behavioral differentiation through which it is manifested, is the 'causal' connection between physiological differentiation on the one hand, and differentiation in the social values, socialization, and institutions we wish to explain on the other.

4.  Suggesting this conclusion is a recent study of demographics in the government of the state of California which finds among thousands of work groups that when the ratio of women increases, men's identification with and attachment to the group decreases (Tsui, Egan & O'Reilly, 1992).

5.  Thus there is a different basis and kind of solidarity in women's and men's groups. Men forge solidarity in status competitions confirmed by steady rule. Their other-directed psyches fix on finding a place in the group as high up as possible. Boys play games of sport and imagine adult games of politics and war while their fathers play games of politics and war and think wistfully of games of sport (perhaps while watching them on television). Women forge solidarity in shared interests confirmed by exchange. Their inner-directed psyches dwell on choices of a mate, on the rhythms and changes of gestation, and on tending the brood. They come to social life with powerful interests and enter relations to serve those interests. Girls fantasize about baby dolls, schoolroom, and hospital while their mothers work as mother, teacher, and physician. While difficult to compare the strength of men's and women's solidarities—so different are they in basis and form—one might guess the ritually-based solidarity of men is more sure-footed and stable whereas the resource-based solidarity of women is more intense and volatile.

6.  On occasion, women's ways of grouping rise to the level of political consciousness. Farrell (1994) describes the attempt of editors of *Ms. Magazine*, a feminist, mass-circulation, commercial periodical, to create a non-hierarchical collective-type organization—in short, a "woman friendly" workplace. The successes, failures, stresses, and strains of this effort reveal interesting tensions between feminist ideology and the practicalities of profit oriented business in deciding how work should be done.

7.  It was Tiger's achievement to identify the male group as a crucial element of this secondary social order. But Tiger is correctly faulted for making too much of this one element and, I suppose, for limiting this element too narrowly to its function in hunting. Armed with a powerful and partly correct hypothesis it is easy to be impressed by examples and evidences that support the hypothesis and to overlook examples and evidences that portend undermining complications.

8.  Evidence that male hierarchy predates the male hunting group appears in a study by Hawkes (1990) on why men hunt. Hawkes examined the nutritional economics of male hunting and female gathering in Paraguay's Northern Ache Indians, a tribe that until recently was a full-time hunter-gather society. Men hunted large game, primarily peccaries and deer, and masses of honey from bees' nests. Women gathered

fruits, insect larvae, and pounded starch from palm leaves. To her surprise, the expected return from male-hunting, measured in total calories, was *lower* than the expected return of female gathering. Nutritionally speaking, the group would be better off if the men did not leave home to hunt, but stayed home to gather alongside the women. Hawkes hypothesized that Ache men do not hunt to "bring home the bacon," so to speak, but to impress females and win mating opportunities. She then asked Ache women to name the potential fathers for their children (their sex partners around the time of conception). She found for a group of 66 children an average of 2.1 men named for each child. Furthermore she found that women named good hunters more often than poor hunts as their lovers, and they named good hunters as potential fathers of more children.

9.     There is question about how unique humans are on this count. In an ingenious series of studies on primate role-taking, Povinelli (1993) shows that among non-human primates chimpanzees can produce something that looks like formal organization. Chimpanzees, like humans, can see how parts of a social arrangement relate to each other and to the whole. Trained in one role of a two-role cooperative task, chimpanzees, like humans and unlike other primate species, can assume or quickly learn the other role without training. They understand the complementarity of the two roles and the need to combine them a certain way to complete the task. This suggests that chimpanzees, like humans and unlike other primate species, can form an idea of the group and of actors in relation to it. We also do not know, however, whether they develop and employ this idea in nature. If chimpanzees do possess the rudiments of a capacity for formal organization we are led to the hypothesis that this capacity presaged and perhaps potentiated the move of hominid species from trees to open savannah.

10.     For men, particularly, it appears also to be a biological fact. There is reason to believe that men's brains are specially evolved for this sort of self-concerned grouping. Based on evidence widely scattered in anthropology, linguistics, psychology and neural-biology, Jaynes (1976) hypothesized that human subjectivity—the ability to think of oneself in relation to others—appeared with a specialization of the brain that located the faculties of speech and language in the left cerebral hemisphere. This specialization, he supposed, freed early humans from the powerful yoke of unthinking obedience to leaders by separating the commanding voice of the group leader from the inner voice of personal thought. This hypothesis is of particular interest here in light of recent brain imaging studies that indicate greater hemispheric specialization of speech and language functions in men (Blum, 1997; Pugh et al., 1997; Shaywitz et al., 1995).

11.     In this we have a decisive discontinuity between animal societies and human societies. Animal and human groups share hierarchy and division of labor, but they do not share self-awareness. Some attach little significance to this, seeing in hierarchy and division of labor an overriding continuity. Others, such as Langer (1962) and me, attach great significance to this difference, seeing in self-awareness a qualitative difference making for a great leap in human social life from animal social life.

12.     Viewing individual and bureaucracy as cognates, we take a position contrary to those such as Freud (1922) who make bureaucracy a result of individual psychology (Freud fashions bureaucracy from aim-inhibited longings of individuals), and to those such as Jung (1990) who make individual psychology a result of bureaucracy (Jung attributes individual sexual conflicts to impersonal bureaucratic roles). Individual and bureaucracy are twin sons of one mother culture.

13.     Academic feminism has been a campaign to encourage people to do just this, thereby to put females and males on the same individual footing. One tactic has been to

refuse body differences between male and female in order to deny a biological basis for sex roles. Failing this, a second tactic has been to subordinate body differences to intellectual argument and theory. Today a leading edge of feminist scholarship takes on pornography to find the logic and theory behind it. That which cannot be denied shall be mastered by theory.

14. It was, after all, a man—Rene Descartes—who famously divided the realms of mind and body, thus to persecute philosophy ever since with the Humpty-Dumpty problem of reconciling the two.

15. Given the intent and effect of the public-private distinction to define a social world of individuals beyond the sexes, in which being male or female is irrelevant to ones place or fate, it is ironic that feminist writers object to it so strongly. They argue that it is oppressive to women to have to shed their biologic femaleness in order to get along and get ahead in public intellectual, economic, and political spheres dominated by men. But this is to forget that this very biologic femaleness is most often used to justify exclusion of women from these public spheres. It is for this reason that some complain of feminists, reasonably I think, that they seem to want the impossible, that is, to have their cake and to eat it too.

16. It is possible that individuality relates also to sexual orientation. If individuality varies with development and integration of male and female elements, we might expect those who are most individual to have more varied and complex sexual preferences. It is a cliche and perhaps true that homosexuality and bisexuality are more common among artists and intellectuals whose lives of mind are set substantially apart from the body. It is also a cliche and perhaps true that "real men" and "real women" whose lives are clearly anchored in male and female bodies tend for that reason to have little interest in the rarified atmosphere of theory or aesthetics.

17. The existence of female elements in the male individual and male elements in the female individual is confirmed by a few personality psychologists in the West who have come to think of the cultural categories of masculinity and femininity not as opposites but as independent dimensions more or less present in all persons (e.g., Bem, 1996).

18. Ghiselin (quoted in Symons, 1979) emphasizes the point to by noting what an accomplishment it is for a free-thinking and truth-seeking individual to emerge from the biological substrate of reproductive concerns and values.

> Man's brain, like the rest of him, may be looked upon as a bundle of adaptations. But what it is adapted to has never been self-evident. We are anything but a mechanism set up to perceive the truth for its own sake. Rather, we have evolved a nervous system that acts in the interest of our gonads, and one attuned to the demands of reproductive competition. If fools are more prolific than wise men, then to that degree folly will be favored by selection. And if ignorance aids in obtaining a mate, then men and women will tend to be ignorant. In order for so imperfect an instrument as a human brain to perceive the world as it really is, a great deal of self-discipline must be imposed.

# Chapter 6

1. Aggressive female sexuality oriented to sensual pleasure rather than procreation, and retiring or irresponsible male sexuality adapted to shared sexual initiative are fearful for three reasons. First, they upset the dynamic of male competition by taking away its aim—why should men play hard and fairly among themselves when woman becomes the pursuer and when she no longer grants the prize of paternal

certainty? Second, they undermine monogamous pair bonding which depends on her exchange of paternal certainty for his commitment to offspring. And third, they confound the physically essential masculine sexual posture of energetic pursuit through competition, perseverance, wooing, and erection, and the physically essential feminine sexual posture of momentous choice, attuned receptivity, and responsiveness to male initiative—at some point it becomes impossible to enact sexual intercourse in a mutually satisfying way.

2.    Lasch (1979, p. 72) takes note of this change in advertising in this new economy:

> In a simpler time, advertising merely called attention to the product and extolled its advantages. Now it manufactures a product of its own: the consumer, perpetually unsatisfied, restless, anxious, and bored. Advertising serves not so much to advertise products as to promote consumption as a way of life. It "educates" the masses into an unappeasable appetite not only for goods but for new experiences and personal fulfillment. It upholds consumption as the answer to the age-old discontents of loneliness, sickness, weariness, lack of sexual satisfaction ...

3.    For reasons now familiar, Goodman (1960, p. 13) finds this a problem primarily for boys and men:

> I say the "young men and boys" rather than the "young people" because the problems I want to discuss in this book belong primarily, in our society, to the boys: how to be useful and make something of oneself. A girl does not have to, she is not expected to, "make something" of herself. Her career does not have to be self-justifying, for she will have children, which is absolutely self-justifying, like any other natural or creative act. With this background, it is less important, for instances, what job an average woman works at till she is married. The quest for the glamour job is given at least a little substance by its relation to a "better" marriage. Correspondingly, our "youth troubles" are boys' troubles—female delinquency is sexual: "incorrigibility" and unmarried pregnancy. Yet as every woman knows, these problems are intensely interesting to women, for if the boys do not grow to be men, where shall the women find men? If the husband is running the rat race of the organized system, there is not much father for the children.

4.    One result of the absence of opportunities to pursue the heroics of the hunt natural to them is invention of substitute heroics less healthy for themselves and for the species. At the same time men of the 1950s were losing their manhood to the corporation they were reclaiming it in "cold-war" crises of their own making—McCarthyism, Sputnik, arms race, Bay of Pigs fiasco, Cuban missile crisis, and the space race. It has perhaps always been true that men will keep themselves important in the life of the group, by whatever means are necessary, including making war with neighboring groups (Tiger, 1969).

5.    With colleagues on the staff at *Fortune Magazine*, Whyte (1956) interviewed 215 business executives at various ages and levels in various corporations, including fifty-five CEO's and senior vice presidents, to find men so completely involved in their work that they cannot distinguish between work and the rest of their lives.

> To the executive there is between work and the rest of his life a unity he can never fully explain, and least of all to his wife. One of the few secrets many an

executive manages to keep from his wife is how much more deeply he is involved in his job than in anything else under the sun. Thus he can never really explain to his wife that what he is doing is not overwork, for the explanation would be tactless. "Overwork as I see it," says one company president, "is simply work don't like. But I dearly love this work. You love only one time and you might as well do something you like." He was not talking about his wife. (P. 162)

6.   Friedan of course sees more in the feminine mystique than a symptom of a bygone era. She sees it an actively pursued political ideology formulated by social scientists and implemented by educators and by advertisers and their business clients to keep women in their place and to deny women their right to grow and develop as individual human beings:

> The new mystique makes the housewife-mothers, who never had a chance to be anything else, the models for all women; it presupposes that history has reached a final and glorious end in the here and now, as far as women are concerned. Beneath the sophisticated trappings, it simply makes certain concrete, finite, domestic aspects of feminine existence—as it was lived by women whose lives were confined by necessity to cooking, cleaning, washing, bearing children—into a religion, a pattern by which all women must now live or deny their femininity. (P. 43)

Calling this idea of feminine existence a "religion," Friedan likens it to an opiate of the masses that hides or denies a deeper and more dangerous truth about women.

> It is my thesis that the core of the problem for women today is not sexual but a problem of identity—a stunting or evasion of growth that is perpetuated by the feminine mystique. It is my thesis that as the Victorian culture did not permit women to accept or gratify their basic sexual needs, our culture does not permit women to accept or gratify their basic need to grow and fulfill their potentialities as human beings, a need which is not solely defined by their sexual role. (P. 77)

Friedan finds that women, like men, thrill to the great projects of human destiny, and like men find the meaning in life in these as well as in home and family. Thus, if the feminine mystique was ever true, it was true when that mystique placed women squarely in the great drama of human existence.

> The material details of life, the daily burden of cooking and cleaning, of taking care of the physical needs of husband and children—these did indeed define a woman's world a century ago when Americans were pioneers, and the American frontier lay in conquering the land. But the women who went west with the wagon trains also shared the pioneering purpose. Now the American frontiers are of the mind, and of the spirit. Love and children and home are good, but they are not the whole world, even if most of the words now written for women pretend they are. Why should women accept this picture of a half-life, instead of a share in the whole of human destiny? Why should women try to make housework "something more," instead of moving on to the frontiers of their own time, as American women moved beside their husbands on the old frontiers? (Pp. 66-67).

One can imagine, with Friedan, that women were healthier and better balanced among pioneering Americans than among middle-class suburban Americans of the late 1950s, without believing it was because women were happier to be part of a great pioneer movement. As I suggest below, I believe it is more accurate and meaningful to suppose that if both sexes were in better order then than today it is because the non-negotiable demands of pioneer life joined men and women in closer more mutually reinforcing relations. Men and women of that era may have been more securely and compatibly matched and therefore less troubled about their sexual identity.

7.     This is from Thoreau's "Life without principle" (1861, p. 631):

Let us consider the way in which we spend our lives. This world is a place of business. What an infinite bustle! I am awaked almost every night by the panting of a locomotive. It interrupts my dreams. There is no Sabbath. It would be glorious to see mankind at leisure for once. It is nothing but work, work, work. I cannot easily buy a blank book to write thoughts in; they are commonly ruled for dollars and cents. An Irishman, seeing me making a minute in the fields, took it for granted that I was calculating my wages. If a man was tossed out of window when an infant, and so made a cripple for life, or scared out of his wits by the Indians, it is regretted chiefly because he was thus incapacitated for—business! I think that there is nothing, not even crime, more opposed to poetry, to philosophy, aye, to life itself, than this incessant business.

8.     This article of faith is well expressed by Beat poet Michael McClure:

I did not fear obscurity in my poetry because I had come to believe that the way to the universal was by means of the most intensely personal. I believe that what we truly share with others lies in the deepest, most personal, even physiological core—and not in the outer social world of speech that is used for grooming and transactions. (1982, p. 26)

9.     In a few larger and more socially conscious communes, such as Twin Oaks in Virginia and Gaskin's "Farm" in Tennessee, marriage and family were regarded as instances private property and thus were rejected on ideological grounds as instruments of economic capitalism and male domination (Wagner, 1982). In other instances, marriage and family were frowned upon more simply because they were alternative units of organization that fragmented the larger group (Kanter, 1972).

10.    Another case in point is the kibbutz movement in Israel. Here was a radically egalitarian social movement begun in the late 1940s under the most favorable circumstances of a clear and stridently liberal ideology, a subsistence economy, and at the birth of a new nation. As conceived and arranged by founding ideologues, kibbutzim were not to have any sexual division of labor or family. All persons were to participate equally to the kibbutz as individuals. And all children were to live apart from their mothers and fathers in community childcare. Measured against these ideals the kibbutzim have failed. Today there is a clear traditionally focused division of labor and today children live and are nurtured by their parents, especially by their mothers. Evidently there are social-sexual arrangements that no amount of well-intentioned social engineering can overcome. See Spiro (1996) and Tiger & Sheper (1975).

11.    Friedan, for her part, saw the excesses of this more radical and divisive feminism for what they were, a grave political and moral mistake:

From the totality of our own experience as women—and our knowledge of psychology, anthropology, biology—many feminists knew all along that the extremist rhetoric of sexual politics defied ad denied the profound, complex human reality of the sexual, social, psychological, economic, yes, biological relationship between woman and man. It denied the reality of woman's own sexuality, her childbearing, her roots and life connection in the family. (1981, p. 51)

12.    Data reported in "The State of Our Unions: The Social Health of Marriage in America." Rutgers University Marriage Project, July 1, 1999.
13.    "The trouble with men," *Economist*. September 28, 1996, pp. 23-26.
14.    "U.S. colleges begin to ask where have the men gone?" *New York Times*, December 6, 1998.
15.    "The fall of man," *New York Times*, January 21, 1996.
16.    Weldon, F. "Where women are women and so are men." *Harper's Magazine*, May, 1998, pp. 65-69. Anticipating her critics, Weldon presses her case as follows:

Roundly I am chastised for such heretical views. The perception remains that women are the victims, that men are the beasts. Women are the organizing soft-centered socialists, the nice people, the sugar-and-spice lot, identifying with the poor and humble; men are snips and snails and puppy-dog tails, and rampant, selfish, greedy capitalists. No wonder conservative and puritanical politicians, for such ours are, adopt female masks. It's the boys who these days are said to suffer from low self-esteem, don't speak in class, lack motivation, hang around street corners, depressed and loutish. It is the men, not the women, who complain of being slighted, condemned by virtue of gender to casual and automatic insult. "Oh men!" say the women, disparagingly. Males hear it all the time, in the workplace and in the home, at the bus stop and over the dinner table, and suffer from it. No tactful concessions are made to male presence. Men, the current female wisdom has it, are all selfish bastards; hit-and-run fathers; potential abusers/rapists/pedophiles; all think only with their dicks, and they'd better realize it. So men shrink, shrivel, and underperform, just as women once did. So where'd the bloody men go? (P. 66)

17.    It is ironic that while the champions of the individual would never intend today's neurotic narcissist, their thinking was instrumental in his or her development. Today's narcissist is the grandchild of Emerson's self-reliant man and Nietzsche's superman. In trumpeting a life beyond the group, individualists held the person apart from the roles he/she played in the group, *including those played in the sexual life of the species*. The individual is a person of indefinite sex concerned only to extend and develop his or her *human* capacities—in Goldstein's phrase, to "self-actualize." A just society puts no constraint or limitation on growth. Thus the silence about sex in humanistic psychology. Maslow's (1954) self-actualizing person is not recognizably male or female, only human. Self-actualization is not a question of being all the man you can be, or being all the woman you can be, it is a question of being all the human you can be. Thus a self-actualizing man might grow by developing feminine sensibilities that complement his own, while a self-actualizing woman might grow by developing masculine sensibilities to complement her own. Man incorporates woman, and woman incorporates man, into a self-sufficing human whole. Humanism literally *confuses* (fuses with) the sexes by assimilating them to an androgynous ideal that no developed man or woman could understand or seek.

18.     It is a testimony to the power of the self-consciousness of the age that many students of the humanities today put the idea of gender at the center of their conception of society. And though few dare say it directly, by their uncompromising politics one can tell they think gender has nothing to do with sex, that culture defines all and biology has no part. This is the apotheosis of a sexless self-consciousness that flies fully over the facts of nature. It is neurotic and narcissistic.

19.     One of the perversities of many of today's well-intentioned codes and statutes relating to sex in schools and in the workplace is that they make sexual relations between man and woman ever more self-conscious and therefore ever more unnatural and untenable. A few years ago Oberlin College in Ohio attracted national attention for implementing a code of sexual conduct which required would-be partners to ask for permission before making each overture in the sex act. Failure to do so was presumably grounds for defining the overture as unwelcome and could be grounds for a charge of sexual assault or harassment. Orwellian as this code of conduct may seem, it is not unusual. A recent *New York Times* article by Phillip Weiss ("No sex please, this is a workplace," May 3, 1998) found that a quarter of American companies, concerned about the expense and disruptions of sexual harassment lawsuits, have policies to restrict or otherwise discourage sex in the workplace, and particularly between employees of unequal power. The intended chilling effect of these policies has been to define sexual harassment down to make people think twice about any sexual overture or relation they might make or welcome in the workplace. There is a presumption built into many of these policies that there can be no genuine consent for a sexual relationship between persons of unequal power. To say that these policies have made the sexes more self-conscious and have made relations between the sexes more awkward would be an understatement.

20.     Ours is a neurotically self-conscious age in which, women and especially men measure their sexual worth in minute and obsessive metrics of breast and penis size, number and intensity of orgasms, number and durations of erections, and numbers of conquests. At a time when it has become casual, indeed because it has become casual, sex, the most natural act in the world, has become a problem. Self-consciousness's twin perils of frigidity and impotence threaten the act at every turn, making it hard to relax and thus hard to accept and appreciate stimulation. Indeed, one may wonder, if not for the dis-inhibiting and sense-dulling effects of alcohol, which allow men and women to lose themselves briefly, if the act could come off at all.

21.     According to Kinsey (1948) oral sex emerges in the United States as a common practice only in the 1920's, with well-educated middle class whites leading the way. If oral cravings indeed reflect the narcissistic character, as Lasch (1979) supposes, then this is the time period and group in which we'd expect to find interests in oral sex to begin.

22.     Data reported in "Population implosion worries a graying Europe," *New York Times*, Friday, July 10, 1998. Similar changes in fertility rates are reported throughout Europe, and excepting times of war, famine and disease, have reached all time lows in Germany, Italy, and Spain.

23.     Lewis Lapham ("In the garden of tabloid delight: Notes on sex, Americans, scandal, and morality." *Harper's Magazine*, August, 1997, pp. 35-43) notes how this commodity mentality infects the current age with persecuting questions and a dangerous soullessness.

    We classify human sexuality as a commodity, like cereal, that can be crowded onto the shelves in the supermarkets of desire. ... The commercial presentations allow us to have it both ways from the end and all ways from the middle—to meet the demands for hard-line feminist theory and the Victoria's Secret catalogue, for Robert Bork's sermons and Tony Kushner's plays, for breast or penile implants and software programs blocking out displays of nudity on the Internet, for as many different kinds of marriage (homosexual, heterosexual, open, closed, Christian, pagan, alternative, frankly perverse) as can meet with the approval of a landlord. ...

As might be expected of people engulfed in a haze of quasi-pornographic images, the subsequent confusion raises questions to which nobody has any good answers but which in the meantime provide the topics for the best-selling books of ethical self-help. What is moral, and where is virtue? Who is a man and who a woman, and how do I know the difference? Is marriage forever, or is it another one of those institutions (like the churches and the schools) wrecked on the reefs of progress? Do the doors of the future open only to people who observe the rules and watch their diets, or must we, as true Americans and therefore rebellious at birth, knock down the walls of social convention? Suppose for a moment that we wish to obey the rules: What do they mean and where are they written? ...

Human beings who tailor themselves to the measure of the market float like numbers across the surface of the computer screen. Without the strength and frame of a moral order—some code or rule or custom that provides them with a way and a place to stand against the flood of their own incoherent desire—they too often lose the chance for love or meaning in their lives, unable or unwilling to locate the character of their own minds or build the shelters of their own happiness.

24.   The decadent similarity of the sexes is favorable not only to sexual inversion, but also to sexual perversions such as sadism and masochism. In sadism and masochism we have psychically twisted masculinity and femininity made possible by loss of contact to male and female bodies. While sadist and masochist may seem made for each other, they enact sex in an uncontrolled way satisfying to neither. Neither in fact wants anything to do with the other. The sadist takes selfish narcissistic pleasure in dominating another person, with whom he or she identifies unconsciously. But this is an empty pleasure if the other person seeks to be dominated. Likewise, the masochist takes selfish narcissistic pleasure in being dominated by another person, with whom he or she likewise identifies unconsciously. This too is an empty pleasure if the other seeks to dominate. Thus the relationship of sadist and masochist defeats itself as partners seek impossible satisfactions in more and more severe and perverse cruelties.

25.   "Southern Baptists declare wife should 'submit' to her husband, " *New York Times*, June 10, 1998, p. 1.

26.   Suggesting the flavor of the new men's magazines, here is publisher Felix Dennis explaining how the top brass of Dennis publishing came to select the title of their magazine, *Maxim*:

So how did we come to choose the name Maxim for the world's finest periodical for men?

Allow me to put your mind at rest immediately. *No namby-pamby focus groups whatsoever were involved in this historic decision.* The truth is that the name of our magazine was chosen, not entirely surprisingly, in a London pub called The Ship over a great many pints of warm beer.

Present were the top brass of Dennis Publishing, who had assembled following a so-called board meeting at which a decision had been made to launch the U.K. version of the magazine you currently hold in your hand. As usual, I was buying the rounds—the main function of the chairman at any sensible company. Drunk then, with power if not with ale, we sat in a haze of cigarette smoke and debated dozens of potential magazine names at high volume across The Ship's beat-up rickety tables.

Finally, tired of all the ballyhoo, The Ship's landlord asked what this new magazine was supposed to do. "Murder the bloody competition!" came back the chorus. "What about *Maxim* then?" he suggested. "The Maxim was the first serious machine gun. Single-barreled, water-cooled. Automatically cocked by its own recoil. Invented by Anglo-American engineer Sir Hiram Stevens Maxim. Absolutely murdered 'em for sure."

Thus today, gentle reader, we find ourselves the recipient of an inspired name from that fount of all wisdom ... our local bartender. ...

27.  As Descartes was first to distinguish mind and body as distinct realms, we could perhaps nominate him as the first individual. Be that fair or not, it is no accident that such a philosopher as Descartes came along just as the Medieval world was giving birth to the individual in the flowering of the Renaissance.

28.  Until recently, the only businesses to turn a profit on the Internet have been those purveying pornography. While more respectable business have had trouble convincing customers to part with credit card numbers over computer lines, pornographers have had no such trouble with their customers. This is perhaps a testament to the power of the unconscious to break through everyday scruples.

29.  In an irony of ironies, James Atlas reports in the *New Yorker Magazine* ("The loose canon: Why higher learning has embraced pornography," May 29, 1999) that the leading edge of academic feminism focuses today on the study of pornography. While this research is typically advertised as a window on misshapen male sexuality and as a vehicle to "unmask the hidden face of repression," one wonders if there is not also an unconscious motive at work to enjoy the expression of sex undistorted and unfettered by contemporary inhibitions and political correctness. Judith Butler, Berkeley professor and doyenne of feminist studies of pornography, confirms the point noting that the appeal of pornography lies mainly in its allegory of masculine willfulness and feminine submission. That academics themselves might be taking pleasure in this art is suggested by Atlas who notes that "not content with merely theorizing about pornography, academics from the ranks of English, philosophy, and sociology departments around the country are also writing it." (P. 61).

30.  Social life, according to Brown (1966), is a recurring male movement away from and return to female. Sexual intercourse enacts this drama in miniature as the upright individual penis returns triumphantly and self-identically to penetrate and rub up against the womb, then to be reduced and subordinated in form (once again a citizen of the whole). This drama is made myth in the story of the return of the prodigal son and in the stories of great religious figures such as Buddha, Mohammed, Moses, and Christ. And this drama is enacted hourly in the corporation, church, and

university. To stand up as manager in a corporation, or as minister in a congrega-
tion, or as professor in a class, is to stand up as penis before the womb. Separated,
leader and group are incomplete, castrated; but together they make a whole. Hierarchy everywhere is projection of male power in the female group.

31.    Much as we might like to believe this a case of altruism on a massive scale, it lacked
the public awareness and collaboration to count as a genuine social movement. A
plainer fact was that those involved in the economy had better things to do with their
time and money than raise children. In family after family, a generation of families
of 4 and 5 children was met by a generation of families of 1 or 2 children. It is hard
to believe that sons and daughters were more altruistic than their parents. Much
easier to believe these sons and daughters were more self-involved and economically greedy than their parents.

# References

Abram, D. 1997. *The spell of the sensuous*. New York: Vintage.

Acker, J. 1990. Hierarchies, jobs, bodies: A theory of gendered organizations. *Gender and Society, 4*, 139-158.

Adler, A. 1978. *Cooperation between the sexes*. Trans. by H. L. Ansbacher and R. R. Ansbacher. Garden City, NY: Anchor Books.

Allport, F. 1927. *The group fallacy in relation to social science*. Hanover, NH: Sociological Press.

Archer, J. 1991. The influence of testosterone on human aggression. *British Journal of Psychology, 82*: 1-28.

Argiolas, A. & Gessa, G. L. 1991. Central functions of oxytocin. *Neuroscience & Biobehavioral Reviews, 15(2)*: 217-231.

Arnheim, R. 1962. *Picasso's Guernica; the genesis of a painting*. Berkeley, CA: University of California.

Arrow, K. 1994. Methodological individualism and social knowledge. *American Economic Association Papers and Proceedings*, May: 1-9.

Axelrod. R. 1984. *The evolution of cooperation*. New York: Basic Books.

Baker, R. & Bellis, M. H. 1995. *Human sperm competition: Copulation, masturbation, and infidelity*. London: Chapman & Hall.

Baumeister, R. 1991. *Meanings of life*. New York: Guilford Press.

Bellah, R. N. et al. 1986. *Habits of the heart: Individualism and commitment in American life*. New York: Harper & Row.

Bem, D. J. 1996. Exotic becomes erotic: A developmental theory of sexual orientation. *Psychological Review, 103(2)*: 320-335.

Berlyne, D. E. 1968. Laughter, humor, and play. In G. Lindzey & E. Aronson (eds). *The handbook of social psychology, 2e.*, pp. 795-852. Reading, MA: Addison-Wesley.

Berger, B. 1971. *Looking for America; essays on youth, suburbia, and other American obsessions*. Englewood Cliffs, NJ: Prentice-Hall.

Berman, P. W. 1980. Are women more responsive than men to the young? A review of developmental and situational variables. *Psychological Bulletin, 88*: 668-695.

Blau, P. 1955. *The dynamics of bureaucracy*. Chicago: University of Chicago.

Blum, D. 1997. *Sex on the brain*. New York: Viking.

Booth, A., Shelley, G., Mazur, A. Tharp, G. & Kittok, R. 1989. Testosterone, and winning and losing in human competition. *Hormones and behavior, 23*: 556-571.

Bouchard, T. J. Jr., Lykken, D. T. & McGue, M. 1990. Sources of human psychological differences: The Minnesota study of twins reared apart. *Science, 250*: 233-8.

Brothers, L. 1995. Neurophysiology of the perception of intentions by primates. In M. Gazzaniga (ed.) *The cognitive neurosciences*, pp. 1107-1115. Cambridge, MA: MIT Press.

Brothers, L. 1997. *Friday's footprint.: How society shapes the mind.* New York: Oxford University Press.

Brown, N. O. 1966. *Love's body*. Berkeley, CA: University of California Press.

Browne, K. R. Sex and temperament in modern society: A Darwinian view of the glass ceiling and gender gap. *Arizona Law Review, 37*, 971-1106.

Budrene, E. O. & Berg, H. C. 1991. Complex patterns formed by motile cells of Escherichia coli. *Nature, 349*: 630-633.

Burroughs, W. S. 1986. "Women: A biological mistake?" In *The adding machine*. New York: Seaver.

Buss, D. M. 1994. *The evolution of desire*. New York: Basic Books.

Buss, D. M., Larsen, R., Westen, D., & Semmelroth, J. (1992). Sex differences in jealousy: Evolution, physiology, and psychology. *Psychological Science, 3*, 251-255.

Buss, D. M. & Schmitt, D. P. 1993. Sexual strategies theory: An evolutionary perspective on human mating. *Psychological Review, 100*: 204-232.

Cairns, R. B., Cairns, B.D., Neckerman, H. J., Ferguson, L. L. & Gariepy, J. 1989. Growth and aggression: 1. Childhood to early adolescence. *Developmental Psychology*, 25, 320-333.

Campbell, J. 1973. *The mythic image*. Princeton, NJ: Princeton University Press.

Carter, C. S., DeVries, A. C., & Getz, L. L. 1995. Physiological substrates of mammalian monogamy: The prairie vole model. *Neuroscience & Biobehavioral Reviews, 19(2)*: 303-314.

Charlesworth, W.R., & Dzur, C. 1987. Gender comparisons of preschoolers' behavior and resource utilization in group problem solving. *Child Development*, 38, 329-336.

Chodorow, N. 1989. *Feminism and psychoanalytic theory*. New Haven, CT: Yale University Press.

Clutton-Brock, T. H. 1991. *The evolution of parental care*. Princeton, NJ: Princeton University Press.

Collaer, M.L. & Hines, M. 1995. Human behavioral sex differences: A role for gonadal hormones during early development? *Psychological Bulletin* 118(1): 55-107.

Corporael, L. R., & Baron, R. M. 1997. Groups as the mind's natural environment. In J. A. Simpson & D. T. Kenrick (Eds.), *Evolutionary social psychology*, pp. 317-344. Mahwah, NJ: Erlbaum.

Crano, W. D. & Aronoff, J. 1978. A cross cultural study of expressive and instrumental role complementarity in the family. *American Sociological Review, 43*, 463-471.

Crick, N. R., & Grotpeter, J. K. 1995. Relational aggression, gender, and social psychological adjustment. *Child Development*, 66, 710-722.

Daly, M. & Wilson, M. 1983. *Sex, evolution, and behavior*. Boston: Willard Grant.

Daly, M. & Wilson, M. 1990. Killing the competition: Female/female and male/male homicide. *Human Nature, 1*: 81-107.

Dawkins, R. 1989. *The selfish gene, 2nd Ed.* Cambridge: Cambridge University Press.

de Beauvoir, S. 1952. *The second sex*. New York: Alfred A. Knopf

de Rougement, D. 1940. *Love in the western world*. New York: Harcourt.

de Waal, F. 1989. *Chimpanzee politics*. Baltimore, MD: Johns Hopkins University Press.

de Waal, F. 1993. Sex differences in chimpanzee (and human) behavior: A matter of social values? In M. Hechter, L. Nadel, and R.E. Michod (eds.) *The origin of values*. New York: Aldine de Gruyter.

Diamond, J. 1997. *Why is sex fun?* New York: Basic Books.

Dinnerstein, D. 1976. *The mermaid and the minotaur*. New York: Harper.

Donaldson, S. (Ed.) 1979. *On the Road: Text and criticism*. New York: Viking Press.

Dunbar, R. I. M. 1993. Co-evolution of neo-cortical size, group size and language in humans. *Behavioral and Brain Sciences, 16*, 681-735.

Durkheim, E. 1893/1933. *The division of labor in society*. Trans. by G. Simpson. New York: Macmillan.

Eagly, A. H. 1995. The science and politics of comparing women and men. *American Psychologist* 50(3): 145-58.

Eagly, A. H. & Karau, S. J. 1991. Gender and emergence of leaders. *Journal of Personality and Social Psychology* 60(5): 685-710.

Eagly, A. H., Karau, S. J., Miner, J. B. & Johnson, B. T. 1994. Gender and motivation to manage in hierarchic organizations: A meta-analysis. *Leadership Quarterly* 5(2): 135-159.

Eagly, A. H., Mladinic, A. & Otto, S. 1991. Are women evaluated more favorably than men? An analysis of attitudes, beliefs, and emotions. *Psychology of Women Quarterly*, 15(2): 203-216.

Eibl-Eibesfeldt, I. 1989. *Human ethology.* New York: Aldine de Gruyter.

Ellis, A. 1961. *The American sexual tragedy.* New York: Grove Press.

Eme, R. F., & Kavanaugh, L. 1995. Sex differences in conduct disorder. *Journal of Clinical Child Psychology, 24*: 406-426.

Erikson, E. H. 1963. *Childhood and society, 2ed.* New York: W. W. Norton.

Etzioni, A. 1999. *The limits of privacy.* New York: Basic Books.

Fagot, B. I. 1994. Peer relations and the development of competence in boys and girls. In C. Leaper, Ed., *Childhood gender segregation.* San Francisco: Jossey-Bass.

Fairfield, R. 1972. *Communes USA; a personal tour.* Baltimore, MD: Penguin.

Faludi, S. 1991. *Backlash.* New York: Crown.

Farrell, A. E. 1994. A social experiment in publishing: Ms. Magazine, 1972-1989. *Human Relations, 47*, 707-730.

Ferguson, K. 1984. *The feminist case against bureaucracy.* Philadelphia: Temple University Press.

Ferris, C. F., & Delville, Y. 1994. Vasopressin and serotonin interactions in the control of agonistic behavior. *Psychoneuroendocrinology, 19(5-7)*: 593-601.

Fisher, H. E. 1982. *The sex contract: The evolution of human behavior.* New York: William Morrow.

Foster, E. H. 1992. *Understanding the Beats.* Columbia, SC: University of South Carolina Press.

Fox, R. 1994. *The challenge of anthropology.* New Brunswick, NJ: Transaction Publishers.

Freud, S. 1922/1959. *Group psychology and the analysis of the ego.* Trans. J. Strachey. New York: W.W. Norton.

Freud, S. 1930/1961. *Civilization and its discontents.* Trans. J. Strachey. New York: W.W. Norton.

Freud, S. 1963. *Sexuality and the psychology of love.* New York: Macmillan.

Friday, N. 1973. *My secret garden: Women's sexual fantasies.* New York: Simon & Schuster.

Friedan, B. 1963. *The feminine mystique.* New York: W. W. Norton.

Friedan, B. 1981. *The second stage.* New York: Summit Books.

Fromm, E. 1955. *The sane society.* Greenwich, CT: Fawcett.

Fukuyama, F. 1999. *The great disruption.* New York: Free Press.

Furstenberg, F. F. & Nord, C. W. 1985. Parenting apart: Patterns of child rearing after marital disruption. *Journal of Marriage and the Family, 47*, 893-904.

Geary, D. C. 1998. *Male, female.* Washington: American Psychological Association.

Geertz, C. 1965. *The social history of an Indonesian town.* Cambridge, MA: MIT Press.

Gesell, A. et al. 1940. *The first five years of life.* New York: Harper.

Ghiselin, B. 1955. *The creative process.* New York: Mentor.

Giddens, A. 1979. *Central problems of social theory.* Berkeley, CA: University of California Press.

Gilligan, C. 1982. *In a different voice.* Cambridge, MA: Harvard University Press.

Ginsberg, A. 1977. *Journals: Early fifties early sixties.* New York: Grove Press.

Goldberg, S. 1993. *Why men rule.* Chicago: Open Court.

Goleman, D. 1996. *Emotional intelligence.* New York: Bantam.

Golombok, S. & Fivush, R. 1994. *Gender development.* New York: Cambridge University Press.

Goodman, P. 1960. *Growing up absurd.* New York: Vintage.

Goren, C., Sarty, M., & Wu, P. 1975. Visual following and pattern discrimination of face-like stimuli by newborn infants. *Pediatrics, 56:* 544—549.

Gouldner, A. 1960. The norm of reciprocity. *American Sociological Review, 25(2):* 161-178.

Gray, J. 1992. *Men are from Mars, women are from Venus: A practical guide for improving communication and getting what you want in your relations.* New York: Harper-Collins.

Gross, C., Bender, D., & Rocha-Miranda, C. 1969. Visual receptive fields of neurons in inferotemporal cortex of the monkey. *Science, 166:* 1303-1306.

Haldane, D. S. 1932. *The philosophical basis of biology.* London: Hodder & Stoughton.

Halpern, D. F. 1992. *Sex differences in cognitive abilities.* Hillsdale, NJ: Lawrence Erlbaum.

Hamilton, W. D. 1964. The genetical evolution of social behavior, I and II. *Journal of Theoretical Biology 7:* 1-52.

Hamilton, W. D. 1975. Gamblers since life began: barnacles, aphids, elms. *Quarterly Review of Biology, 50:* 175-180.

Harris, J. A., Rushton, J. P., Hampson, E., & Jackson, D. N. 1996. Salivary testosterone and self-report aggressive and pro-social personality characteristics in men and women. *Aggressive Behavior, 22:* 321-331.

Hawkes, K. 1990. Why do men hunt? Benefits for risky choices. In E. Cashdan (ed.) *Risk and uncertainty in tribal and peasant economics.* Boulder, CO: Westview Press.

Hedges, L. V. & Nowell, A. 1995. Sex differences in central tendency, variability, and numbers of high-scoring individuals. *Science 269:* 4045.

Herdt, G. 1996. *Third sex, third gender.* New York: Zone Books.

Hobbes, T. 1651/1958. *Leviathan.* Reprint. Indianapolis, IN: Bobbs-Merrill.

Hochschild, A. 1989. *The second shift.* New York: Viking Press.

Hochschild, A. 1997. *The time bind.* New York: Metropolitan.

Hoffman, M. L. 1977. Sex differences in empathy and related behaviors. *Psychological Bulletin, 84:* 712-722.

Holland, J. 1992. Genetic algorithms. *Scientific American,* July: 66-72.

Homans, G. C. 1950. *The human group.* New York: Harcourt, Brace & World.

Horney, K. 1967. *Feminine psychology.* New York: W.W. Norton.

Hrdy, S. B. 1981. *The woman that never evolved.* Cambridge, MA: Harvard University Press.

Hughes, T. 1997. *Tales from Ovid.* New York: Farrar, Straus, Giroux.

Huizinga, J. 1950. *Homo ludens.* Boston: Beacon Press.

Hyde, J. S. & Linn, M. C. 1988. Gender differences in verbal ability: A meta-analysis. *Psychological Bulletin, 104:* 53-69.

Isaac, B. 1992. Throwing. In S. Jones, R. Martin, & D. Pilbeam (Eds.), *The Cambridge encyclopedia of human evolution,* (p. 358). New York: Cambridge University Press.

Jackall, R. 1988. *Moral mazes.* New York: Cambridge University Press.

Jardine, R., & Martin, N. G. 1983. Spatial ability and throwing accuracy. *Behavioral Genetics, 13:* 331-340.

Jaynes, J. 1976. *The origin of consciousness in the breakdown of the bicameral mind.* Boston: Houghton Mifflin.

Jung, C. G. 1990. *The basic writings of C. G. Jung.* Trans. by R. F. C. Hull. Princeton, NJ: Princeton University Press.

Kanter, R. M. 1972. *Commitment and community; communes and utopias in sociological perspective.* Cambridge, MA: Harvard University Press.

Kenealy, A. 1920. *Feminism and sex-extinction.* New York: Dutton.

Kerouac, J. 1972. *Visions of Cody.* New York: McGraw-Hill.

Kinsey, A. C. 1948. *Sexual behavior in the human male.* Philadelphia: Saunders.

Kinsey, A. C. 1953. *Sexual behavior in the human female.* Philadelphia: Saunders.

Koch, P. B. and Weis, D. L. 1998. *Sexuality in America.* New York: Continuum.

Koolhaas, J. M., Van den Brink, T. H., Roozendaal, B., & Boorsma, F. 1990. Medial amygdala and aggressive behavior: Interaction between testosterone and vasopressin. *Aggressive Behavior, 16(4):* 223-229.

Lacey, R. & Danziger, D. 1999. *The year 1000.* Boston: Little Brown.

Lamb, M. E., Frodi, A. M., Hwang, C. P. & Frodi, M. 1982. Varying degrees of paternal involvement in infant care: Attitudinal and behavioral correlates. In M. E. Lamb (ed.). *Nontraditional families: Parenting and child development*, pp. 117-137. Hillsdale, NJ: Lawrence Erlbaum.

Langer, S. 1962. *Philosophical sketches.* Baltimore, MD: Johns Hopkins University Press.

Langer, S. 1967. *Mind: An essay on human feeling, Vol. 1.* Baltimore, MD: Johns Hopkins University Press.

Langer, S. 1976. *Mind: An essay on human feeling, Vol. 2.* Baltimore, MD: Johns Hopkins University Press.

Lasch, C. 1979. *The culture of narcissism.* New York: W.W. Norton.

Laumann, E. O., Gagnon, J. H., Michael, R. T., and Michaels, S. 1994. *The social organization of sexuality.* Chicago: University of Chicago Press.

Lever, J. 1972. Sex differences in the games children play. *Social Problems* 23: 478-487.

Lever, J. 1978. Sex differences in the complexity of children's play and games. *American Sociological Review, 43,* 471-483.

Maccoby, E.E. 1998. *The two sexes: Growing up apart, coming together.* Cambridge, MA: Belknap.

Maccoby, E.E. and Jacklin, C. N. 1974. *The psychology of sex differences.* Palo Alto, CA: Stanford University Press.

Mailer, N. 1959. "The White Negro," In *Advertisements for myself.* New York: Putnam.

March, J. G. & Simon, H.A. 1958. *Organizations.* New York: Wiley.

Maslow, A. H. 1954. *Motivation and personality.* New York: Harper.

May, R. 1980. *Sex and fantasy.* New York: W. W. Norton.

Mayo, M. 1948. *The American square dance.* New York: Sentinel.

Mayr, E. 1991. *One long argument.* Cambridge, MA: Harvard University Press.

Mazur, A., Booth, A. & Dabbs, J. M. Jr. 1992. Testosterone and chess competition. *Social Psychology Quarterly, 55(1):* 70-77.

McClure, M. 1982. *Scratching the Beat surface.* San Francisco: North Point.

McDougall, W. 1909. *An introduction to social psychology.* Boston: Luce.

Mead, M. 1949. *Male and female.* New York: William Morrow.

Mencken, H. L. 1918. *In defense of women.* Garden City, NY: Garden City Publishing.

Meyerson, D. & Fletcher, J. 2000. A modest manifesto for shattering the glass ceiling. *Harvard Business Review, 784,* 127-136.

Millett, K. 1970. *Sexual politics.* Garden City, NY: Doubleday.

Mills, C. W. 1951. *White collar.* New York: Oxford University Press.

Mitchell, J. & Oakley, A. 1986. *What is feminism?* Oxford: Blackwell.

Moscovici, S. 1997. *The invention of society: Psychological explanations for social phenomena.* Cambridge, MA: Blackwell.

Moss, H.A. 1974. Early sex differences and mother-infant interaction. In Friedman, R. C., Richart, R. M. and VandeWiele, R. L. (Eds.). *Sex differences in behavior*. New York: Wiley.

Moyer, K. E. 1974. Sex differences in aggression. In R. C. Friedman, R. M. Richart, and R. L. Vande Wiele (eds.) *Sex differences in behavior.* New York: Wiley.

Paglia, C. 1990. *Sexual personae*. New Haven, CT: Yale University Press.

Paglia, C. 1994. *Vamps and tramps*. New York: Vintage.

Paglin, M. & Rufolo, A. M. 1990. Heterogeneous human capital, occupational choice, and male-female earnings differences. *Journal of Labor Economics, 8*, 123-144.

Palmer, C. T. & Tilley, C. F. 1995. Sexual access to females as a motivation for joining gangs: An evolutionary approach. *Journal of Sex Research*, 32, 213-217.

Parke, R. D. & Slaby, R. G. 1983. The development of aggression. In P. Mussen, ed., and E.M. Hetherington (vol. Ed.). *Handbook of child psychology, vol. 4, Social, personality, and social development*, pp. 547-641. New York: Wiley.

Perrett, D. I., Heitanen, J., Oram, M., & Benson, P. 1992. Organization and function of cells responsive to faces in the temporal cortex. *Philosophical Transactions of the Royal Society of London Series B, 335*: 23-30.

Piaget, J. 1932. *The moral judgment of the child*. New York: Free Press.

Pitcher, E. G. & Schultz, L. H. 1983. *Boys and girls at play: The development of sex roles*. South Hadley, MA: Bergin and Garvey.

Plato 1892. Phaedrus. *The dialogues of Plato*. Trans. By B. Jowett (1871). Oxford: Clarendon Press.

Plomin, R., Owen, M. J. & McGuffin, P. 1994. The genetic basis of complex human behaviors. *Science, 264*: 1733-1739.

Povinelli, D. 1993. Reconstructing the evolution of mind. *American Psychologist, 48*, 493-509.

Pratto, F. 1996. Sexual politics: The gender gap in the bedroom, the cupboard, and the cabinet. In d. M. Buss & N. M. Malamuth (eds.). *Sex, power, conflict: Evolutionary and feminist perspectives*. (Pp. 179-230). New York: Oxford University Press.

Pryce, C. R. 1995. Determinants of motherhood in human and non-human primates: A biosocial model. In C. R. Pryce, R. D. Martin, & D. Skuse (Eds.), *Motherhood in human and nonhuman primates: Biosocial determinants* (pp. 1-15). Basel, Switzerland: Karger.

Pugh, K. R., Shaywitz, B. A., Shaywitz, S. E., Shankweiler, D. P., Katz, L., Fletcher, J. M., Skudlarski, P., Fulbright, R. K., Constable, R. T., Bronen, R. A., Lacadie, C., & Gore, J. C. 1997. Predicting reading performance from neuroimaging profiles: The cerebral basis of phonological effects in printed word identification. *Journal of Experimental Psychology: Human Perception and Performance, 23*, 299-318.

Putnam, R. D. 1993. *Making democracy work: Civic traditions in modern Italy*. Princeton, NJ: Princeton University Press.

Reik, T. 1957. *Of love and lust*. New York: Farrar, Straus & Cudahy.

Reisman, D. 1949. *The lonely crowd*. New Haven, CT: Yale University Press.

Roberts, R. E. 1971. *The new communes; coming together in America*. Englewood Cliffs, NJ: Prentice-Hall.

Rolls, E. T. 1995. Learning mechanisms in the temporal lobe visual cortex. *Behavioural Brain Research, 66*: 177-185.

Rousseau, J. 1762/1950. *A discourse upon the origin and foundation of the inequality among mankind*. Reprint, Boston: Harvard University Press.

Roszak, T. 1969. *The making of a counterculture; Reflections on the technocratic society and its youthful opposition*. Garden City, NY: Doubleday.

Rymer, R. 1993. *Genie: An abused child's flight from silence*. New York: Harper-Collins.

Sachs, J. 1987. Preschool boys' and girls' language use in pretend play. In S. U. Phillips, S. Steele, and C. Tanz, (Eds.), *Language, gender, and sex in comparative perspective*, pp. 178-188. Cambridge: Cambridge University Press.

Sandelands, L. E. 1994. The sense of society. *Journal for the Theory of Social Behaviour*, *24(4):* 1-33.

Sandelands, L. E. 1997. The body and the social. In. J. D. Greenwood (ed.), *The mark of the social*, pp. 133-152. Lanham, MD: Rowman & Littlefield.

Sandelands, L. E. 1998. *Feeling and form in social life.* Lanham, MD: Rowman & Littlefield.

Sandelands, L. E., Ashford, S.J. & Dutton, J.E. 1983. Reconceptualizing the over-justification effect: A template-matching approach. *Motivation and Emotion*, 7, 229-255.

Scheinfeld, A. 1943. *Women and men.* New York: Harcourt, Brace, and Co.

Schwartz, H. 1997. Psychodynamics of political correctness. *Journal of Applied Behavioral Science, 33*: 132-148.

Sears, R. R., Rau, L. & Alpert, R. 1965. *Identification and child rearing.* Stanford, CA: Stanford Press.

Shanahan, D. 1992. *Toward a geneaology of individualism.* Amherst, MA: University of Massachusetts Press.

Shaywitz, B. A., Shaywitz, S. E., Pugh, K. R., Constable, R. T., Scudlarski, P., Fulbright, R. K., Bronen, R. A., Fletcher, J. M., Shankweiler, D. P., Katz, L., & Gore, J. C. 1995. Sex differences in the functional organization of the brain for language. *Nature, 373*, 607-609.

Sheets-Johnstone, M. 1990. *The roots of thinking.* Philadelphia: Temple University Press.

Singh, D., Vidaurri, M., Zambarano, R. J. & Dabbs, Jr., J. M. 1999. Lesbian erotic role identification: Behavioral, morphological, and hormonal correlates. *Journal of Personality and Social Psychology, 76(6)*: 1035-1049.

Skuse, D. H., James, R. S. & Bishop, D. V. M. 1997. Evidence from Turner's syndrome of an imprinted X—linked focus affecting cognitive function. *Nature* 387: 705-8.

Smuts, B. 1985. *Sex and friendship in baboons.* New York: Aldine de Gruyter.

Smuts, J. C. 1926. *Holism and evolution.* London: Macmillan & Co.

Sober, E. & Wilson, D. S. 1998. *Unto others.* Cambridge, MA:   Harvard University Press.

Spiro, M. E. 1996. *Gender and culture: Kibbutz women revisited.* New Brunswick, NJ: Transaction Publishers.

Stumpf, H., & Eliot, J. 1995. Gender-related differences in spatial ability and the k factor of general spatial ability in a population of academically talented students. *Personality and Individual Differences, 19*: 33-45.

Symons, D. 1979. *The evolution of human sexuality.* New York: Oxford University Press.

Theweleit, K. 1987. *Male fantasies.* Trans. by S. Conway. Minneapolis: University of Minnesota Press.

Thibaut, J. & Kelley, H. 1959. *The social psychology of groups.* New York: Wiley.

Thompson, H. 1936. The dynamics of activity drives in young children. *Psychological Bulletin, 33(9)*: 751-63.

Thoreau, H. D. 1861/1947. Life without principle. In C. Bode (ed.) *The portable Thoreau.* New York: Viking Press.

Thornhill, R. & Gangestad, S. W. 1996. Human female copulatory orgasm: a human adaptation or phylogenetic holdover. *Animal Behaviour*, 52: 853-5.

Thornhill, R. & Palmer, C. T. 2000. *A natural history of rape: Biological bases of sexual coercion.* Cambridge, MA: MIT Press.

Thurber, J. & White, E. B. 1929. *Is sex necessary?* New York: Harper Perennial.
Tielhard de Chardin, P. 1959. *The phenomenon of man.* New York: Harper and Row.
Tiger, L. 1969. *Men in groups.* New York: Free Press.
Tiger, L. 1999. *The decline of males.* New York: Golden Books.
Tiger, L. & Shepher, J. 1975. *Women in the Kibbutz.* New York: Harcourt Brace Jovanovich
Trivers, R. L. 1971. The evolution of reciprocal altruism. *Quarterly Review of Biology, 46*: 35-57.
Trivers, R. L. 1972. Parental investment and sexual selection. In B. Campbell (Ed.), *Sexual selection and the descent of man* (pp. 136-179). New York: Aldine de Gruyter.
Tsui, A., Egan, T. D., O'Reilly, C. A. III. 1992. Being different: Relational demography and organizational attachement. *Administrative Science Quarterly, 37*: 549-579.
Uvnas-Moberg, K. 1994. Oxytocin and behaviour. *Annals of Medicine, 26(5)*: 315-317.
Waddington, C. H. 1962. *The nature of life.* New York: Atheneum.
Wagner, J. E. (Ed.). 1972. *Sex roles in contemporary American communes.* Bloomington: Indiana University.
Wagner, W., Elejabarrieta, F. & Lahnsteiner, I. 1995. How the sperm dominates the ovum—objectification by metaphor in the social representation of conception. *European Journal of Social Psychology, 25*: 671-88.
Watson, N. V. & Kimura, D. 1991. Non-trivial sex differences in throwing and intercepting: Relation to psychometrically-defined spatial functions. *Personality and Individual Differences, 12*: 375-385.
Weber, M. 1964. *The theory of social and economic organization.* New York: Free Press.
West, M. M. & Konner, M. J. 1976. The role of the father: An anthropological perspective. In M. E. Lamb (ed.), *The role of the father in child development* (pp. 185-217). New York: Wiley.
White, D. R. & Burton, M. L. 1988. Causes of polygyny: Ecology, economy, kinship, and warfare. *American Anthropologist, 90*: 871-887.
Whiting, B.B. & Edwards, C.P. 1988. *Children of different worlds: The formation of social behavior.* Cambridge, MA: Harvard University Press.
Whiting, B. B. & Whiting, J. W. M. 1975. *Children of six cultures: A psycho-cultural analysis.* Cambridge, MA: Harvard University Press.
Whyte, W. F. 1943. *Street corner society.* Chicago: University of Chicago Press.
Whyte, W. H. 1956. *The organization man.* New York: Simon & Schuster.
Wiederman, M. W. & Allgeier, E. R. 1992. Gender differences in mate selection criteria: Sociobiological or socioeconomic explanation? *Ethology and Sociobiology, 13*: 115-124.
Williams, G. C. 1966. *Adaptation and natural selection: A critique of some current evolutionary thought.* Princeton, NJ: Princeton University Press.
Williams, G. C. 1975. *Sex and evolution.* Princeton, NJ: Princeton University Press.
Williams, G. C. & Williams, D.C. 1957. Natural selection of individually harmful social adaptations among sibs with special references to social insects. *Evolution, 11*: 32-39.
Willingham, W. W. & Cole, N. S. 1997. *Gender and fair assessment.* Hillsdale, NJ: Lawrence Erlbaum.
Wilson, G. D. 1978. *The secrets of sexual fantasy.* London: J. M. Dent & Sons.
Wilson, D. S. 1975. A general theory of group selection. *Proceedings of the National Academy of Sciences, 72*: 143-6.
Wilson, D. S. 1989. Levels of selection: An alternative to individualism in biology and the social sciences. *Social Networks, 11*: 257-72.
Wilson, D. S. & Sober, E. 1994. Reintroducing group selection to the human behavioral sciences. *Behavioral and Brain Sciences, 17*: 585-608.

Wilson, E. O. 1975. *Sociobiology: The new synthesis.* Cambridge, MA: Harvard University Press.

Wrangham, R. & Peterson, D. 1996. *Demonic males.* New York: Houghton Mifflin.

Wright, S. 1945. Tempo and mode in evolution: A critical review. *Ecology, 26*: 415-419.

Wynne-Edwards, V.C. 1962. *Animal dispersion in relation to social behavior.* Edinburgh: Oliver & Boyd.

Yamori, K. 1998. Going with the flow: Micro-macro dynamics in the macrobehavioral patterns of pedestrian crowds. *Psychological Review*, 105, 530-557.

Zajonc, R. 1965. Social facilitation. *Science, 149*: 269-274.

Zicklin, G. 1983. *Counter-cultural communes.* Westport, CT: Greenwood.

# Index

control power of, 93
risk-reward ratios, 92
sexual discretion in, 93
universality of, 93
Women's movement. *See* Feminist
   movement
*Working Women,* 150

*You Just Don't Understand,* 151
Youth movements
   epochal idea of, 130-131
   failures in, 131-132
   individuality vs social convictions,
      131
   sexual relations in, 132
   successes in, 131
   types of, 130